STRAWBERRY

Earn more. Save more. Give more.

FIELDS

Neil Schober

FOREVER

Jaquith Creative / Kirkland, Washington

© 2012 by Neil Schober. All rights reserved.
neilschoberconsulting.com

Published 2012
Jaquith Creative, Kirkland, Washington
jaquithcreative.com
Printed in the United States of America

ISBN 978-0-9849082-0-2
19 18 17 16 15 14 13 12   1 2 3 4

Cover and book design by Andrew Chiu
two-floors.com
Cover image by Tanner Wendell Stewart
todaymightbe.com

Unless otherwise indicated, all Scripture quotations are taken from the Holy Bible, New Living Translation, copyright © 1996, 2004, 2007 by Tyndale House Foundation. Used by permission of Tyndale House Publishers, Inc., Carol Stream, Illinois 60188. All rights reserved.

Scripture quotations from The Message. Copyright © by Eugene H. Peterson 1993, 1994, 1995, 1996, 2000, 2001, 2002. Used by permission of NavPress Publishing Group.

Scripture quotations marked NKJV are taken from the New King James Version. Copyright © 1982 by Thomas Nelson, Inc. Used by permission. All rights reserved.

Printed on acid-free paper.

Endorsements

"I have known Neil Schober for twelve years, and I can say without reservation that he lives what he teaches. Over the years, Neil has invested countless hours and funds into the Dream Center. His passion for using his resources to change lives is inspiring. Neil's generosity has made a deep and lasting impact on my church and ministry, as well as on my own life.

"Neil is a visionary and a realist—an uncommon combination—and this book represents both sides of him well. It is a summary of biblical truth and hard-earned life lessons that will challenge you to achieve more in every area of your life."

—Tommy Barnett, author, senior pastor of Phoenix First Assembly of God, and co-pastor of the Los Angeles Dream Center

"I have been in the fitness business now for over sixty years. I have been given many national awards and a unanimous resolution by the California Legislature for my over fifty years of dedication to the fitness of the citizens of California.

"However, what I am most proud of are the many people I have mentored. Of all of these people, Neil Schober was by far the fastest learner I ever worked with. I remember mentoring Neil when he was a very young man, now over 35 years ago; he was very smart and driven.

"If you want to glean a lifetime of experience and wisdom, I would recommend reading this treasure. I found Neil's book to be very inspiring and very interesting. In fact, I couldn't put it down."

—Ray Wilson, designer of the LifeCycle Exercise Bike

"Neil Schober has been a great inspiration to the businesspeople at The City Church. We have observed the way he responds to the storms and testings in his life and family, and we have learned from him. He is a great example: a hard worker, diligent in business, faithful in church attendance, and generous in giving.

"Marlene and I value his friendship and input in business matters. It is our joy to be called his 'business pastors.'

"This book will be a textbook to anyone wanting to succeed in business. His wisdom is invaluable!"

—Don Ostrom, business pastor at The City Church, Seattle

"I have worked for and been mentored by Neil for over twenty-two years. His teachings have been instrumental in transforming me into the successful person I am today. He challenged me to be great not just in business, but to be successful in all aspects of life. You will not find a more transparent and candid person in leadership to learn from. I thank God that he sent him into my life to be my coach. I would not be where I am without him."

—Eric Stearns, CEO, Emerald City Athletic Clubs

"Strawberry Fields Forever is truly inspiring and life changing. I couldn't put it down. It grabs you from the first paragraph and pulls you into a life filled with God's possibilities! I have known Neil for over sixteen years and have witnessed the miracles of God in and through his life and business as he lived the principles in this riveting book. Neil is a leader in the marketplace and within the local church, and he is a bridge between the two. In this book, Neil lays out that the marketplace was and is the focal point for the church to bring about a reformation of our society. It is a must read for pastors and entrepreneurs alike."

—Jude Fouquier, lead pastor at The City Church Ventura

"God has truly gifted Neil with not only the ability to make money, but to use his gift to extend the kingdom of God all over the world. We have personally been the recipients of his and his wife's generosity as they have given to our mission in Mexico. One of our churches, which seats seven hundred people, is the direct result of his generous gift.

"This masterpiece is a great testimonial to God's faithfulness and provision to the Schobers through their lifestyle of faith, work ethic, obedience, and spirit of generosity. These truths need to be taught to businesspeople, churches, and anyone who has money come through their hands all over the world!"

—Phil Jaquith, missionary, pastor, and church-planter in Mexico

To my loyal wife and best friend, Gina

Contents

	Foreword	1
	Introduction	2
01	Everything I Learned, I Learned in the Strawberry Fields	6
02	Who Is That Man in the Mirror?	24
03	From Rags to Riches	36
04	Falling Off the Cliff	64
05	Black Ice	76
06	Do the Right Thing, at the Right Time, All the Time	90
07	Discovering the Spirit of Generosity	106
08	Catching a God-Vision	128
09	The Building of a Champion	136
10	Building a Company That Lasts through Organized Effort	176
11	Love Never Fails	222
12	The Perfect Storm	248
13	Building a Solid Foundation	276
14	Take Your Land!	286
	Conclusion	308

Foreword

By Judah Smith
Lead Pastor, The City Church

I have had the privilege of knowing Neil Schober for over ten years, and in my mind, he is the epitome of a business leader. He has extraordinary faith, passion, and integrity. He is a gifted businessman who has prospered even in a very difficult economy.

Even more importantly, he is a committed husband and father. His marriage has lasted three decades, and his four children are successful, secure, and love their father deeply. That's a level of success that can't be argued with.

Neil and his wife Gina are some of the most generous people I know. They love people, and they never hesitate to use their resources to be a blessing. They will probably never know the extent to which their giving has made a positive impact around the world.

Neil is the perfect person to talk about earning more, saving more, and giving more—he does all three better than perhaps anyone I know. I regularly ask his advice on business matters in our church, and he has mentored many young people in business and financial matters.

Strawberry Fields Forever is half autobiography, half training manual for a new generation of businesspeople. It is a fascinating story of success, failure, and persistent faith.

Whether you are an entrepreneur, an executive, or an employee, this book will inspire you to believe for more and achieve more by the grace of God.

Introduction

Over the last few years, I have shared pieces of my story in various settings around the world. I have a passion to help others learn and apply the principles that were foundational to my success, so I usually talk about my journey: how I made and lost great sums of money and what I learned along the way.

After I finish speaking, inevitably someone will come up and ask me how they can get into the fitness business and make as much money as I have.

They have missed the point. The fitness industry isn't the key to success. And making millions of dollars is the wrong goal in the first place.

This book, then, is what I wish I could tell people. It's about how to discover your calling, why you need to be smart and work hard, and what it means to achieve success in every area of life.

My objective in writing this book is to show you how to achieve personal and financial success. I hope to blend the old-fashioned work ethic and commonsense principles I learned from my parents, my forty years' worth of experience in business, and ancient biblical truths that transcend time.

You'll discover a few things about me as you read, so I might as well spell them out up front.

First, I am a Christian. Christianity is more than a religion or a set of rituals to me—it is a relationship with Jesus that colors every aspect of my life. That's why this book contains references to God, the Bible, and morality.

I came to know Jesus after I was already involved in business, and it took me more years than I care to admit to really live out my Christianity in business. Had I understood the value of spirituality and morality earlier on, I am convinced I could have built a billion-dollar business and avoided incredible heartache and lost time.

You don't need to be a Christian to apply the principles I will share here, however. As a matter of fact, I know non-Christians who do a better job at some of these things than most Christians, and the results in their lives are very positive. I respect all beliefs, but I won't shrink back from sharing the truths and values that I believe business leaders need to know.

Second, I think God and man are supposed to work together. I don't believe for a minute that I deserve the credit for my successes, but I also know I would not have achieved the same level of success if I had sat around and done nothing. God works through us, not instead of us.

Third, I am a visionary. I appreciate people who are detail-oriented, but I don't have a lot of patience when they get so bogged down dealing with problems that they can't see the possibilities around them.

Fourth, I am pragmatic to a fault, so this book is full of straightforward and practical instruction. I might even come across as arrogant or outspoken. I'm really not that way. But at nearly sixty years of age, I am not as concerned about getting people to like me as I used to be. I'm more interested in what works. And I've learned a few things that work! And finally, I believe success is not measured by net worth.

If you make millions but lose your family, health, or relationship with God, your wealth and accomplishments will mean nothing.

I will share very personal experiences—some good, some bad. As you will probably pick up, I am a bit hardheaded; so a lot of what I know, I learned the hard way. I want to help you avoid the mistakes, anguish, and lost time I experienced.

I built a company in my early twenties that did nearly $100 million in sales annually. By my early thirties, we were broke and tens of millions of dollars in debt. By my forties and fifties, I had rebounded and built several successful companies that sold for many millions of dollars. But in the middle of my success, I nearly lost my family to divorce.

I believe that these real-life experiences and the lessons I gleaned along the way will benefit you. It is my hope that this book will encourage and empower you to discover your purpose and then fulfill it, bringing you much joy.

01

Everything I Learned, I Learned in the Strawberry Fields

Fifty years ago, my mom and dad sat me down and broke the news that I would start my first real job the next morning at five o'clock.

My father, always the enthusiastic worker, was excited to have his firstborn son join the work force of America at the ripe old age of eight. Back in 1961, the starting age for strawberry picking was about ten, but he told me I was going to get the jump on my competitors.

From his point of view, I was more than ready to attack and succeed, since he had started me a couple of years earlier working for ten cents an hour pulling weeds in the yard. He had bought me a leather pouch that attached to my belt buckle, and he would give me shiny silver dimes that I was free to spend on whatever I wanted, including my favorite treat, penny candy.

I loved penny candy, but I liked even more the sound of those silver coins clinking against each other. I guess it made me feel rich.

Mom sat silently as Dad explained that he would be waking me up about four in the morning, which is when he woke up every day, and that Mom would prepare a lunch consisting of a couple of sandwiches and some Hostess Twinkies. I was short and skinny even for an eight-year-old, but he instructed me to walk tall and get on the bus quickly and without hesitation.

The next day, my mom and dad saw their young son, the oldest of their five kids, out of the door before five o'clock. It was dark, cold, and scary, but kind of exhilarating, too.

I followed my dad's advice to walk confidently. I found a seat at the back of the bus. Most of the kids were several years older than I, so I just sat by myself and kept my mouth shut. It was an hour-long bus ride from Portland to Gresham, where the farm was. It was still dark when we arrived, but I could dimly see row after row of strawberry bushes.

We shuffled off the bus, one by one, and were appointed rows. We were instructed to pick all the berries, even the very small ones.

That was emphasized because the little ones were harder to pick and didn't fill up the crate as quickly as the big ones, so you made less money.

It was cold, damp, and miserable at first, but soon the sun came up. We began peeling off layers of clothing to keep cool. It was hard work, but things were going well.

I finished filling my first crate of berries and took it up to the checker who inspected it. It passed inspection, and to my delight I received a half-dollar coin—real silver back then.

"Wow!" I remember thinking to myself excitedly. "I just made fifty cents in an hour, five times more than I made pulling weeds!"

I went back to my row determined to pick my next crate of berries in less time. What seemed to be only a few minutes of work passed, then a whistle went off, letting us know that our thirty-minute lunch break had started.

That was when my nightmare began.

The big kids decided to have some fun with the little punk kid—that being me. First they stole my lunch. Then they surrounded me, hands full of strawberries, and moved in for the kill. They crammed berries in my eyes, ears, mouth, and, of course, huge amounts down my pants. I fought hard, but to no avail; they simply overpowered me.

Somehow I didn't shed a tear—at least in front of them—and went back to my row frightened, humiliated, and determined never to return.

I walked into my house around four in the afternoon, dejected and discouraged. My mom greeted me. She could tell by my berry-stained clothing and sour attitude that things hadn't gone so well. She helped clean me up, scrubbing my hands with Clorox to remove stains. Then she prepared dinner while I retreated to my room to lick my emotional wounds.

As usual, my father walked through the door at 6:15 p.m. He summoned me to give him a glorious report of how well I had done on my first day on the job. Over dinner, I described in detail the horrors of my day and firmly informed him that I was not going back for further punishment.

But I was no match for my father. My mother remained quiet as he stated unequivocally that I would return tomorrow and face my adversaries. His point, if I remember clearly, was that I had no broken bones, only a bruised ego. He said all little kids must endure this type of initiation from the big kids, and in time, if I didn't show fear, they would let up on me. He told me that this was the highest form of bravery and courage, since at that point in my life I wasn't able to defend myself.

The next day I was on the bus.

Baseballs and Bicycles

To my relief and surprise, the older boys left me alone and in time treated me kind of like their little brother. A strange comradeship was born between us. Maybe they respected me because I continuously picked more then them and therefore made more money.

Every season, the person who picked the most berries won a fifty-dollar cash bonus. Winning that money quickly became my burning desire. My biggest threat was a group of girls who simply could move their fingers faster than I.

I concluded that the only way I could achieve my goal was to work longer than them. I was the first one off the bus in the morning, I worked through lunch, and I was the last to leave, many times barely catching the bus as it pulled out.

The strawberry season drew to a close. I can't remember who won the prize (that season, anyway—I won it many of the following seasons), but I was making more money than I could believe—usually four or five dollars a day in glorious silver half-dollars.

After the strawberry season ended, we moved on to raspberries and blackberries, then finished up the summer picking beans.

One day my mom asked me if I wanted to open a savings account to protect my money. I had accumulated a couple of hundred dollars from my work, and the thought that it could be stolen was instantly horrifying.

Together we walked downtown to the bank, a mile or two from our house. Back then, most average-income families only had one car, which the father usually drove to work.

The bank looked like a fortress to me. It was made of solid red brick, had high ceilings, and seemed impenetrable.

My mom led me up to the bank teller. She was pleasant and professional. I told her that I wanted to open a savings account. She had my mom and me fill out the paperwork, and then she explained that I would receive interest on my money. She gave me a green passbook that she had filled out with $200.00 under the "deposit" column.

After leaving the bank, I asked my mother what the bank lady meant when she said the bank would pay me interest. My mom carefully explained to me a couple of fundamentals about interest and about the difference between simple and compound interest. She told me the bank would pay me compound interest at 4 percent on my money. In other words, I would begin to earn interest on my interest. It was kind of like babies having babies.

The idea that I could make money without working captured my imagination. "How can banks afford to protect my money if they also pay me so much money?" I asked.

"Trust me, they make a lot of money by loaning to people who want to build houses and other things. They charge much higher interest when they loan out money." She looked at me seriously, like this mattered a lot, and continued. "You loan your money to the bank, and they loan it to others. Most people would rather borrow and get what they want right away, even though it costs them more than saving up and paying for it with cash. Most people don't have the discipline and the patience to save."

I got her message loud and clear. Saving was smarter than borrowing. Then she changed gears and said, "Let's go shopping!"

We went to my favorite stores: the sporting goods store and the bicycle store. My dream at the time (and for years to come) was to take the place of my hero, Mickey Mantle, playing center field for the powerful and then-unbeatable New York Yankees.

We entered the store, and my eyes were drawn like magnets to the most beautiful baseball glove I had ever seen. It had a price tag on it for twenty-five dollars. I wanted to run back to the bank that instant, withdraw my money, and buy the mitt of my dreams. I rationalized it in my mind, reasoning that it was so big that I would never need to buy another, and that surely it would help me become a major league ball player and help me make even more money.

My mom told me that the money in my bank account was mine, and I could do with it as I wished; but she warned me not to buy out of emotional impulse. She said it would be wise to sleep on it, and if I still wanted it the next day, I could buy it. I was afraid the glove would be sold, but I agreed.

Then we wandered over to the bicycle store. And there, of course, was the bike of my dreams: a powder blue, banana-seat Schwinn Sting-ray. I imagined how cool I would look doing wheelies through the neighborhood on that bike.

My mom said I could buy it if I chose, even though it cost fifty-nine dollars—a huge amount in those days. But again, she asked me to sleep on it first.

Looking back, one of the things I appreciate the most about my mom was that she continuously imparted wisdom to me but never forced it down my throat.

Grandpa Bill

On our way home, she shared details about her father, my Grandpa Bill. I was fascinated by the story.

He grew up on a farm in North Dakota with eleven brothers and sisters. When he was in sixth grade, his father made him quit school so he could work twelve to fourteen hours a day on the farm. He was paid very little for his work.

One day, he decided to leave. He hardly had any money, but his discouragement and the idea of working on the farm the rest of his life were motivation enough to head out on his beat-up motorcycle.

Eventually he ended up in Great Falls, Montana, where he learned carpentry and became a journeyman carpenter. He saved his money zealously. He married his wife, Ann, and had three children.

Shortly after the birth of their third child—my mom—the Great Depression hit. The construction business came to a standstill. From 1930 to 1933, my grandfather made a total of $938. Amazingly, his family never missed a meal, had plenty of heat in a severely cold climate, and had a nice home to live in, all because he saved and was prepared for the worst to happen.

He had invested his savings in what he knew best—houses. He owned three houses, and the rent he received from them got his family through those rough times, maybe the toughest and bleakest days America has ever faced. He spent most of his time while unemployed volunteering as a handyman for his church.

Eventually things got better, and in time he started his own home construction company. It was not the biggest company around, my mom told me, but he built some of the nicest custom homes in his city. Over the years, he developed a good reputation as a quality builder.

I remember Grandpa Bill taking me around town as a young boy, showing me the different homes he had built and telling me who lived in them. He had a great sense of accomplishment. It's inspiring to me that he accomplished all this with only a sixth-grade education. His family never wanted for anything; they always had more than enough.

After my mom finished the story of my grandfather's life, she reiterated the importance of savings. For some reason, that story and her advice stayed with me the rest of my life, and they saved me more than once from financial ruin.

The next morning, after sleeping on it and taking into account all that my mom had said, I announced to my parents that I would buy both the baseball mitt and the bike and still have over 50 percent left in savings. They looked at each other and shrugged their shoulders. That was approval in my mind, and I was out the door before another word could be said.

I ran to town, withdrew the money I needed to the penny, and within an hour was speeding through the neighborhood on my shiny new Schwinn bicycle. I tried to be cool, but I couldn't help smiling. I was so proud of my bike! I had purchased it through hard work and saving my money, and I still had plenty left in my savings account.

I always felt sorry for friends of mine that were forced to save everything. Their parents would not allow them to spend the money they earned on anything for themselves. In the end, I think it damaged their motivation to work hard and save.

Every summer, I looked forward to getting out of school and getting back to making money in the strawberry fields. As I got older, clothes became important to me; so after I saved 50 percent of what I made, that was mainly what I spent my earnings on. I always looked forward to the first day of school when I could sport my new purchases.

Although I was free to purchase the clothes I wanted, my mom influenced my opinion of what was a good deal and what was not. Her advice was, "Look for the best value, not just what is on sale." Value was always stressed over price.

She showed me how to identify quality material that wouldn't wear out and to pick conservative styles that would endure the changes in style. She took me into her closet and showed me an array of beautiful cashmere sweaters that she had owned for many years. Any of her acquaintances could attest that she always dressed with class. It was her opinion that colorful wool Pendleton shirts were warm, stylish, and best of all, would last a lifetime. I have to laugh because my son (who believe me is up to date on today's fashions) still wears the same kind of shirts.

Tough Love

As the oldest son, I was brought up with tough love. My parents loved me, but they didn't coddle me. They made sure to correct and discipline me as needed.

I remember being reprimanded by my dad for getting in a fistfight. He asked somewhat rhetorically, "How is it that I grew up in the streets of New York City and never got in a fight, and yet you get in fights all the time?"

Shortly after this, I came home and told my mom that my friend and I backed down from a fight.

She said, "You did what? No son of mine is ever going to back down from a fight!"

Yes, there was a bit of a mixed message there. Even she would admit it if she were alive today. What I think she was saying is that life is tough, and you better be prepared on all levels to defend yourself.

I am thankful for my father—a talented, principled, and disciplined man and a committed father. He worked hard and long to provide enough for our family so that my mother would not have to work.

I am also thankful for my mother, who was determined to raise children with strong character. Much of the wisdom I learned in life came from my mother's instruction. She was honorable in every way, and her primary goal was to raise quality, responsible children who were not dependent on anyone, except of course God. She taught me to always do my best. Although she was affectionate, she was careful not to create weakness in her children by fostering self-pity.

My only regret is not adhering to all the wisdom she taught me in my early years. She practically could have written the book of Proverbs. Maybe that is why it has become my favorite book in the Bible.

Young Man of Character

One hot July day toward the end of the strawberry picking season stands out in my mind. After a ten-hour day picking berries, I got off the bus and walked down the street to my house.

My mother met me at the door. To my surprise, she was nearly hysterical. I remember her hollering something to the effect that she "didn't raise a dishonest thief."

My response was an indignant, "What in the world are you talking about?"

It turned out the owner of the strawberry fields had called the house and accused me of stealing strawberries. She told my mother that in all her years as an owner, no one had picked as many strawberries as I had in one season. It was simply impossible to pick that much, she said, and somehow I must be stealing. So I was fired.

I told my mother that I would call her and clear things up. My mom handed me the phone, and I called the owner and explained that, in fact, I had not picked all the strawberries myself. A lot of the kids who went out there were not interested in making money, so they spent the whole time talking. The owner knew that was true. I told her that when my friends would wander over to where I was, I would encourage them to pick berries and put them in my crate while we talked.

There was a long hesitation; then she basically apologized for jumping to a wrong conclusion. I asked her to talk with my mother and assure her that my behavior was not dishonest. Both my mom and I were relieved that this situation was cleared up and that my name and our family's reputation were not marred.

My mother then talked to me at length about being a young man of character. She emphasized that honesty, truthfulness, integrity, and upright behavior in all I did were much more important than anything I could accomplish.

I wish I could say I took that counsel to heart as much as her teaching on savings and wise spending. But it took a colossal business failure a few years later to drive home the value of personal and business integrity.

Dirty Money

In time, I graduated from the strawberry fields to working in fast food restaurants. That included flipping burgers at Jack in The Box, where I made $1.35 an hour; after tax and food deductions, I received $1 an hour.

That was better than picking berries, but my friends' fathers had landed them construction jobs that paid as high as ten dollars per hour, and it aggravated me that my father would not use his influence to get me a high-paying job. He believed that hunting down the job myself was more valuable than the wages themselves. He also told me it was wiser to work for commission than an hourly job, because you weren't limited in what you could make. At the time, these ideas seemed conflicting, and they frustrated me; but now they make sense.

After working fifty hours one week and clearing only fifty dollars, I was thoroughly motivated to find a better job. Then I saw an advertisement at the school office for janitorial work that offered $2.85 per hour, more than double what I had been making.

I jumped in my car and was soon standing in front of my soon-to-be employer, Mrs. Harriet Wily. The reason I remember her name so well is because she was ten steps beyond a perfectionist. Every night I would receive a handwritten note critiquing my performance in detail. Those notes drove me crazy. It was impossible to please that woman!

But the pay was good. I learned how to wash huge numbers of windows quickly and without leaving streaks. I could strip and wax floors so well that I could see my face reflecting in twenty thousand square feet of floor. The worst part of the job was every day having to clean hundreds of ashtrays and all the toilets and urinals. To this day it aggravates me when I see someone spit tobacco into a urinal—if they only knew how much work and time it takes to remove that disgusting stuff.

Never once did Mrs. Harriet Wily ever compliment me on my work, but she gave me something more valuable than a compliment—she taught me excellence, a gift I would carry with me the rest of my life. She taught me what my mother had often preached, that, "A job worth doing is a job worth doing well."

Every May, when I was finishing my spring quarter at college, she would call to ask me if I would work for her. I always accepted her offer, knowing that this was the best compliment I could ever receive.

Over the years, I earned pay raises and stretched my hours by learning to clean carpets as well. But I wanted to make more money. It occurred to me I could strip and wax floors at doctors' and dentists' offices on my own and make some additional money.

I asked Mrs. Wily if I could use her big stripping machine from time to time to do these special projects if my idea worked out. Hesitantly she agreed, warning me that her jobs came first and that the quality must not suffer or the deal was off. Down deep, I think she admired my tenacity and creativity to increase my earnings.

I began my quest, and soon I had my first taker, a dentist. He said if I could guarantee him that I could get the job done during the weekend and have everything sparkling clean by seven o'clock Monday morning, we had a deal. He asked me how much I charged, and courageously I told him $300, knowing that my costs would be about $100. He accepted on the spot.

I had a hard time holding back a smile. This was my first successful business deal, and it was more than exciting to me.

I completed the job on time and with excellence. He was elated with the shine I put on his floor and told me that he knew many other doctors and dentists who would love to hire me. Word spread quickly about my expertise on stripping and waxing floors, and the customers came.

There must have been a lack of quality service in that occupation back then because thirty years later, my wife took one of my daughters to get braces and the orthodontist asked, "You aren't married to Neil Schober, are you?"

She said, "Yes, I am. Do you know him?"

He replied, "He waxed my floors many years ago. Never in all my years of practice has someone done such a good job." It turned out that he was that first dentist who had hired me for $300.

I was soon forced into hiring a work force that consisted mainly of my sisters and friends. My sisters were excellent workers because they were trained by my mom and dad. My friends were not quite up to par and really didn't like taking orders from their buddy, but even though at times I had to work side by side with them to get an excellent final product, we got the job done. In the future I learned—painfully, at times—not to hire friends and not to make employees your friends.

I was not yet twenty, but I had increased my income to over thirty dollars per hour, which was very good money in the early seventies. All it took was hard, excellent work, along with a little imagination and the courage to act on an idea.

When people asked what my profession was, I stated proudly that I was a janitor. Never once did I think that doing janitorial work was below me. Had I not gone into the fitness business, I would have built maybe the best janitorial company ever.

I bring this up to illustrate an important point that my parents taught me: all work is good. My mother often emphasized to me that I must do my best, whether as janitor, garbage collector, or president of the United States.

Many times I have encountered employees who for some reason thought certain jobs were below them or were not part of their so-called destiny. My real pet peeve is when a lackluster employee says he will do a great job for me when I promote him to manager. I always think, "That will be a cold day in hell."

Old-Fashioned Work Ethic

My parents had their disagreements, like most married couples do, but they stood united on the value of self-reliance. They believed that until a person could effectively take care of themselves, they had no business thinking about getting married and having a family.

The so-called "golden rule" in our family was to never expect or take anything from the government. They believed it was a trap, that it created weakness of character and slothfulness.

I tested those beliefs once when I thought I would take a quarter off from college. I let my dad know that I was going on unemployment. Thank God I was on the other end of the phone, or I would have ended up in the hospital—at best. He was outraged. I tried to tell him that I probably would never be unemployed again, so what was the big deal? But none of it went over too well.

Now, years later, I understand how easy it is to fall into the insidious trap of dependency. Don't get me wrong—I will devote a large portion of this book to the importance of giving and helping the impoverished of the world, beginning with your next-door neighbor, if the need arises. But it is one thing to receive aid in time of need, and quite another to have a lifestyle of living off of the work of others.

I was about twenty years old when I was approached by a friend who was a hard worker, a straight-A student, and one of the smartest guys I knew. He wanted me to meet this guy who had invented a new type of refrigeration process for milk and juices that would allow these perishable products to be transported without keeping the temperature low. It was going to revolutionize the cooling process, like pasteurization had done many years ago.

The minimum investment was $5,000, and the promise was that within a year, we would get a return of at least ten times—and maybe up to one hundred times—our investment.

I only had $3,000 because I had just purchased a brand new Volkswagen for $2,200. So I asked my parents to meet this person and see if they thought it was a good deal. My parents said they would listen, but it sounded kind of fishy to them. We met with the individual, who was both the inventor and the marketer. He was smooth, and within a few minutes my parents had become at least neutral to the idea.

My mom agreed to lend me $2,000 at simple interest of 7 percent, and I agreed to pay her back at $107 per month until it was paid. The kicker was that she wanted the title to my car as collateral in case I failed to make payment.

Six months later, the guy disappeared. That was the first time I was burned and probably the most painful!

I put my beloved car up for sale and received more money then I paid for it—the first and last time I would ever make money on the sale of a car. It was a painful, memorable day for both my mother and me. Years later, she told me that that was one of the hardest things she ever did, especially when I walked out of the door on my way back to college, hitchhiking over a hundred miles each way.

Although I would make more foolish investments over the years, I am sure this early, very painful lesson saved me millions of dollars in the long run. But the best lesson, even beyond the need for good judgment, was the principle of taking full responsibility for my actions.

Both my mother and father believed in working and playing hard. Principles relating to money and responsibility were very clear to them. Now, looking back over fifty years, what they taught me has been tested and proven.

One of my favorite books in the Bible is Proverbs. My parents weren't too big on reading the Bible, but they adhered to many of its concepts and precepts without knowing it.

The operative word here is "adhered." I wouldn't describe my parents as religious, although we were raised Catholic, but they knew what they believed, and they lived it. Many people know what is right, but they just don't do it.

In this book, I will answer many questions about creating a life of personal and financial freedom. I hope to inspire you to pursue and achieve success.

More importantly, I want to motivate you to begin a personal quest toward finding real truth for your life. What worked for me may not work for you. Success isn't a formula that can be taught; it is the result of a lifestyle of right choices and wise actions within the unique context of every person's life.

Through introspection and inspiration, we can find what brings us personal satisfaction on the deepest, most spiritual level. No matter your age or life situation, it is never too soon or too late to start your journey toward truth.

I am eternally grateful to have had parents who believed in tough love. They took parenting very seriously and realized that equipping their children for life in this sometimes cruel world is more important than fun and games.

That's not to say that we never had fun. One of my mom's favorite statements was, "Let's get all this work done so we can go play." My mom loved competitive games more than just about anyone I've ever known. But building in her children a solid foundation of frugality, prudence, industriousness, personal responsibility, enthusiasm, optimism, and courage under fire took precedence over all else. Although I wandered far from these ideas at times, they were always there, trying to guide me back on track.

I am certain I would never have made it without their wise instruction, and I am blessed to have had them as parents.

02

Who Is That Man in the Mirror?

I reached over and turned off the alarm clock off, then picked up ten hits of speed from my nightstand and swallowed them with some water. Slowly, I felt my body come back to life.

I stumbled into the bathroom, hung over and sick, trying to get it together. I looked in the mirror and my own bloodshot, swollen eyes stared back. It jolted me. Who was that man? Who had I become?

It was 1973, the fall quarter of my senior year at college, and for the first time in a long time, I was really scared. Somehow, I had lost all concept of who I was. My identity had been stolen or had just melted away without me being aware of it.

I lay back down and began to think about what had gone wrong.

Don Juan Is Born

It started in ninth grade. We were about to play the last game of the football season. For the first time in the history of our school, we were undefeated. That afternoon, we would play the other undefeated school for the championship.

In the locker room, the coach personally wrapped my ankles—a great honor—and told me that I would be starting on both offense and defense. He said that because of my enthusiasm and hustle, he was promoting me over the faster guy on the team. He looked me straight in the eyes and assured me that I would do well. I was so nervous I felt like I was going to be starting in the Super Bowl.

That game was magical for me. I intercepted four passes and ran one back for a touchdown. We won the championship. I was floating on absolute elation.

That evening, some of my teammates and I walked a few miles to where another team was going to play a game. On the way, they stopped off at their favorite corner store and stole a few bottles of wine. I had seen them do this before. They had their strategy down, and it worked without fail.

Like usual, they tried to get me to drink some of the wine. I had always turned them down before. I didn't see why they needed alcohol or marijuana to have fun.

But this time, in my excitement over winning the championship, I said, "Sure, give me a drink!"

Immediately, I "got it." No inhibitions. Rush. Brotherhood. And . . . girls. I had always been shy around girls, but suddenly I felt like Don Juan!

I remember walking home that night, arm in arm with my teammates, singing, "We are the Rams, the mighty, mighty Rams! Everywhere we go, people want to know who we are, so we tell them..." We must have repeated that dumb song a thousand times that night.

After that, I never even considered socializing without at least a beer in my hand. Beer, pot, girls, and fighting soon became my focus. The only exception was work—somehow I was able to separate parties and work, regardless of how hung over I was.

My ego centered on the girls in my life and the countless fistfights I won. Fighting gave me a thrill that I sought to fulfill every chance I had. I wasn't very big, but while juiced up on some form of alcohol, I would somehow come out the victor. This was almost a sport in my neighborhood, so there were always takers who wanted to prove their courage and manhood.

I wasn't a good student because I couldn't read well. Years later I found out I had dyslexia, but at the time people thought I was dumb or lazy. Teachers couldn't understand why I stumbled over the easy words when they asked me to read aloud. The deep humiliation I felt in front of my classmates had a negative effect on my self-esteem for years.

Even today, though I probably read more books than 95 percent of people, I would sound pretty stupid if someone had me read out loud. The reading disorder never goes away unless it is corrected at an early age through brain exercises, as my son Ian was able to do years later. But when I was growing up, not many teachers even understood dyslexia, let alone knew how to cure it.

Instead of overcoming my limitation, I took the easy way out and started to cheat. My grade point average was a 3.0 only because I mastered the art of cheating. When I applied for college, I probably had an eighth-grade education.

My sports involvement fell apart since practicing took too much time, and before long I had completely given up sports. My senior year in high school, I didn't even turn out for baseball, a sport I had always loved. Partying, fighting, girls, and work dominated my time.

To the Moon and Back

As I lay there that morning, hung over and sick, those memories brought me pain and shame. I had hurt so many people—my parents, my friends, some really nice girls. Broken relationships and missed opportunities littered my high school career.

In my mental journey, I started thinking about my freshman year in college. After high school, I had decided to attend Western Washington University in Bellingham, Washington, about a hundred miles from where my family was living at the time.

It was the height of the Vietnam War. Absolutes were despised and rebellion was valued. We created a culture of dissent. Our famous battle cry was "sex, drugs, and rock & roll." John Lennon, who declared that he was more important and popular than God, was my hero.

Drugs were commonplace. We could even smoke pot in some of our classes. For a dollar we could "take off to the moon" on LSD. We would land in about twenty-four hours if we didn't lose our mind, like a friend of mine did right in front of me. It was insanity mixed with naiveté. That was the most dangerous part—we thought we had it all figured out.

By the end of my freshman year, I had flunked out with one D and four Fs. This was a sobering reality for me, because I never saw myself as a college flunk-out.

The summer after my freshman year, I drove from Seattle up to Bellingham to try to convince the dean of students to give me one more chance. He compared my good grades in high school and my low grades on my college entrance exams, and he asked me why I had scored so low. I lied and told him I didn't do well on tests. Actually, I was nearly illiterate.

Through some great salesmanship, I convinced him to give me one quarter to get my grades up to a C average, or a 2.0. If I failed to accomplish this, I would take his advice and go to a vocational school. That was a great motivator, since doing anything mechanical completely confused me.

Driving back from Bellingham to Seattle, I made up my mind that I would never cheat again. No matter how hard or long I had to study, I would achieve my goal of getting a 2.0.

School started, and so did my new lifestyle of studying. I began showing up at the library when it opened at seven in the morning, carrying my books and a thirty-two-cup coffee pot. I would set up shop in one of the glass-enclosed cubicles, studying all day and leaving only to attend class. I usually stayed until the library closed at ten o'clock at night.

Looking back, I was pathetic. I could hardly take notes while the professor lectured. I would look around, and it was a breeze for everyone but me.

Finally I came upon a lifesaver that was actually legal—Cliffs Notes. They even sold them in the student bookstore. These notes summarized books on Shakespeare so I could understand them, and they cut my reading time in half.

I became good friends with the librarians. They would help me find books so I could write my own term papers. Before, I had always bribed my friends to write these papers for me—so to write a paper all on my own was a big deal. Thank God for my English 101 teacher, who spent countless hours teaching me how to write. I remember getting my first essay paper back: a C minus. I was overjoyed because I passed with no illegal help from anyone.

I built friendships with my professors, and they helped tutor me. I began to get passing grades. At the end of my fall quarter, I barely accomplished my goal of straight C's in all my classes. Truthfully, that was one of the greatest accomplishments of my life.

But there was one problem.

Over the Rainbow

A friend of mind had introduced me to a substance called speed—white, crisscross pills that helped hyperactive people like me slow down and concentrate for long periods of time. It was wonderful. I could study for twenty-four hours at a time without getting tired.

My grade point increased to over a 3.0 average; one quarter I got an unbelievable 4.0.

But like all drugs, I began to build up a tolerance and had to increase my dosage. Then I wouldn't be able to fall asleep, so I would drink some form of alcohol in order to pass out. And the next day, I would start the cycle again. It was a daily routine.

I kept my heavy partying confined to the weekends, when I would use an assortment of drugs and alcohol to get as high as possible. For nearly four years, I don't think I had one day of complete sobriety.

During my senior year, something strange began to happen to me. I got two D's during my fall quarter, after getting straight A's the summer quarter before. I went to both of my professors, who were now my friends, and asked what the deal was with the D's.

Both responded the same way, saying essentially, "Did you read the garbage you turned in?" They were serious, so I reread my essay exams, and it was like a third-grader had written them.

Without realizing it, I had gone "over the rainbow," as we called it. My behavior had become erratic. I was no longer a stoned-out, peace-loving hippy: I spent every weekend at some kegger, drinking heavily and getting into fistfights.

I was out of control, and I knew it.

Chased by God

Lying there in my bed, strung out on drugs and alcohol, with sirens going off in my mind, I suddenly began to think about God. I was raised a Catholic and knew a lot about God and how He sent His son to earth to die for our sins, but it had never really resonated with me. It was a neat little story, but that was it.

Once during the peak of my rebellion, my father tried to talk some sense into me about going back to church. I told him to take his God and put him where the sun didn't shine. My father reacted by telling me I wasn't welcome in his home and to stay away from the rest of the family because he didn't want me to influence them. I had become the prodigal son—minus the inheritance.

Strangely, after I got up from my bed that day, I couldn't stop thinking about God. That afternoon I went to The Ram, a tavern a couple of miles away, but my heart just wasn't in it. Around midnight, I put down my pool stick and ran all the way home in my cowboy boots, with God on my mind.

During Christmas break I travelled down to Vancouver, Washington, where I had grown up. I went with a friend of mine, Bob Sims, and we stayed at his parents' house for about a week. Every night we went out partying, and I would somehow get in a fight. He was a hippy type and thought fighting was barbaric, so he didn't appreciate this kind of behavior.

Each afternoon about one o'clock, I would wake up hung over. Bob's mom always had coffee and breakfast ready for me. She and I would spend the entire afternoon talking about God, and she would try to explain the difference between knowing all about God and knowing him personally.

She did not condemn me for my behavior. I shared the raw and ugly reality of who I was, and all she showed me in return was love and acceptance.

I never saw her after that week, but she was an angel sent to me from heaven. The strange thing, looking back on it, was that whenever the subject of God came up, Bob excused himself.

Then came winter quarter of my senior year. One day at the library, I bumped into an old girlfriend by the name of Tina. She was a hotheaded Italian who was never afraid to let me know what was on her mind. She had broken up with me shortly after my twenty-first birthday. At the time, she called me a drunk and a loser. She said that I would make the worst husband and father, and she didn't want to waste any more time with me.

We began to talk. She seemed different, more peaceful. She asked me for forgiveness for how she treated me and other personal issues. I sensed the same spirit that I had felt with my friend's mom.

I asked, "Tina, what's different about you?"

She replied. "I got born again this summer."

I kind of knew what she was referring to but wanted her to spell it out. So I asked with a little cynicism in my voice, "Oh, so you're a Jesus freak now?"

Instead of reacting to my insult like she normally would have, she began talking about her relationship with Jesus.

I said, "Come on. We were both brought up Catholic. What's the difference?"

She opened her little Bible to John 3:16 and read, "For God loved the world so much that he gave his one and only Son, so that everyone who believes in him will not perish but have eternal life."

She went on to tell me the story of a Jewish Pharisee named Nicodemus who had a secret conversation with Jesus late at night. Although Nicodemus was well-educated and had even memorized great portions of the Old Testament, Jesus said that unless he was "born again" by the Spirit of God, he would not be saved. Jesus continued by saying that the Spirit is like the wind—you can't see it, but it is very real.

Tina told me that it doesn't matter how much you know about God or even how good you are—what is important for eternal salvation and an ongoing relationship with God is believing that Jesus is the son of God, that we are sinners, and that He died for our sins.

My immediate reaction to this was negative: if I remember right, I rolled my eyes in contempt and left. Knowing Tina, I'm sure she wasn't fazed.

My mind screamed no, but my heart screamed yes. I couldn't get God off my mind or heart. It was like he was chasing me down. No one knew it, but there was a battle going on inside of me.

One bitterly cold and rainy night, I rang the bell of Tina's apartment and asked if I could come in. I'm sure she was suspicious of an old boyfriend showing up at her door, but she reluctantly let me in anyway.

Without introduction or hesitation, I told her, "I want to know Jesus."

She looked at me and took my hand, and we knelt down together, and she helped me say my first real prayer ever. I am sure my words weren't too articulate, but my heart was pure and humble before God.

That was the most defining moment of my life.

Without understanding it at the time, I had been changed from the inside out. Although I would face many personal struggles in the coming years, my inner self and my perception had been renewed.

It is the Christian belief that at the point of conversion, the Holy Spirit actually takes residence inside of you. In other words, God himself lives in this invisible place we call our hearts.

I can't prove it scientifically, but after nearly forty years, it is even more real to me today than it was that cold, rainy evening.

Some might say, "It's the same old story of a weak person, strung out on drugs and alcohol, who needed a crutch to make it through life." There is some truth to that, actually, because we all need help in life. But I had everything I could want—popularity, parties, money, girls, fights. I was strong and self-confident. But until I found God, I was empty, searching, and dissatisfied on the inside.

Clearing My Head

Overnight, I had a new life. Within days I was able to quit all forms of drugs and alcohol. I even quit smoking.

I went back to working out at the gym and running five miles a day. Most mornings at daybreak, I would mix protein with a couple of raw eggs and go for a run, breathing the clear, clean air and loving a life of sobriety for the first time in years.

My school studies were a breeze. It was now my spring quarter, and all I had left were easy elective classes. I had enough credits accumulated for majors in both economics and sociology, so I spent most of my free time studying the Bible, sometimes ten to twelve hours a day.

I had tried to read the Bible before and was bored by it, but now it seemed electric to me. I couldn't get enough of it. The story that captured my imagination the most was how the God of the universe loved humankind, his prized creation, so much that he sent Jesus to die a brutal death on the cross at the hands of his own creation.

I was amazed to learn that Jesus' birth, life, death, and resurrection had been predicted three hundred times over a period of thousands of years by many different prophets in the Old Testament scriptures. To me the evidence was overwhelming.

What really moved me was that the maker of all things chose to introduce himself to mankind through his son Jesus in such a humble way. I couldn't believe he would be born in a cold barn, surrounded by farm animals and filth. Or that thirty-three years later, after healing the sick, restoring sight to the blind, and even raising the dead, he would be beaten, abused, insulted, spit upon, slugged in the face, and whipped. Then, he suffered an excruciating death nailed to a cross.

What kind of God would allow this to happen when he could have stopped it at any moment? As I read and studied, I saw that God loves mankind so much that he reached out to us. He passionately desires that we recognize his love and the gift of salvation through his son.

This simple but profound realization of God's love for humanity has been an anchor for me on several occasions when my life was in chaos and bad things were happening everywhere I looked.

03

From Rags to Riches

My new life was good. I went to class, read my Bible and attended church regularly, and worked out like a fanatic.

I was a member of an athletic club called Family Fitness Center. Physical fitness, especially weight lifting, had been my hobby ever since junior high. I was undersized for sports like football, but lifting heavy weights helped me pack on up to fifty pounds of muscle, enabling me to be more competitive in sports. Now I worked out as a release and for physical discipline.

It was May of 1974, and spring quarter was almost over. All I had left after that was to write a paper on a project I had recently done in a group home for troubled teenagers. I planned to write it during the summer or fall quarter. Although I was happier than I had been in years, I had no idea what I was going to do after I graduated.

I had thought about going into social work. That was why I did the project with troubled teenagers. However, I didn't think I had the patience for it, plus the pay was low, and there was little financial future. Those things wouldn't have mattered so much if I were passionate about that career, but the bottom line was, I wasn't.

The only idea I had was starting my own janitorial company. Money was important to me, and I knew I could make a lot doing janitorial work—mainly because most people looked down on it, which created a large demand for quality service. But the idea of scrubbing dirty urinals and ashtrays the rest of my life just didn't capture my imagination.

I remember sitting in a glass cubicle in the library that might as well have had my name on the door, since I had occupied it nearly nonstop for the last three years. I lowered my head, closed my eyes, and asked God to give me a job where I could help people and make good money.

I think I was hoping to hear a loud voice from heaven tell me what to do with my life, but I heard nothing. Somewhat discouraged, I packed my books and headed for the gym.

Like usual, I started with sit-ups to strengthen my abdominal muscles. Just as I was finishing my last repetition, a woman tapped me on the shoulder. It was one of the club managers. She got right to the point. "Would you like a job here at Family Fitness Center?"

I was caught off guard, but I replied, "How much do you pay?"

"Two dollars per hour."

That was less than motivating, but her next words struck a chord deep inside me. "It's obvious that you know more about exercise than anyone else here. I will give you free rein to teach and educate members on fitness any way you would like."

I didn't even hesitate. "You've got a deal."

Built for This

To this day, I'm surprised I agreed so quickly to such a low-paying job, especially since I almost had my college degree and could easily make thirty dollars per hour stripping and waxing floors. Somehow, intuitively, I knew it was the right decision.

I began to teach exercise to men on Tuesdays, Thursdays, and Saturdays. Back then, men and women used the gym on alternate days. The club was equipped primarily with passive equipment—vibrating machines that supposedly jiggled off the fat, or rollers that people leaned against that rolled off the excess weight. However, there was a limited amount of weight machines and some dumbbells and benches, so I could use those to design effective workout programs.

The first day I arrived on the job, I knew that I would do this the rest of my life. Everything about it charged me up. I knew more about exercise and nutrition than anyone else there, and I was passionate about fitness. It was like God had been preparing me for this type of work my whole life.

Many of my college professors used the gym, and it was gratifying to see the tables turned. Now they were listening intently to me and depending on my knowledge and instruction to achieve their fitness goals. It was also kind of funny to see them dressed down in white T-shirts and shorts instead of their distinguished suits. Most of them had skinny little arms and legs and potbellies. Ironically, these were the men that I had felt intimidated by for the last four years.

I started out as a part-time employee, but once summer came, I wanted to work full-time. They couldn't give me enough hours as a fitness instructor, so we worked out a deal where part of the time I did janitorial work and part of the time I taught fitness.

I loved it. Even though I wasn't earning much money, I was full of enthusiasm from the minute I arrived to when I left twelve hours later.

I worked with stroke victims, hugely overweight people, and young guys who wanted to gain muscle for sports or just feel better. Many of them achieved wonderful results through my inspiration, education, and accountability. They began to refer their friends, and my following increased.

My First Club

In August of 1974, I was promoted to general manager of the club. A couple of months later, I had to make one of the biggest decisions of my life up to that point.

The owner of the club, Fred Sessions, offered me a promotion: manager at another Family Fitness Center club he had just built, in Lynnwood, Washington. I would have to quit college and move a hundred miles south.

To the absolute displeasure of my father, I accepted the job. He believed that anything you started you should finish, especially since I had spent so much time and money on my education. He also wasn't excited that I was going to receive just $300 a month plus 10 percent of the profits—which, I admitted after he asked, were zero. He thought I had lost my mind.

My reasoning was that I could finish college anytime, and I was only going to do janitorial work after I graduated anyway. So to do something that excited me and that I was good at was an easy decision. In retrospect, you could say I was following my destiny. I didn't think of it that way at the time—I was just responding to my heart's desire, illogical though it was.

I moved down to Lynnwood, filled with excitement, and started my job. I was the enthusiastic general manager of a tiny fitness club—less than five thousand square feet—with very little exercise equipment. The walls barely had paint on them. The locker rooms and showers had cement floors and picnic benches as seats. The only real plus was that we had locker rooms for both men and women so they could use the club facilities every day except Sundays, when we were closed.

Fred, the owner, sat me down and basically said, "Here are the keys to the club. Do your best to make a profit, and I'll see you in a month." He wasn't too big on training or motivational speeches.

We had a total of thirty members. I had no money to advertise, though it probably wouldn't have done me any good since I didn't know the first thing about advertising or even sales, for that matter.

It was so slow that between one and four o'clock in the afternoon, there wouldn't be a single person in the club. My staff of two people was depressed, and so was I. One of my staff, the owner's daughter, calculated that I was making even less than they were. I worked twelve hours a day, five or six days a week, for just $300 a month. That worked out to eighty-six cents an hour, since there were no profits.

As the days passed, the energy and drive to be successful were sucked out of me. One day, Fred showed up. He asked how I was doing. I muttered something, but the defeated look on my face answered his question the clearest.

He took me out to breakfast. He hardly spoke a word during the meal, but as he paid the check, he matter-of-factly said that I had thirty to sixty days to show a profit, or he would replace me or shut the club down. His hobby was riding motorcycles, and he told me he would be traveling around for a while, and my performance would determine his decision when he got back.

We went back to the club, then he drove off. I had no direction or answers. I just knew that I loved the fitness business, but I was failing miserably at it.

Minutes later, to my surprise, a friend of mine whom I hadn't seen in years walked through the door. We greeted each other and talked about the good old days in high school, and then he asked me how I liked the fitness business.

I answered truthfully, "Great! Except for one problem—I am failing horribly, and I'll probably either get fired or the club will be shut down because of the terrible job I'm doing."

He looked at me kind of oddly and said, "Wait a minute. Someone gave me these two books. I haven't read them, but they might help you. I'll run out to my car and get them."

The Other Dimension

After he left, I stared at the books. They were *The Power of Positive Thinking*, by Norman Vincent Peal, and *Think and Grow Rich*, by Napoleon Hill. I had nothing to do for the next few hours because the few members we had wouldn't show up until around four o'clock, so I began reading.

I couldn't have imagined it at the moment, but those books and others like them would change my life. They taught me that God gave me a mind with huge creative powers, and through him, I could create just about whatever my heart desired.

I can't overemphasize the importance of this principle. The power found in creative thinking was a key catalyst in going from failure to success, from making $3,600 a year to making millions.

Creative, positive thinking enables average people to accomplish extraordinary things. It has little to do with intellectual power but much to do with "imagination power." If anything, I have seen that those with a very high IQ have the hardest time wrapping their minds around the concept of creative thinking.

These principles are accessible to anyone willing to take the time to learn them and put them into practice. In sad irony, the friend who gave me those first two books never read them himself. He was smart, good-looking, and had one of the most charismatic personalities I have known. But he died of acute alcoholism at the age of forty-five.

I often refer to this principle of creative, faith-filled thinking as the "other dimension." It is a place where the world of imagination is manifest in the physical world, where dreams become reality. I believe that this dimension can be inspired by God, the devil or evil, or by man himself.

These ideas are straight out of the Bible, but more has been written about them in secular writing than in Christian writing. Christians might call this type of thinking the "Law of Faith"; secular writers often refer to it as the "Law of Attraction." They are in essence talking about the same principle, although for Christians, the primary source of power and transformation is God, not one's one mind.

If you are interested in knowing more about biblical teaching on the power of faith and positive thinking, the following passages are a good starting point.

Hebrews 11:1 "Faith is the confidence that what we hope for will actually happen; it gives us assurance about things we cannot see."

Hebrews 11:3 "By faith we understand that the entire universe was formed at God's command, that what we now see did not come from anything that can be seen."

Romans 4:17 "[God] gives life to the dead and calls those things which do not exist as though they did." (NKJV)

These principles were understood and practiced by some of the earliest patriarchs, including Abraham, some four thousand years ago. Other Bible authors, including Paul and the author of the book of Hebrews, both writing about two thousand years ago, describe this way of thinking in detail.

Throughout my life, I have studied the most successful people in many fields, and I have discovered that most of them practice this philosophy in one form or another. I see more than enough evidence in the Bible, in my experience, and in simple logic to convince me that disciplining our thoughts and releasing our imagination is the most powerful secret that lies within human beings.

I want to take a moment to outline the steps of this process in the hope that it will enable you to achieve the success that God has destined for you.

Step 1: Get quiet.

Be still. Let your mind be at peace. Relax and try to become emotionless. Take deep breaths if necessary and imagine your body floating away. Go to the most relaxing place for you in your mind.

I used to imagine I was on a sailboat in the middle of a large body of water, sailing slowly along, lying on the deck as the sun warmed my entire body and melted away all my problems and anxieties. Why my mind took me there, I have no idea—I don't think I had ever been on a sailboat back then. It is amazing how your mind can teach you how to relax if you allow it to.

One of my favorite verses in Psalms says, "Be still, and know that I am God" (Psalm 46:10). It is framed as a command because stillness and peace are not human nature. Getting absolutely quiet is nearly impossible for many people in our culture. If that is you, you will have to work at it at first. In time, you will find that these quiet times become your favorite part of the day.

Step 2: Dream.

Use your imagination to create the life you would like to lead. Be comprehensive. Include all aspects of your life: relational, physical, spiritual, and material.

Note that this can be done on a selfish or evil level, or it can be done on a selfless and moral, or godly, level. I suggest that you ask God what He wants for you and analyze whom your life is meant to benefit, not just what would make you the most comfortable.

I strongly believe that God is best described by the word love. He is a good God, and we are His prized creation. He created us with a specific purpose that will bring us maximum joy and abundance in life. If you are interested in scriptures that support this view, take a look at Jeremiah 29:11, Matthew 7:11, and John 10:10, to list a few.

Incidentally, God is not a cheap God, either. In 1 Kings 5–6, God describes to Solomon how He wanted his temple built: no corners were cut and no expenses were spared.

This step is like building your dream home exactly the way you want it. Recently I had dinner at the newly-built home of a friend of mine on Lake Washington. The house sits on two acres of beautifully landscaped lawn. A hundred yards away, a private dock juts into the water, boats bobbing in the waves. The entrance to the house is majestic and absolutely breathtaking.

Inside, he and his wife designed each room in detail. The beauty flows from one room to another with luxury and taste. It fits perfectly with their Norwegian personalities—a little flair, but not too much; simple elegance; and (best of all) paid for with cash.

He left Norway as a young man, hoping to achieve success in America, where taxes were lower and opportunities greater. Now, thirty years later, he is living in his dream home.

Building and furnishing a luxury home is a good example of the process involved in creating the specific life that you (and hopefully God) want for yourself. Think of yourself as the architect of your life. Ask questions of your creative mind in that other dimension:

Do I want to be married? To what kind of person? What will my spouse look like? What personality will he or she have? How do

I want us to interact and communicate? Do we want children? If so, how will they be raised? How important are mutual religious beliefs? How will our personality, financial needs, and goals and desires complement each other?

What is my dream job? What complements my natural gifts and talents? Would I enjoy running my own business? What kind of business would it be? How big?

What kind of material things do I like? What type of house? What kind of car? What style of clothing?

What relationship do I want with my children and their children? What sort of parent and grandparent will I be for them? What will my friendships be like? What fun things will we do? Who will speak into my life? With whom will I share my deepest secrets?

What role will I play in each potential sphere of influence, such as church, neighborhood, and government? What charities will I support and be actively involved with?

What kind of person do I want to become—positive, optimistic, enthusiastic, outgoing, peaceful, quiet, self-controlled?

What do I want to look like physically? How important is it to me to be physically fit?

Some things you imagine will instantly resonate with you, and these will typically be easier to manifest into the physical world. It is important to evaluate your gifts and talents and find what ignites passion within you.

For the most part, people with naturally laid-back personalities aren't interested in taking over the world and will be happy with a nice, peaceful life. On the other hand, warrior types will never be happy unless they are creating a company that conquers the world, like a Bill Gates and Microsoft.

What you imagine won't always be easy, but that doesn't mean it's wrong, either. I am by nature a very high-strung individual, a triple type A. To morph my natural personality into a peaceful, laid-back person is a stretch for even the most creative thinker. But to a certain degree, it can be accomplished.

Design your life the way you and God want it, no bigger and no smaller. Don't allow stereotypes, wrong expectations, or past experiences to cripple your dreams.

Step 3: Write the dream.

Take detailed notes about what you see. Describe your vision in full color, bringing emotion and passion to your words.

What you are doing is beginning with the end in mind, rather than improvising as you go. No one would build a house without first laying out detailed plans. Yet too many people don't give any thought to their lives. At best, many have just a raw sketch of what they hope to accomplish.

Write your dreams down as if they already happened, using past tense. The ancient prophet Habakkuk said, "Write my answer plainly on tablets" (Habakkuk 2:2). This process of writing with clear and concise words will bring life to your vision.

Step 4: Speak the dream.

Declare your vision out loud, with as much emotion as possible. The combination of a quiet mind, a detailed vision, and a voice of conviction will begin to create that substance known as faith, which is the invisible connection between the tangible and the invisible. Reading and declaring your vision, preferably morning and evening, will begin to build faith and, in time, bring your dreams into the physical realm.

There are things that will try to kill your faith. You might fight doubt or fear, physical suffering, or debt. No matter what, you must continue to declare your dreams with as much authority as possible. In this day-to-day fight against unbelief, I believe that those who find their strength in God have a distinct advantage over those who just believe in themselves.

A friend of mine ran a men's shelter for years in downtown Seattle. His purpose was to get men off the streets. Ninety percent were alcoholics, drug addicts, or both. He would take anyone sincere about getting free of their addiction through rehabilitation.

His program, which was free, followed a similar process as the well-known and expensive Betty Ford program in southern California that serves many wealthy people with addiction problems. It included changing nutrition and eating habits.

The biggest difference between this men's shelter and the plush Betty Ford clinic were the results. He told me that only a small percent of those who went through the Betty Ford program were clean and sober after one year, compared to 85 percent of those who went through his program. The difference, according to him, was that the men he worked with made a sincere declaration of faith in Jesus Christ.

This invisible power of God is real—I have experienced it firsthand. I know that self-generated faith can also create miracles, but I believe the power we generate on our own is not as great as that of God working through the determined will of man.

Step 5: Conceive the dream.

After the devastating Korean War, a pastor named Dr. David Yonggi Cho started a church in South Korea with a handful of people. Today, it has grown to nearly one million members. In describing his success, Dr. Cho refers to the principle of being impregnated with your vision, like a woman is pregnant with a child.

Envision your future; meditate with complete mental focus on it. Speak your vision with absolute authority until you have assurance in your heart that it has been done in the invisible world. Then continue this process until you see physical evidence of your dream.

Step 6: Be patient.

When a farmer plants his seeds, he believes that with enough water, sun, nutrients, and time, the plants will begin to poke out of the ground. He would be foolish to go out every day and dig up the seeds to see how they are progressing. The farmer must have the faith to keep watering his crop until the plants spring up.

The same is true for us. We must act and imagine as if we were going to have a huge crop, all in good time.

Step 7: Talk to yourself.

We must reprogram the thoughts and words that flow through our mind second by second, minute by minute, hour by hour. Our internal words have to be positive and affirm what we believe.

We are like magnets—we attract what we most think about. Focus on changing your thoughts, and before you know it, you will bring into your life what you really want instead of what you are used to having.

Passionate faith is one of the most powerful creative forces in the world. When you believe something deeply enough and for long enough, your dreams will almost fulfill themselves.

On the other hand, when you fear something, the thing you try to shield yourself from frequently seems to find you. That's not to say that all negative circumstances are due to our fears, because good and bad things happen to us all. But I have seen many instances of fear crippling people and skewing their judgment to the point that they experience exactly what they were trying to avoid. As Job says in the Bible, "What I always feared has happened to me. What I dreaded has come true" (Job 3:25).

I suggest you write down short, faith-filled statements to counteract doubts, negative thoughts, or contradictory circumstances. Carry them around on three-by-five cards in your pocket, and every free minute you have, recite them to yourself.

Some of the best power thoughts can be found in the Bible. "I can do everything through Christ, who gives me strength" (Philippians 4:13) is a good example of a phrase you can use to defeat doubt.

My favorite passage, one that reminds me to continue in a state of strong faith, is Mark 11:22-24. Jesus says, "You can say to this mountain, 'May you be lifted up and thrown into the sea,' and it will happen. But you must really believe it will happen and have no doubt in your heart. I tell you, you can pray for anything, and if you believe that you've received it, it will be yours."

Whether you use power verses out of the Bible or other positive and affirmative words you find or create yourself, make sure to carry them with you so that in times of weakness you can recite them to yourself.

Another suggestion is to write out statements of positive self-affirmation. Begin with the words "I am." These "I am" declarations will change how you see yourself, which in turn will change your negative thoughts and your reactions to difficult situations.

These seven steps—get quiet, dream, write the dream, speak the dream, conceive the dream, be patient, and talk to yourself—are not difficult to understand, but they require some honest introspection. Before jumping back into the rest of my story, I encourage you to take a moment to think about how to apply these steps to your life.

What negative beliefs have you accepted as reality? What have you given up on? Are your thoughts about yourself and your circumstances predominately negative or positive? Are you focusing on past failures or future possibilities?

Remember that like any spiritual truth, the principle of creative thinking doesn't always operate within our desired time frame. So, you can't just "try it out" for a while; you have to allow yourself to be transformed from the inside out, and that takes time.

But it's worth it!

When Dreams Become Real

My heart burned for success. I loved what I was doing and truly thought the fitness business was my life destiny, yet I was failing miserably.

As I read those two books, my mind was captured by the examples of "normal" people achieving amazing successes. I learned that nearly all of the great industrialists of the early twentieth century, people like Henry Ford and Andrew Carnegie, practiced the Law of Attraction or the Law of Faith, even though many of their religious or philosophical perspectives differed.

I thought, it can't hurt, especially in light of my current situation. I have heard it said that the definition of insanity is doing the same thing over and over again and hoping for a different result. So I jumped in all the way and embraced this new type of thinking.

Every afternoon, I would go into my office, lie on the floor, and sail away to that peaceful place in the sea, the warm sun shining down on me. At the time, I had one sales office and two lackluster employees—but I envisioned four full-time sales staff, all with big smiles and their own offices. I saw my club full of members, with salespeople handing me one new membership agreement after another, until my hands were so full I could hardly hold them. I saw my members losing hundreds of pounds and telling their friends how great our club was. I saw my total membership grow to thousands. I saw us adding racquetball courts and a beautiful swimming pool.

It was all a fantasy, of course. As soon as I opened my eyes, I was back to reality: a tiny, ugly club; no members; and two very negative employees who were just passing time, maybe hoping to get a job somewhere else or thinking I would get fired and somehow things would get better.

I was kind of in a pickle because one employee was Fred's daughter and the other had been my roommate in college for four years. The few members we had liked them better than they liked me because I was so worried about how bad things were that I walked around uptight all the time.

One day, after meditating on my dreams for a better life, I thought seriously about firing them both. The idea frightened me, and yet it was kind of freeing.

The next day, I lay down as usual and started my meditations. As I imagined a new life with happy members and employees and a higher income, again the thought came strongly that I needed to fire my staff.

This time I got up, opened my door, and invited my assistant manager into my office. I looked him in the eye and told him to pack his belongings and hit the road.

He looked at me kind of dazed and said, "You're not serious, are you?"

"I'm as serious as a heart attack," I replied. I don't think I was even nervous—I had just had enough. I stared at him, he stared back at me, and then he left.

Next came my boss's daughter. I don't think she really cared one way or another about her job. She was eighteen and loved riding motorcycles with her dad. When I told her she was finished, she just giggled nervously and left.

About an hour later, her mother called me up and told me that I had no right to fire her daughter.

I replied simply, "Take it up with your husband," and hung up, knowing that I had probably just cut my throat.

My total staff now consisted of me, myself, and I.

Soon after, I saw a guy drive into my parking lot. He had a couple of bicycles strapped to his car and several TVs inside on the seats.

The club was empty, and I thought maybe it was a guest and I could sign him up. No such luck.

Instead, he started trying his best to sell me a bicycle. He was sure I could somehow use it to get members to sponsor their friends into my club.

He was full of enthusiasm and energy. I'm still not sure what he was so excited about, but it was captivating.

Before I knew it, I asked him if he wanted a real job. "I'll give you a guarantee of $500 a month," I told him. "But you have to work bell to bell with me, twelve hours a day, six days a week."

Without a second's hesitation, he stuck out his hand. "You've got a deal!"

Rick Clark was the first person who ever believed in my vision of building a prosperous fitness club. He would work for me in different capacities over most of the next thirty-six years. Together we were magic.

The next day, I got a phone call from an old college friend, Patti Patterson. She was calling from somewhere in the middle of Mexico. I had seen her about a year earlier and offered her a job. The connection was so terrible I could barely hear her, but it sounded like she was asking me if that job offer was still open.

I told her it was if she could get there in a week. We agreed on ten days. She, too, started at $500 a month.

Without knowing it, I had just hired my first dream team in the fitness business.

They thought I was a little odd because every day, I would go into my office and meditate and pray for an hour or so. But my vision got clearer and more concise.

I began writing down what I saw in my dreams. I developed strategies on how to sign up potential members on their first visit by creating a sales presentation that my employees would memorize. This would make them better salespeople and enable them to sign up a higher percentage of guests who were inquiring about memberships. Instead of enrolling two new members a day, we started enrolling four—an improvement of 100 percent, but not nearly enough to make a profit.

After two weeks of working with my new staff, Fred walked through the door. I hadn't talked to him since I fired his daughter, and I figured there was a good chance I was history.

Instead, he stuck out his hand and said, "Now you've got a chance—at least you can make a decision."

Then he handed me the ugliest advertisement I had ever seen. It was illustrated with a combination of road signs—Stop, Curves Ahead, and so on—and it advertised a special of twenty dollars for six weeks. We had run ads before but had never had much success, and I didn't see how this would be any different.

But Fred said, "Take this to the newspaper and run it on Wednesday." He said his friend from Chicago told him the phone would ring off the hook. So I did what I was told, and a few days later the advertisement broke in the Lynnwood Enterprise. To my surprise, within four hours I got eighty-five calls on that special of twenty dollars for six weeks. It was unbelievable! That month, we signed up three hundred of these mini-memberships and began to convert them over to two-year contracts.

We were now really busy but still not showing a profit. I knew my time was short: it looked like Fred was going to close the club within thirty days. He owned six small Family Fitness Center clubs around Washington State, and his Lynnwood club was by far his worst-performing club. In fact, our nickname was "Limping Lynnwood." Just imagine what my follow managers would have thought if they knew I spent an hour a day meditating on this great vision I had for our club!

Idea Magnets

Things were changing—I could tell. I was reading my three-by-five cards almost hourly. My mind was being reprogrammed. I was no longer negative and despondent: I was full of enthusiasm and excitement, and so was my big two-person staff. They believed in me and did what I asked them to do, and together we knew that somehow we would succeed.

One morning, I showed up for work early and told my staff that I was going to increase our sign-up fee by 300 percent, from $200 to $600. They thought I had lost my mind, but they were getting used to me doing the unusual on a regular basis, so they just shrugged their shoulders.

I took the first tour of the day. The little lady I toured couldn't have been nicer and was excited to become a member and get great results. I told her it would be $600, and she didn't bat an eye. I wrote up her agreement and walked out of my office with a big smile on my face.

That month was the first month we didn't lose money. Even though we profited a skinny amount, $836 to be exact, we now knew we could run a profitable company. I took my staff out and celebrated. We were so happy you would think we had just won the Super Bowl.

My daily meditation on the new vision became an idea magnet. Creative strategies started to pop into my head. My staff started thinking creatively, too. They began coming to me every day with innovative ideas to increase our guest traffic, which was our most important economic indicator—the more guest traffic we created, the more new members we could sign up.

To give you an example of the creativity that broke out: one day we were sitting in a McDonald's having a cup of coffee. They had just come out with their famous Big Mac. I looked at the yellow box it came in, and the idea of making it into a lead generator box came to me.

I said to my team, "Let's cut a slit in these boxes, stick flags in them with our name, and put them out at local businesses. We'll advertise that if people give us their contact information, they'll have a chance to win a free one-year membership."

At the time, the idea was new to us. We weren't aware of anyone in any company that was doing this. In time, we got a little more sophisticated and created our own lead boxes that were professional and attractive.

Within months, this small idea produced thousands of quality leads at a very low cost. Every month, we would go around and collect the leads—garbage bags full of them. We gave away a free membership every month. We also contacted each person who had filled out a card and offered them a free thirty-day trial.

Our guest traffic increased by about two hundred people per month. We converted at least a hundred of those into sales for a net revenue increase of approximately $30,000 a month. I estimate that eventually, just at that one club, that idea would increase my own income by $10,000 a month.

It is hard to describe where meditation and prayer stop and "real life" begins. You become so creative in your quiet times that it begins to bleed over into your conscious reality. In a very real sense, you begin to create twenty-four hours per day. Ideas fly at you like small magnets attracted to a larger magnet.

I have taught myself over the years to wake up slowly. It seems that somehow during the night, your mind and maybe the Holy Spirit are at work, bringing you creative ideas that will help you innovate or solve important issues. The key is to keep relaxed and allow the deeper mind of God to talk to you before you engage your conscious mind.

Sometimes our conscious mind overrides our creative mind. That is why just concentrating harder when you need to be creative is self-defeating. Instead, you must go to that quiet place of creativity, the "other dimension."

As our revenue grew, we continued to practice financial frugality, even though money was flying at us. In under a year, we increased our profits from less than zero to over $40,000 per month. I now received 50 percent of the profits because I had become the owner's most valuable employee. All of his other clubs combined didn't make half of what we were making.

My personal income had gone from nothing to $250,000 a year, and I had barely turned twenty-five. All the way through college I could live on $125 a month, including rent. Since I had lived on so little for so long, increasing my monthly expenses to $600 was like becoming a millionaire. Now I had my own apartment, a nice car, and decent clothes, and I was saving $15,000 to $20,000 per month.

Partners and Profits

One of the visions I had been meditating on was becoming an owner in the fitness club industry. So I saved every extra dollar, waiting for the opportunity that I somehow knew would appear.

I wouldn't say I am a very confident person, but I usually seem to make up for that deficiency with courage and tenacity. So one day, I got up the courage to approach my boss and ask to become his partner. I offered all my savings, about $100,000, to purchase 25 percent of all his clubs. I said I would run them as I had run my profitable Lynnwood club.

He accepted my proposal without hesitation, and I became his partner.

One of the biggest keys to the Lynnwood club's profitability was a management system that I had developed with my team. I called it PSROPS. That's pronounced pis-rops—a bit awkward, I know, but people remember it! It stands for Personality, Service, Results, Obligation, Promotion, and Sales.

I'll explain this in detail in a later chapter, but in essence, PSROPS was about creating an exciting club atmosphere with employees who were helpful and enthusiastic and who provided a humble, knowledgeable, professional service that produced great fitness results. Providing a service that was of more personal value to our members than what they paid created a psychological obligation toward us, and they were happy to help us build our business by sponsoring their friends and family members. Incidentally, this service and sales system will work for just about any business.

For example, we enrolled a husband and wife, Al and Evelyn Christensen. We provided them with wonderful service, and they loved the results, our employees, and our club. Al was the superintendent of the Edmonds school district, and one day he approached me and told me he wanted to get his teachers and their spouses to start on a fitness program at our club. Inside of a year, we signed up over two hundred teachers and probably another thousand of their friends and family members. All of that came because we gave Al and Evelyn a quality product that they could wholeheartedly recommend.

My system is a hybrid of the spiritual law of sowing and reaping. Provide a great product, and you'll receive customer loyalty and eventually financial growth. The human tendency is to try to get before you give, which never works, especially long-term.

When I became Fred's partner, I enthusiastically began to implement the systems and procedures I had created in our Lynnwood club. I thought it would be simple duplication of a winning formula. I could imagine my income doubling or tripling in the next year.

But I quickly realized that if the people you are teaching are not interested in learning, changing, and implementing, it doesn't matter what you know or how motivated you are. You might as well be pouring your heart and enthusiasm into a rock.

The managers I was training were certainly smart enough, and they had more experience than I. But everything I did met with resistance. They wouldn't do what I told them, despite the fact that my commissions were $20,000 a month and theirs were less than $2,000. Most of them were five to eight years older than I, with ten years in the business compared to my two, and I couldn't convince them to change their thinking.

After trying my best for a couple of months to pound valuable knowledge into these people's minds and producing terrible results, I decided to act decisively like I had before. I told my boss (now my partner) that I had decided to fire every manager I had except the manager I had trained in my Lynnwood club. Although I'm sure he was surprised by my radical decision, he replied simply, "You've got to do what you've got to do."

I drove from club to club, firing managers and replacing them with managers who had less experience but better attitudes. I call it OMPA: Opened-Minded Positive Attitudes. Within a couple of months, and after a lot of long, hard work, all of our clubs were producing growing profits. In six months, I put over 36,000 miles on my car. It wasn't unusual for me to leave my Lynnwood club, head 150 miles east to my Yakima club, and finish the day in Spokane, another 175 miles away. I remember once or twice catching a couple of hours of sleep there in Spokane and then opening my club in Bellingham, 300 miles away, beating my manager to work.

No one was ever quite sure where I would end up or when. This kept everyone on their toes and created a sense of excitement, because nothing motivates employees more than a boss who talks a good game and plays a better one.

I continued to meditate on a new life of prosperity, and the results began to come so quickly it felt magical. We built a relationship with a savings-and-loan bank that financed about twenty brand-new clubs. These were thirty- to forty-thousand square-foot clubs (at the time, the normal size for our industry was about five thousand), fully equipped with racquetball, basketball, swimming, indoor jogging tracks, and a host of other facilities. We owned the real estate in all of these new clubs instead of paying rent. We were setting industry records for signing up new members. In some of the new clubs, we would enroll 2,500 members in one club in one month during the grand opening. Within a couple of years, we were opening almost a new club a month.

The excitement was palpable, and money was rolling in. We cut all of our managers in on the profits to varying degrees. Some employees who had started at minimum wage were now making $250,000 per year.

We purchased the finance company that owned our membership contracts so we would pick up the profits that they made by financing our contracts. It was an easy deal, since we retained the great executives that ran the company and cut them in on the profits as well. They were making more money than they had ever made before, so they became more excited, innovative, and profitable.

The banks freely extended our lines of credit to help finance our finance company, and within a few years we had a revolving line of credit of $15 million just to finance membership contracts. We purchased companies that leased exercise equipment, tanning machines, cars, and whatever else we thought we could make money on. We entered into a partnership in an advertising company that produced great profits. We even acquired a printing company.

Within seven years, we went from a company that was on the verge of shutting down to owning and operating over fifty full-facility, full-service clubs in Washington, Oregon, Idaho, and northern California, along with owning multiple related companies. We had over 250,000 members, employed over 4,000 employees, and did close to $100 million a year in total revenue. All of us as partners had fulfilled our dreams of becoming multimillionaires.

This success all came before my thirtieth birthday. I was sure it was just the beginning!

Not Just Another Lunch

One day when I was visiting our Bremerton, Washington club, I noticed a beautiful, dark-haired girl working at the club. She was the prettiest woman I had ever seen and full of spunk and passion. I remember thinking to myself as soon as I saw her, that's the person I'm going to spend the rest of my life with. Her name was Gina.

I can't say I did much to further the relationship at the beginning, despite my attraction to her. If anything, the situation made me kind of uncomfortable and standoffish, as I was careful to separate my business and personal life.

It was my habit to take employees to lunch and spend a couple of hours mentoring them one-on-one. One day, when I was at the Bremerton club, Gina stopped me. She looked me in the eye and said, "You've taken every other employee out to lunch but me. Why won't you train me?"

I couldn't argue with that, so that day we had lunch together. Afterward she said, "Since you're in town and you don't have anything planned this evening, why don't we have dinner together?"

From that moment, we were together, and we have been until today. We were married about three years after we first met. Soon a beautiful baby girl, Crystal, was born; our second daughter, Rachel, followed two years later; four years after that came our third daughter, Leslie; and after another four years came Ian, our son.

Gina is truly my soul mate, and our love has stood the test of time. Our relationship hasn't been without severe storms, which I'll share about in another chapter. But I wouldn't be where I am or who I am without her.

04

Falling Off the Cliff

My vision—or maybe my obsession—soon became taking out our main competitor, European Health Spa, which had about two hundred clubs across the country. In our market, they owned twenty clubs. Their clubs were nice but didn't have coed facilities with dual locker rooms, Olympic-size swimming pools, indoor jogging tracks, basketball and racquetball facilities, or the other amenities we offered.

We strategically built large clubs within a mile or two of this national competitor's clubs. Our employees were better trained, and they were highly motivated because they shared in our monthly company profits. Our beautiful facilities, great training programs, and profit-sharing programs were effective recruitment tools to capture the best employees our competitors had.

In time, we dominated at least 85 percent of the market share in our region, reducing our competitor to a skeleton of what they once were. Eventually they had no choice but to either shut down or sell their clubs in order to cut their losses.

After a few months of negotiations, they gave us their clubs, equipment, membership dues, and other income at no cost and with no strings attached. We could do with their clubs whatever we wanted—run them or shut them down.

Once the deal was decided, I called an emergency meeting with all of our managers to give them the good news. I purposely showed up a little late, which was unusual for me since I am obsessive about being on time.

I walked into the meeting, tossing a huge set of keys up in the air over and over again, not saying a word. My team probably thought the pressure had gotten to me, and I had lost my mind. I paused for effect, looked out over our army of great warriors, and announced that these keys were the keys to our competitor's clubs.

At first there was no response. I don't think they could believe what they were hearing, since we had battled day and night against them for years. Then I declared in a commander's voice, "The clubs are ours, and they cost us nothing!" After the shock passed, elation and the greatest sense of victory and pride I had ever experienced filled the room.

Success and Excess

We had somehow captured that elusive thing called momentum. Everything we did turned to gold.

But insidiously, we had grown arrogant, especially me. I was making as much money as elite professional athletes. I believed that my mind had grown so wise that I needed no one's advice, that I was a genius and could overcome any and all obstacles that were thrown before me.

I remember my boss, Fred Sessions, trying to warn me. "You have a golden thumb, Neil. Everything you do turns to gold. But someday, it's going to turn to crap."

At one point, I was approached by the biggest name in the fitness industry, Ray Wilson. Ray, who came from a very poor background and didn't even go to school until he was fifteen, had built the most successful fitness empire around when he was in his twenties—267 clubs. Then, through a series of youthful mistakes, he had lost everything and was broke by the time he was thirty-two years old.

He didn't stop there, though. He started a group of athletic clubs that became one of the most successful fitness companies ever. He ended up selling that company for $46 million to a company on the New York Stock Exchange. He was also the inventor of Lifecycle, the first electronic cardiovascular exercise machine, which revolutionized the industry and went on to be a billion-dollar business.

Ray told me he thought I had a lot of promise but that I was ignorant. "You are going to make the same mistakes I made," he predicted, "and you will probably rebound like I did—but I can save you ten years of your life."

He offered to become our consultant, and he asked for 20 percent of the company. In his words, he would be our "insurance policy" to protect us from committing the mistakes he had made and losing everything.

Ray was more than twenty years older than I and far wiser, but I couldn't see that. I was at the top of my game, and everything I touched succeeded. I didn't need him, or so I thought.

"Thanks, but no thanks," I told him. "I'll do just fine."

He replied, "I expected that. But I like you. You remind me more of myself than anyone I've ever met." He wished me luck, and he left.

In retrospect, I wish I had accepted his offer!

I was good at business—I knew intuitively how to make decisions, build team spirit, and out-strategize the competition. Within four years, we owned 55 clubs and had 4,000 employees. Our new member enrollments and annual income were far beyond the industry average. To all outside observers, we were a huge success.

But through it all, I had become arrogant and self-centered. I hurt many people during that four-year period, something I regret to this day.

My relationship with God had become non-existent. I couldn't remember the last time I had prayed or read the Bible. My personal behavior had deteriorated to the point where I was embarrassed to even refer to myself as a Christian. I had two little girls at the time and a wonderful wife whom I treated with disdain and even contempt.

The company, starting with our key staff, was morally bankrupt. I had focused too much on talent and not enough on character. We ended up with executives and employees with rampant moral failures, addictions, and greed. We spent $100,000 putting some of our executives through rehab. I lost five key employees to addiction-related causes.

The work environment turned sour. We had to deal with frequent interpersonal conflicts, unhealthy competition between employees, and even accusations of sexual misconduct and other morality issues. Our reputation with both our members and the community was ruined.

My mother used to say that Rome fell due to immorality. I can personally attest that a company rises and falls on its character and morality, because I watched it happen with mine.

Moral weakness is tricky because it is insidious and slow to act. Things can look great on the outside, but underneath, the foundations have been compromised. Excesses, addictions, conflicts, greed, arrogance, and selfishness undermine the things that made you successful in the first place. And when outside forces like economic downturn occur, you find yourself unable to respond wisely, quickly, and in a unified manner.

Downfall

Nearly every major religion agrees on one doctrine: "What you sow, you will reap"; or, "Whatever you put on the wheel of life will revisit you."

The downfall started in the early eighties, when inflation grew out of control. Eventually it rose to nearly 14 percent. To combat inflation, the Federal Reserve increased interest rates, and within eighteen months or so, prime interest grew from 7 percent to 21 percent.

In early 1980, we were in the middle of a presale in Boise, Idaho, and had presold about two thousand memberships before the club had even broken ground. Then I got a call from the developer in Boise who was going to build our club. He was the top developer in the area, but he gave me the bad news that he had lost his financing and was pulling out of the deal.

I told him that he couldn't do that, but he pointed out that in fact, he had an escape clause in the lease based on his ability to land financing.

After some negotiation, we agreed to put up $2 million in cash and he would throw in his property in order to get the club built. We would be fifty-fifty partners in the real estate. We had the cash in our reserves, but barely. So we went forward, and the club was built.

I couldn't foresee the future, so I thought, no big deal—we will replenish our cash reserves, and things will be fine.

But within a few months, unemployment grew to about 12 percent in our region, causing our sales production to falter. People just couldn't afford a gym membership.

We borrowed money on our $15 million line of credit at two points above prime. Instead of the 9 percent interest we had before the economic decline, we were now paying a whopping 23 percent. Soon, it was costing us nearly $300,000 a month in interest to run our finance company.

Our real estate contributed to our woes. All of the buildings we had built and owned were on variable rates tied to some kind of interest indicator like prime. In some cases, our mortgage payments increased by as much as 50 percent.

We closed most of our competitor's clubs, thinking that their sixty thousand members would just love our clubs because of the additional facilities and services we offered. To our surprise, they had grown accustomed to men and women using the clubs on alternate days. Many of the men liked using the spa facilities nude, but in our clubs, the spa area was coed. Some of the older male members rebelled to the point of using the whirlpool, steam, and sauna in the buff anyway. You can imagine the commotion this created!

Soon, many of our competitor's members began to demand that we reimburse their initiation fee. Those fees had gone to our competitor, not us, but that didn't matter to them—as far as they were concerned, we owed them a refund. We took a hard stand on this and would not refund money we hadn't received.

We thought this was a reasonable decision, but many people were upset and complained to the attorney general's office. Then the newspapers picked up on it, and like a forest fire, it grew out of control. People who had joined our clubs on two-year memberships but who were not using the club saw a chance to get their money back or at least stop paying on their membership contracts, so they also complained to the attorney general's office. Before we could catch our breath, the attorney general of the State of Washington sued us for illegal business practices. The allegation was untrue, but the bad press that came out of it was irreparable.

I have heard time and again that there is no such thing as bad press; that in the long run, all press, whether positive or negative, is good for your company. That is one of the biggest stupidities ever circulated. My mother taught me as a young man, "It takes a lifetime to build a good reputation, and a moment to destroy it; so guard your actions with your life, and your reputation will stay intact." Had I had the wisdom and humility to negotiate peaceful settlements with the disgruntled members, we could have spared ourselves a great deal of pain.

Then our lead bank called us in for a special meeting. They informed us that they were reclassifying our $15 million line of credit as "special credits" because we were out of covenant with our loan. I was not well-versed, to say the least, in all the rules and regulations of banking institutions, but they made it clear that they were not going to renew the lines of credit that had been so easy to get in good times. It seemed our debt-to-equity ratio was out of balance, and therefore we had broken a covenant that I had ignorantly agreed to.

I argued to the best of my ability that we had never missed a payment and that the only significant thing that had changed on our profit and loss statement and balance sheet was that we were now paying them $300,000 per month in interest instead of $100,000. I pointed out that as interest rates lowered, so would that expense—which was going directly to them anyway—and we would be back in covenant. I added that if they refused to renew our lines of credit, it would force us out of business, and over 250,000 members would lose their memberships.

They responded that between our real estate and membership contracts they had enough collateral to go ahead with their plan. Plus they had our personal signatures that they would be made whole on what we owed them.

My feeble reply was, "But we are paying you, and you are going to ruin us and our entire company. That doesn't make sense!"

We left the meeting in shock. We fought to save our company for three more painful years, but to no avail.

Eventually my partners and I split the remaining assets in a last-ditch attempt to save the company. I took our ten clubs in California, they took the clubs in Washington, and we sold the clubs in Oregon. Under my oversight, the California clubs began to show a profit again. But since we were centrally run, all the finances went north to Washington and nothing came back. I couldn't get my bills paid on time, and the electric company was about to shut off our electricity.

So I started a local bank account and deposited our profits there. This enraged one of my partners, who then told our bank in California that I was siphoning company funds into a personal account. That wasn't true, of course. Everything I had done was completely legal. I could prove the funds were being handled correctly, and I was making the promised bank payments without fail. But it was enough to turn the bank against me.

The board forced me out of my role, although I still owned 50 percent of the clubs. To make matters worse, the clubs went downhill again, and they didn't pay the bank loan payments or employee federal withholding taxes.

By early 1986, nearly all of our clubs were closed.

This Is Your Mess

At this point, my personal indebtedness exceeded $35 million. As one of the signers on our loans, I was personally liable. We owed everybody.

The IRS and the Washington State Revenue Department came after me for millions of dollars in back taxes. The Federal Justice Department accused me of fraud, saying that because I was president, I was responsible for half a million dollars of unpaid federal withholding taxes—even though I had no vote or involvement with the company during the time those taxes were not being paid.

Over the next few years, I was sued nearly fifty times by leasing companies, banks, customers, vendors, and the Washington State attorney general. One representative of the state revenue department, maybe the most vicious human being I have ever met, told me it was his goal to see us live in the projects of Seattle the rest of our lives.

It was like being buried alive in an avalanche, yet not dying. My name was ruined; my credit was ruined. I watched our hard-earned properties get foreclosed on, one at a time. Everything I had worked for, everything I had been so proud of, was lost.

I would not wish that experience on my worst enemy. The pain, fear, and humiliation were unbearable. Personal relationships were destroyed. One partner committed suicide. For four months I couldn't sleep at night. There was emotional trauma and complete devastation on all levels.

The Humble Road

Eventually, we were able to sell off our business properties and assets and cover all the debt except for the IRS and the state taxes. I negotiated payment plans with them that stretched over ten years. The Justice Department dropped the fraud charges when I proved I was not involved in the company when the taxes weren't being paid.

But we were broke, in every sense of the word. In the long, hard fight to save the company, I had even used up all my personal savings. I had no idea what I would do to provide for my young family.

A few years before losing everything, I had recommitted my life to God, hoping that he would jump in and help me overcome my problems. I began to read large portions of the Bible and pray fervently for grace, mercy, and protection. I tried to visualize success once again, but all to no avail. God had gone silent on me. It was like he was saying, "Hey big shot, where was I in your life when you took all the credit for your success?"

I read in the book of Psalms how King David cried out to God after he sinned so badly against him. I slowly began to understand my selfishness toward God and man. In my pain and tears, I learned humility.

I had used my God-given gifts and talents and the spiritual understanding of the law of faith to benefit me and me alone. I was like a spoiled child who needed to be firmly disciplined.

An old friend of mine once said, "He who cannot see must feel." I felt the correction of God in a way I find hard to describe. But it was real, and it lasted a very long time—until I learned the most valuable lesson of my life: "The fear of the Lord is the beginning of wisdom" (Proverbs 9:10, NKJV).

I believe wholeheartedly that we have a merciful God who loves his children so much that he sent his son to die for our sins. I believe his love and mercy for us outweighs his justice. However, just saying we are sorry, or even repenting from our sins and changing our actions, does not mean that we are free from the consequences of past failures.

As the great writer and philosopher Emerson said in his essay Compensation: "Cause and effect, means and ends, seed and fruit, cannot be severed; for the effect already blooms in the cause, the end preexists in the means, the fruit in the seed."

Although my mother and father had stressed the importance of honesty, truthfulness, and right behavior, these precepts did not stick like others they had taught me. So through the tough love of my heavenly father, God, I had to learn by way of some very hard consequences.

These consequences did not just affect me, but all those who were following me, especially my wife. Some of us are born to lead; it is an awesome gift, but a huge responsibility and not to be taken lightly.

One day my mother called. She told me how sorry she was for my misfortune and that she was praying for my young family and me. Then she added words that I would never forget. "Neil, you got yourself and your family into this mess, and I want you to know that even if your father and I had the financial wherewithal to help you out, we wouldn't. You caused this problem, and you need to solve it. So you better pick yourself up and figure it out. Goodbye."

She felt my pain, but she didn't offer me any pity—just motivation to get up, brush myself off, and somehow take care of my family. A conversation that lasted no longer than sixty seconds sobered me up and got rid of the most paralyzing emotion of all: self-pity. Not until I took 100 percent responsibility for my failings and stopped blaming them on the economy, interest rates, and the banks did I begin to heal and grow again.

05

Black Ice

Over time, we lost almost everything. I was desperate to find a way now just to take care of my wife and two little girls.

I read the Bible, prayed, and hoped that God would instantly rescue me from my dire situation. But there was nothing instant about it. Over the next couple of years, God took me on an intense process of inner transformation. I learned to value character, something that before had meant little to me.

Growing up, my parents taught me a great deal about work, responsibility, and business. They also tried to teach me moral character, but I didn't learn those lessons as well. My ego got in the way, in part because I achieved success so quickly.

I am truly a different person than I was before that difficult season. I was forced to confront the moral deficiencies that had contributed to my downfall. It was a painful—but somehow liberating—experience.

In hindsight, I am convinced that I could have built a billion-dollar company if I had understood how to run a business that was as wise and moral as it was competitive. But I had to learn the hard way.

That's one of the main reasons for this book. I hope to impart some of the lessons that cost me millions of dollars and years of wasted effort to learn.

Let me start with an illustration. One January, years ago, I decided to drive across the mountains from Seattle to Spokane in a blizzard. It was eleven at night, and I was in my new Porsche—not exactly an off-road vehicle. I thought that if I could make it over the mountain pass, it would be smooth sailing after that.

The snow was coming down hard, the wind was blowing, and it was very scary; but true to my personality (especially at the time), it was an adventure. I kept on, even though many cars were pulling over or turning around.

Finally, after a couple of hours battling intense weather conditions, I made it over the pass and started down the other side. It was cold, maybe five degrees, but the snow and wind had subsided. I thought it was going to be an easy drive the rest of the way.

I passed the town of Ellensburg, the last place to stop for the next 150 miles or so. About ten miles later, I hit black ice. The road was completely frozen over with a thin sheet of ice that shined eerily in my headlights. Then my car started to spin. I slowed down and barely got it back under control.

I discovered by trial and error that the only way I could keep the car from sliding off the road was to drive 25 mph down the center of the road, straddling the high point between the lanes. If I veered the slightest to the right or to the left, I would start to slide off the road. My concentration had to be nearly perfect.

There were no other cars on the freeway because of the frightening conditions, so although I didn't have to worry about crashing into anyone, there would be no one to find me if I slid off the road. In those days there was no such thing as cell phones, so if you got stranded, you really were stranded. It hit me that if I wrecked and my car turned off, I would probably freeze to death. I was genuinely terrified.

I inched along in those terrible conditions, straining to keep a straight course, for eight hours. By the time I arrived in Spokane, every muscle in my body was unbelievably tense.

The memory of that trip and the effort it took to avoid sliding off either side of the road often comes back to my mind as an illustration of maintaining a healthy tension between two extremes.

When I first became a Christian in my college days, it was easy for me to understand God's grace and love for me. I had no doubt that God loved me absolutely and unconditionally. As I mentioned earlier, what act of love could be greater than the God of the universe giving his life for us?

What I didn't grasp—until I had "driven my car off the road," so to speak—was the fear of the Lord. The wreck I had made of my financial and personal life brought me face to face with some glaring deficiencies in my character, things I had been able to ignore when I was on top of the world.

I think all of us have a tendency to lean in one direction or the other based on our personality type: either toward God's love and grace or toward the obedience of his law. I strongly believe that whatever our natural bent is, we need to work hard to maintain balance. In other words, if the grace of God comes easily for us, we most likely need to work extra hard on keeping his law. If obedience is easy, then we probably need to focus on learning to live in grace rather than relying on our good works.

We need to learn to navigate the road of life with both the grace of God and the fear of God. It's not one or the other, because they are not in opposition to each other; rather, they work together to keep us on the "straight and narrow." Our love for God will be reflected in a lifestyle of obedience, but our obedience is motivated and powered by God's grace.

A New Success Formula

During those agonizing months of material loss and spiritual growth, I spent a lot of time reading my Bible. I wasn't trying to impress God any longer or get a quick miracle—I just desperately wanted to know how to live my life.

I came across a verse that would become my lifelong guide. As I meditated and applied this verse to my life, it changed my perspective and shaped my decisions. The verse was 2 Chronicles 7:14. God is speaking:

> Then if my people who are called by my name will humble themselves and pray and seek my face and turn from their wicked ways, I will hear from heaven and will forgive their sins and restore their land. My eyes will be open and my ears attentive to every prayer made in this place.

This verse became my new "success formula" for a godly, truly successful life. My goal was no longer to have great wealth and power, but to become a wise man of God, a man who fulfills God's destiny. That was no easy chore for me, especially in the beginning, but it got easier as time passed.

I fell in love with the story of King David. He was an adulterer and a murderer, yet somehow God called him "a man after my own heart." He was even part of Jesus's direct bloodline and heritage.

This story gave me hope, because if God would restore David and think so highly of him, maybe I had a chance.

I began to understand why God loved David so much. It wasn't because David was perfect, but because he loved God with all his heart and sincerely wanted to please him.

Every time David failed, he cried out to God in total humility. He didn't rationalize his sin, but instead he asked for forgiveness and God's power to do what was right.

David wrote many beautiful psalms, but I think Psalm 51 best describes his humble heart before God, even as a powerful king. This psalm was written after he had committed adultery with Bathsheba and murdered her husband to cover his misdeed. To call that a "moral failure" is an understatement! Psalm 51 is a beautiful illustration of true repentance.

Have mercy on me, O God, because of your unfailing love. Because of your great compassion, blot out the stain of my sins. Wash me clean from my guilt. Purify me from my sin. For I recognize my rebellion; it haunts me day and night. Against you, and you alone, have I sinned; I have done what is evil in your sight. . . . Purify me from my sins, and I will be clean; wash me, and I will be whiter than snow. Oh, give me back my joy again; you have broken me—now let me rejoice.

Don't keep looking at my sins. Remove the stain of my guilt. Create in me a clean heart, O God. Renew a loyal spirit within me. Do not banish me from your presence, and don't take your Holy Spirit from me. Restore to me the joy of your salvation, and make me willing to obey you. (Psalm 51:1-12)

Passion for Wisdom

My motto became, "Do the right thing, at the right time, all the time." This was my personal definition of wisdom. I learned that wisdom was less about what you know and more about how effectively you use what you know. I began to study the book of Proverbs, writing verses out by hand and memorizing them.

I realized I had to completely renew my thinking patterns. My natural mind had been programmed by my culture and my sinful nature to think, in most cases, exactly opposite of how God wanted me to think.

For example, "turning the other cheek," or not returning evil for evil when people go out of their way in business to harm me, was a challenge for me. It still is. There's nothing easy about it, because in order to be successful in business, you have to be strong and courageous—yet somehow, you can't react to personal attacks.

The book of Romans tells us to give God space to deal with our enemies as he sees fit and warns us not to take matters into our own hands. When I have followed this advice, I have saved a lot of money and heartache. When I have ignored it, it has cost me a great deal of time, distress, and in some cases, millions of dollars.

I have found that the key to living a balanced, godly life is the pursuit of wisdom. When wisdom, not success, is our burning desire, everything falls into place. The only thing greater than our love for wisdom should be our love for the creator of wisdom, God.

I was inspired by the story of Solomon in 2 Chronicles 1, who became king at the young age of nineteen. Instead of praying for security, power, and riches, he prayed for wisdom. God made Solomon the wisest man who ever lived, and through his godly wisdom he became the richest and most powerful king of the day.

Wisdom is fundamental to the fulfillment of God's purpose for us on earth. If we acquire it, it will—in time—bring maximum joy, peace, love, and prosperity into our lives.

I believe wisdom is the intersection where God's sovereignty meets human responsibility. God wants to do miracles on our behalf, and the instrument he usually chooses is—us! Even though he could do everything independently of humankind if he chose to, he would rather involve us in what he is doing. He offers us the power, grace, strategies, open doors, and gifting we need.

Some people get worked up trying to figure out what part God plays in our success and what part we play. I don't pretend to be a theologian or have it all figured out, but I do know what works.

God puts dreams and desires in our hearts, then challenges us to believe that we can accomplish them through him. We demonstrate our faith by responding with excellence and effort. Faith pleases God, and where he finds faith, he does miracles.

It's a partnership. We will probably never be able to define exactly where his part and our part start or stop.

I look at wisdom as being the part I play. It is doing the right thing, at the right time, all the time. I pour myself out emotionally, mentally, and physically, but God does far more than I could ever do.

That is all I can do, actually. I can't control other people, the economy, or many other factors. But I can choose to pay attention to what God is doing and enthusiastically get on board.

The idea of "wisdom" can be difficult to visualize. Proverbs 8 talks about wisdom as if it were a person. Ultimately, I believe Jesus is the fulfillment of that chapter. Jesus embodies the wisdom of God.

The more we think like, talk like, and get to know Jesus, the more our lives will mesh with God's plan for us, and the more his power will be displayed through us. When I am unsure what the "wise" thing to do is in a given situation, I take a step back and try to imagine what Jesus would do.

The principle of acting in wisdom is, at the end of the day, very liberating. I don't have to have everything figured out: God handles that. I just have to do what is right in each situation that presents itself, and do it with all my heart.

Is Money Evil?

In rebuilding my life, I had to decide once and for all what God wanted for me. Did he want me to have a life of success and prosperity?

I realized that many people, especially religious people, react negatively when they hear the word prosperity. They think, often subconsciously, that a life of poverty equates to holiness and that acquiring wealth is evil.

This didn't make a lot of sense to me, so I decided to find out the answer. After all, business is all about creating and accumulating wealth. If God hates money and riches, then everything I had done was misdirected and everything I planned to do needed to be redirected.

As I carefully studied the Scriptures, I saw what seemed to be two opposing viewpoints. For example, 1 Timothy 6:9–11 says:

> "But people who long to be rich fall into temptation and are trapped by many foolish and harmful desires that plunge them into ruin and destruction. For the love of money is the root of all kinds of evil. And some people, craving money, have wandered from the true faith and pierced themselves with many sorrows. But you, Timothy, are a man of God; so run from all these evil things. Pursue righteousness and a godly life, along with faith, love, perseverance, and gentleness."

An apparently opposing view is found in Deuteronomy 28:1–14. Verses 8 and 11–2 say:

> "The Lord will guarantee a blessing on everything you do and will fill your storehouses with grain. The Lord your God will bless you in the land he is giving you. . . . The Lord will give you prosperity in the land he swore to your ancestors to give you, blessing you with many children, numerous livestock, and abundant crops. The Lord will send rain at the proper time from his rich treasury in the heavens and will bless all the work you do."

In my quest to figure out what God wanted for my life, especially when it came to wealth and success in business, I found twenty-eight passages in Deuteronomy that say, in effect, "God will prosper you in all ways, spiritually and materially, if and only if you carefully follow my commandments."

I also came across Matthew 6:33. "Seek the Kingdom of God above all else, and live righteously, and he will give you everything you need."

I realized that this was the answer to what Paul was saying in 1 Timothy and other passages that warn against the perils of wealth. God wants to bless us, just like any good father would want to bless his children, but he wants our priorities in the right order.

The key phrase in the Timothy passage is "the love of money is the root of all kinds of evil." My problem in the past was that I had loved money instead of seeing it as a tool or a commodity to do good. Like Paul said, money is dangerous; but if used with wisdom, it should be and can be a very godly pursuit.

It reminded me of traveling that highway covered with black ice. I had to drive carefully, slowly, staying on the high point in the middle of the road to avoid sliding off either side.

God wants to bless us. We are not to shrink back out of a fear of sinning, but we must acquire wisdom like Solomon, make money, and accomplish great things for God's kingdom. God has given us but one life. We must pour ourselves out, using our gifts and talents to fulfill our God-given destiny in a godly way.

A Crazy Plan

During late 1986, after I had been praying and reading 2 Chronicles 7:14 about how God promised to take care of the humble, a plan began to grow in my mind. It was complicated and had ridiculously low odds of working. I really wasn't sure whether it was God or just some harebrained idea that popped into my head in a time of distress, but I had no other options, so I put it into action.

Step one was to contact two of my partners from Family Fitness Centers who were still fairly friendly toward me and offer them my ownership interest in two clubs in Spokane in exchange for their interests in one club in Everett, Washington. The Everett club was in foreclosure. The mortgage payment had not been made in months because the lessee was failing in the operation of the club and not making his lease payment.

They agreed to quit claim their interest over to me in exchange for me doing the same for them in the two Spokane clubs. They had nothing to lose.

Step two was to contact my not-so-friendly partner in California. He had basically stolen ten clubs from me by turning the bank against me through a set of lies. He and the bank still had one major problem: how to deal with my 50 percent ownership interest in the ten clubs. I offered him all of my interest in the clubs, which at the time were still profitable, for his interest in the Everett club, on the condition the bank release my house as collateral from all loans.

He and the bank jumped at the offer. I flew down to California with all the proper paperwork for the transaction, the papers were signed in minutes, and I was back on the plane a few hours later, returning to Seattle.

Now I owned 100 percent of a building that would be foreclosed on in a couple of months.

Step three was to serve legal papers on the tenant who was not paying, which gave him a few days to either catch up on his lease payments or vacate. Within a week, he chose to leave peacefully.

My first key employee, Rick Clark, and I then took over the operation of the club. We still had one major problem: the impending foreclosure.

Step four was to meet with the bank that was foreclosing on our property. We proposed an idea that would benefit them and possibly us. We would give them back complete ownership in the real estate if they would give us a favorable lease that included some free rent, gradually stepped up rent for another year, and provided an option to buy the building back five years later at a stipulated or preset price.

This worked for them because they could avoid a potentially messy, drawn-out bankruptcy procedure. They would also have complete ownership and could evict us like we had done to the previous tenant if we didn't make payment on the lease. And of course, there was the possibility that we would be successful and pay them rent that would cover the mortgage payment and satisfy the debt owed on the building.

They agreed to the deal. My close friend Dick Hart, who would soon become my new partner, was an expert in legal matters. Without his help and assistance in my idea, I am sure it could not have been completed successfully. We named the new club Hart's Athletic Club.

What we had just accomplished through this elaborate plan probably had less than one chance in a hundred of working. I could have taken the credit like I had done in the past, but not this time. I knew then and now, twenty-five years later, that it was God's divine plan and his power working through all the details that gave us a chance for success.

Now we had just one small problem. How could we build a successful business in a run-down club that needed a major overhaul with only $5,000 in cash, no credit, and millions of dollars in debt?

Partners in Sobriety

For the first time in a very long time, I could sense God's presence in my life. I was now reunited with my original employee, Rick Clark, who helped me build our first company and who, for whatever reason, still believed in me.

Rick and I became accountability partners for each other, making sure that neither of us fell back into old habits.

My first boss once told me that one of the keys to success is to know your strengths and accentuate them, and to know your weaknesses and eliminate them or surround yourself with people strong in those areas.

Personally, my greatest weakness was drinking anything that had alcohol in it. It wasn't that I was a fall-down, hopelessly addicted drunk; it was how I behaved when I drank. It caused me to act in very unwise ways and inevitably led me into a destructive lifestyle.

I had sworn off drinking various times throughout the last few years, always thinking that I could somehow control it and my negative behavior. My resolutions never lasted.

I was determined to build a different kind of company this time around, and I knew alcohol and the excesses associated with the whole bar scene could not be a part of it.

Finally, I asked God to help me quit. I have never taken a drink since. That was over twenty-five years ago, and it was probably the best decision of my life, second only to following Christ.

I have watched countless people destroy their lives through the use of alcohol and other drugs. Five of my dear friends have died prematurely because of substance abuse.

Many of my friends can safely have a drink or two, even daily. They say that drinking a glass of wine or a bottle of beer has no negative effect on them, and I believe them.

However, my response, especially to young people who have never drunk alcohol, is, "Would you put one bullet in a revolver, spin the chamber, and then put the gun to the side of your head and pull the trigger, knowing that you have one chance in six to blow your head off?" The answer any sane person would give is, "Of course not!"

My point is that you don't know whether alcohol will ruin your life or not when you take your first drink. Just because some can use it safely doesn't mean it won't harm you.

I believe this so strongly that my wife and I bribed our children with a significant monetary gift that they would receive at the age of twenty-two if they did not use alcohol or any other harmful drugs. My three older children have all received their reward. My nineteen-year-old son has never drunk and has more fun than any kid I know. I am sure he, like his three older sisters, will get his reward.

I consider this the best investment I ever made. It is reasonable to believe that at least one of my children would have been negatively affected by the use of alcohol, maybe to the point of destroying his or her life. It's just not worth it.

06

Do the Right Thing, at the Right Time, All the Time

As I mentioned before, my definition of wisdom is doing the right thing, at the right time, all the time. This not only became my lifetime pursuit, it is also the hallmark of how my wife and I brought up our children and how we have developed employees, business partners, and the reputations of our companies for the last twenty-five years.

We have made our share of mistakes, but after the failure of our first company, it has always been our intent to do right and to be honest down to the smallest detail in transactions with others, even if hurt us or cost us more money. Never again would our goal of creating a successful company become more important than doing what was right at any particular time.

The moral strength and self-control that had been missing in my leadership of Family Fitness Centers became key components of Hart's Athletic Clubs and, years later, my third fitness club chain, Pure Fitness of Arizona. (I'll describe in a later chapter how that company came to be and how it almost cost me my family.)

In this chapter, I am going to jump ahead of my story and give several examples where this principle of wisdom was tested. Sometimes I failed the test, and it cost me heartache, money, and worst of all, my reputation. Other times, I did the right thing and saw positive results in the long run.

Too Bad for Her

One incident happened not too long ago, in another fitness company I started. There was a woman who had begun as an entry-level employee in Hart's Athletic Clubs. Through hard work and talent, she was promoted to district manager over a number of our clubs. I had worked with her and helped develop her career for fifteen years.

In this new company, I invited her to be a partner. She was the one who would run the day-to-day operations.

We started the company with high expectations and enthusiasm. My wife and I were the major investors. We put up a large amount of cash and signed personally on all of the building leases and bank loans. Our partner put up sweat equity and a minor amount of money.

We grew rapidly, and as we built more clubs, it became more and more apparent to me that our partner was not reaching the financial objectives we had presented to our bank. I was forced to get increasingly involved with day-to-day operations. This put a big demand on my time, since I was also running another fitness company in another state, thousands of miles away.

After a few years of lower-than-acceptable performance by my partner and a general lack of profitability in the company, I needed to make a change. My wife and I had remortgaged our house to satisfy negative cash flows and were getting into a dangerous place financially.

We had brought a few minority partners on over the years who worked directly for our partner over operations, so I offered her and the other partners the opportunity to buy my wife and me out for a below-market price with a very small down payment. They met with our outside accounting firm, and after evaluating the offer, they declined. I had mixed feelings about selling them the company anyway because they had proven that they were incapable of running it without my help and my continuous capital infusions.

A chasm grew between my key partner and me. I was disappointed in the results she had produced over about a five-year period, but she felt she had worked hard and given every bit of her heart and soul to our company and that I was being too harsh.

I made a painful decision, the hardest by far I have ever made with a partner—to exercise my authority to buy her out at a preset price as determined in the management agreement within our LLC partnership. Being realistic and pragmatic in business is fundamental to good leadership and the survival of a company; however, this kind of decision is never easy, especially when it comes to terminating working relationships that were once fruitful or where you have grown close as partners.

I invited her into my office and told her that I wanted to exercise my authority to buy her out and remove her from her executive position. I would continue to pay her salary until the transaction was complete.

It was like I put a spear through her heart. My decision ruined our relationship forever.

Almost immediately, her attorney called our attorney, threatening a sexual orientation lawsuit if I didn't give her an inflated amount of money for her ownership. I was extremely angry over the threat because it was untrue and unfair. She was lesbian, a fact I had known for years, all during the time she worked for me in the previous company. I had continued to promote her and eventually made her a partner. To accuse me of discrimination now was ridiculous.

I gathered myself emotionally and asked her to give me three months to market the company. Hopefully we could sell it and get our money back and a profit. I would continue to pay her salary until I completed a sale.

She agreed, and I contacted potential buyers. To my surprise, I received a more than fair offer that would net her significantly more money than what she and her attorney were demanding.

We worked on the deal with the potential buyer, going through a series of due diligence tests that were very uncomfortable, since they were our main competitor. The deal progressed almost to closing, which took approximately three months—but just before we were to close the sale, for no apparent reason, the buyer pulled out.

It was a crushing blow. Not only was there now turmoil in our partnership, but our employees thought we were being sold to our competitor, so any morale that existed before was gone. We were in chaos as a company.

I didn't know why our competitors had done what they did. I thought maybe it was their way of finding out everything about our company from the inside out, or maybe they were purposefully throwing us into chaos. Whatever their reasoning, they almost sent us over the brink.

I contacted each of our partners and relayed the bad news. I told them that I would continue to search for a buyer and that they should focus on getting their jobs done or we wouldn't have any value left to sell.

When I spoke to my key partner, the one who had threatened to sue me, she exploded. She accused me of somehow purposely blowing up the sale. She demanded the money immediately, or she would go through with her sexual discrimination lawsuit against me.

This was a vicious threat, and I knew it could bring down our company and even my wife and me personally. I asked her to give me twenty-four hours to talk with my wife before I gave her an answer.

Gina and I talked and prayed over this matter and decided to give her the money she was demanding, even though it brought our cash reserves down to almost nothing.

I called my partner the next day and agreed to buy her out at her desired price. Her attorney drew up the agreement and sent it over to us. I made sure to put a strong disclaimer in the agreement that specifically addressed a future sale of the company. If the proceeds of such sale exceeded what we had paid her, she would have no right to further compensation.

Just before she and I signed the deal, the company that had recently backed out of buying us out contacted me and informed me that they wanted to continue toward a possible buyout. They said there were some lease assignment issues that they hopefully could overcome, and if they could, they were confident the sale would close.

I asked them why they didn't close before, and they told me they weren't at liberty to tell me. That didn't make me feel too warm and fuzzy.

At the time, the lease on our most valuable club, representing 50 percent of the value of our company, was about to expire. We had been negotiating with the landlord to extend it or possibly build us a new club. Since the company that was proposing to buy us out was a much stronger credit risk than we were, I was afraid that our competitor would convince our landlord not to renew with us and to lease to them instead, thereby stealing our business. Other competitors had tried to do this a few times, so I knew the threat was real.

Even though I was uncomfortable about reopening negotiations with them since they had "left us at the altar" three weeks prior, I decided to go forward.

I chose not to tell any of my partners about the renewed negotiations, except for my CFO who had been with me for many years. She was very loyal, and I needed her to complete due diligence financial summaries that only she had the knowledge to do. My excuse for keeping the potential sale to myself was that it might fall through again. In reality, though, my bitterness had skewed my judgment.

I went ahead and bought my key partner out, knowing that there was a chance the company would soon sell for a significant profit, and she would lose out on the money. I thought angrily, too bad for her!

About a month later, the sale did close. Instead of taking the high road and telling my ex-partner that I would send her a check for the difference, I said to myself, the heck with her, she did it to herself with all those false accusations.

The next year, she sued me. It was a very expensive lawsuit that I had little chance of winning, because as the managing partner, I had a financial obligation to disclose to her all pertinent financial matters while she was still a partner.

We settled in arbitration for more than what I owed her on the difference, plus I paid all her legal fees and of course mine. That doesn't include the time and heartache I suffered or the humiliation I felt before God for not doing the right thing under pressure.

If I had not returned evil for evil, it would have cost less than I ended up paying, I likely would have preserved a very treasured relationship, and I would have had the positive testimony of being a man of character.

But instead, I failed a very difficult test. In my experience, as we mature we are tested in all ways to see if our beliefs are real. If they are firmly implanted and we remain true to our convictions, we will pass the test; if not, we will fail it. Besides paying a dear price for our failure, we then have to relearn the lesson.

The Tenant

Fast forward a few years to the nightmarish recession our country recently experienced. I'll address this time period later, but I'm going to mention a story that shows how our character is proven through often gut-wrenching situations.

My wife and I had refinanced our house to invest in our business. Incidentally, this was after completely paying it off three different times. Bless my wife for putting up with my entrepreneur spirit! We were operating eleven fitness centers in Arizona. The recession had hit us hard, and to survive we had to put in huge amounts of money.

We also owned a large building in Everett, Washington that we had just completely renovated, at a cost of nearly a million dollars, so we could lease it out to a fitness club operator. We had been making sizable mortgage payments to our bank for nearly ten years, never missing a payment or being late, even though for the past year we had not charged any rent while the club was remodeled and the new tenant built up his membership. We wanted to give him every chance to be successful.

When I approached our bank to refinance our building because the ten-year term was nearly up, they turned us down. This was a shock to us, because this was our lead bank. We had never missed a payment with them with all of our various loans, and we were operating within all of our financial covenants.

If we had to pay the mortgage off, it could cause us to become insolvent and not be able to cover our million-dollar-a-month payroll. It made for some sleepless nights, to say the least.

I decided to be proactive and cold-call other banks. Finally, after being turned down about five times, we caught the interest of a bank we had borrowed from in the past. It helped our case that we had paid them back in full, ahead of time.

We settled on terms, and the loan was scheduled to close within days. As part of the process, I had to sign a document that verified that our tenant's lease payments were current.

This tenant had experience in the fitness business and was running a fairly successful club, but he had missed several payments. I contacted him again, and he promised to make good on what he owed in a couple of weeks—but our loan was closing in just a few days.

I had personal money that would cover the new mortgage payment, and my wife and I would be signing personally. All I had to do was sign the paper that verified current rent payments, and the huge amount that was due would be financed.

I wanted in the worst way just to sign the document. I thought to myself, the lessee will pay, and everything will be okay in the long run. Our six hundred-plus employees and their families will get paid. Our company will survive.

I prayed long and hard about what to do. Did the end justify the means? Was this the right thing to do? The answer to both questions, of course, was no. But the bank was more than collateralized for the loan, so was it really that bad?

After going back and forth with my moral dilemma, I chose to do the right thing even though it could cost us everything. I called the banker who was processing the loan and disclosed to her that our tenant was behind on his rent payments and that in good faith I could not sign the declaration that our lease payments were current.

She responded, "This is a definite problem and will most likely kill the deal." She said she would get back to me in a week or so.

Our lead bank, the one holding the mortgage, heard that the loan was on hold because our tenant had failed to make payment and that I had disclosed it to the bank that had promised financing. They called me and said that I had proved to be a man of high character, but they still expected to be paid in full within the month. I agreed to make payment and hung up, more than sick to my stomach.

Then came a welcome surprise. The new banker called and informed me that because I have had such a good track record and reputation over the last twenty years, and even more importantly because I had proved my integrity in a most difficult time, they would go forward with the loan!

Getting the desperately needed financing wasn't the only positive result. My lead bank extended financing on a couple of other equipment leases and termed out a personal line of credit, due, as they said, "to my personal character."

In the end, our tenant never did make payment. We negotiated peacefully to remove him, and I released the building to my partners of twenty years.

Today, the lease payments are being made in a timely fashion, and we are making a handsome profit on the business. What seemed to be a disaster on the surface turned into one of the best deals I have ever made because I did "the right thing at the right time."

Of Siding and Jewelry

One beautiful August day about five years ago, my wife and I decided to take our boat for a spin around the lake. On the way home, we passed by the home of a friend of ours and noticed they had a construction team tearing all the siding off their brand-new house.

We asked why they were replacing essentially new siding, and they told us that the particular siding they had used turned out to be porous, and water had seeped through it.

My wife looked at me, and I knew what she was thinking. We had used the same product on our new house. We were both sick to our stomachs with the thought of having to replace our siding after living there less than five years. But I thought, with some kind of comfort, that we had insurance that would cover any damage.

Gina called a siding expert to come out and check for water damage. Sure enough, he showed us what our house looked like underneath the siding. It was black, like fire had eaten at the framing of our house. Large beams had rotted almost completely through. The damage was unbelievable.

I called the company who was responsible for the guarantee of the work. To my disappointment, they were no longer in business.

Then I called our insurance adjustor, who came out and reviewed the damage. A week later, the company informed us that they were somehow not responsible and would not be paying to repair the damage. I argued with them for a while, but to no avail.

Next I called our attorney. She said that thousands of people were suffering from the same issue with this type of siding and that most insurance companies were drawing a hard line about not covering the claims. She said if I wanted to fight the insurance company, I should plan on spending at least $100,000, and at best we had a fifty-fifty chance of winning a favorable settlement.

When all was said and done, we decided to adopt a positive attitude and not only redo the siding, but add a beautiful, covered cabana with a fireplace onto our outside patio, which faced the lake. The renovation project cost us an unbudgeted $600,000. Ouch!

Less than a year after this unfortunate situation with our house, my wife lost most of the jewelry that she had accumulated over the years. It was worth a lot of money and had sentimental value for us as well. We searched everywhere, but it was not to be found.

Eventually we turned in a claim to the insurance company— the same one that had turned down our house damage claim earlier— for $85,000. The jewelry was all listed carefully with appraisals and pictures, so there was no argument from the insurance company,

A few weeks later, a check for $85,000 arrived in the mail. My wife was excited to take our daughters out and purchase new jewelry. I think she had already picked a few pieces out while we were waiting for the check to arrive.

Then my youngest daughter spoiled their fun. She found Gina's entire jewelry bag in the trunk of her car when she was cleaning it out.

Now we had an $85,000 check in one hand and the lost jewelry in the other, and the painful memory of how this same insurance company had basically cheated us out of half a million dollars. What should we do?

Trust me, everything inside of us wanted to take the money, rationalizing that we were owed it and much more. All that God had taught us and that we had taught our children was on trial.

Reluctantly, we sent the check back. It was worth it to live with what I feel is the most valuable thing of all: a clean conscience before God and a good reputation before our children. We had passed the test.

An interesting side note is that for years, I kept a picture of my dream house on my desk at work. When my daughters were young and would ask about it, I would tell them that some day we would have that type of house on our property on the lake.

Because I was working so long and hard, when we replaced the siding and renovated the house, I completely delegated the project to my wife. To my amazement, when the house was done, it was almost an exact replica of the house in that picture, down to the siding and color. My wife doesn't remember ever thinking about that picture while she oversaw the remodel. Again, I saw the invisible power of the imagination at work.

The lesson is always the same: in dire situations, do not lean on your own understanding—in other words, don't take matters into your own hands—but trust God to work things out for you by doing the right thing. He will never leave us nor forsake us, and if we learn how to adhere to his righteous ways under all circumstances, he will bless us in ways we couldn't have foreseen.

If My People

In the final analysis, getting wisdom is the primary thing; or as I think of it, "Doing the right thing, at the right time, all the time." I could give dozens of examples of when I made wise decisions; and I could give dozens more of when, out of ignorance or stubbornness or both, I made foolish decisions.

As I said earlier, 2 Chronicles 7:14 has been key in helping me determine right thinking and right acting. It is worth reviewing the wisdom it contains. Hopefully it will help you like it has me.

It begins with, "If my people who are called by my name will humble themselves . . ." In order to be one of God's people, we have to recognize that we are sinners and that God sent his son Jesus to die for our sins. Through the grace of God and our faith in him, we are saved and become his sons and daughters. Jesus freely gives us the power and wisdom we need to do the right thing.

The passage says that God's people must "humble themselves." That means learning to become humble and staying humble. God despises the proud, which is anyone who thinks he can somehow handle all the challenges of life on his own.

We can learn a lesson from the life of David, whose story is recorded in the Bible. As a young man, he had the courage to go up against the nine-foot giant Goliath on the battlefield, defying all odds, and killed him with one well-targeted stone. He went on to become a great general and ultimately one of the most powerful kings who ever lived. Yet this same man cried his eyes out countless times before God, asking for help to overcome his enemies and his own sinful desires. God did not see David's dependency on him as a weakness, but rather embraced it as a strength, calling him "a man after my own heart."

A humble heart is meek and gentle before God. There is no weakness in that. Our culture often confuses humility with weakness and arrogance with courage. God wants to help us, but we must recognize our need for him, putting our confidence in him, not ourselves.

The next part of the verse reads, ". . . and pray and seek my face . . ." I believe that more than anything, God desires a personal, interactive relationship with us. He calls himself our Father and us his children. Jesus says we are his friends, and he describes the Holy Spirit as our comforter. In order to have effective fellowship with God, we must learn his voice and his ways.

I strongly believe God wants to communicate to us his direction for our life. In many passages, the Bible tells us he has a specific plan and purpose for each of us. Our gifts and talents are perfectly suited to that purpose.

True understanding and relationship with God come first from continuous, consistent reading of his words, which are recorded in the Bible. God commanded Joshua to read and meditate on his word day and night. This enables us to better interpret what God is saying to us.

Besides studying the Bible, we also glean knowledge, wisdom, and direction from the time that we spend one-on-one with God in prayer and meditation. We must learn the value of being still during prayer, rather than endlessly talking.

The Bible says that God knows our thoughts and needs before we even ask him, but on the other hand, it says we have not because we ask not. Those are not contradictory statements. The key is to distinguish God's voice from the other thoughts that bombard our minds even during prayer. In order to hear the soft, peaceful voice of the Holy Spirit, we must first learn how to be quiet and listen. This takes time and discipline.

The famous pastor Dr. Yonggi Cho wrote that an hour of effective prayer was worth twenty-four hours of activity. Dr. Cho himself spent five hours a day in prayer. He built a church of nearly one million people and started another five hundred churches around the world.

John 15:7–8 describes the perfect relationship with God, both in prayer and in life. The passage reads, "But if you remain in me and my words remain in you, you may ask for anything you want, and it will be granted! When you produce much fruit, you are my true disciples. This brings great glory to my Father."

Continuing on in 2 Chronicles 7:14, we read, ". . . and turn from their wicked ways." I am living proof that God is a patient God. Just ask my wife! However, if we want to accomplish all that God has in store for us, we must overcome our sinful ways through the grace of God. That includes both the "big sins" and the "little sins," as people like to categorize them in their minds. In reality, it is all sin, and eventually it will bring destruction and loss.

God wants us to experience a complete identity overhaul. We should become who we are meant to be in Christ; in essence, we are to be remade in the image of Jesus. Then and only than will we become truly effective in life.

It starts with "becoming," and that produces the "doing." We cannot overcome our sinful tendencies through willpower alone—it is impossible for something broken to fix itself.

Our will to do right must be joined to the supernatural power of God. Then, through his power, we will turn from wickedness. If we are not empowered by God, it often seems that the harder we try, the harder it is to overcome. Those who have incredibly strong wills might overcome certain wrong behaviors, but the by-product is usually pride, which in time just causes more problems.

So humbly ask God to help you, then let God do what he wants to do in your life.

The passage in 2 Chronicles concludes by saying, "I will hear from heaven and will forgive their sins and restore their land. My eyes will be open and My ears attentive to every prayer made in this place." Humility, prayer, seeking God's face (his ways), and turning from our wicked ways are fundamental to gaining God's favor in our life. As Deuteronomy 28 teaches, faith and obedience come before blessings.

Just as we expect our children to mature as time goes on, so God our Father expects us to mature, which includes growing in integrity. This is proven more by our actions than our words, especially our actions under pressure.

Do not mistake God's firm hand of discipline for a lack of love. Like the book of Proverbs says, a good father disciplines his son or daughter. God is full of mercy and grace, but he refuses to allow us to act foolishly.

God's wisdom helps us know when to proceed with caution and when to sprint forward and seize the opportunity God has given. Sometimes we must go slow to go fast, while other times it is full speed ahead.

Doing the right thing, at the right time, all the time means walking with God consistently, regardless of the storms of life. It is walking circumspectly, always considering what God would do under these exact circumstances. It is listening to God and then acting, knowing that He is far more faithful to us than we are to him.

If, like Solomon, we make wisdom our primary pursuit, success, wealth, and favor will find us, and everything we do will prosper.

07

Discovering the Spirit of Generosity

It was spring of 1987, a little over three months after we had gained possession of Hart's Athletic Club in Everett, Washington. We were all working hard. Gina, who was six months pregnant with our third little girl, was working part-time selling memberships and helping with janitorial work while commuting an hour each way to make sure our three-year-old and five-year-old were being cared for. Gina's parents were a great help with the kids as well.

I stayed at the Motel 6 next to our club Monday through Thursday so I could save time on my commute, allowing me to put in sixteen-hour days. Club membership was growing, but not at the speed we had hoped for. Our financial situation was very difficult, and we had no credit.

One spring afternoon in particular stands out in my memory. I had gone outside to be alone for a few moments. It was a clear, blue-sky day; the air was crisp and the cherry trees were in full bloom. Everything would have been beautiful, except for one major problem: payroll was due the next day, and I was $2,500 short.

My employees were loyal, but they were in pretty much the same sad state of affairs as we were financially. They couldn't afford to go without a paycheck. The club was slow, no potential new members had walked through the door all day, and my faith was at an all-time low.

I had no fancy, faith-filled prayers—just a tearful cry to God for help. I thought, why would he take us this far, only to let us fall now? I gathered myself and went back into the club, a half-hearted smile attempting to cover up my concern. I knew that if something didn't happen soon, we would be out of business within days.

Then, three men I didn't recognize walked in the door. The older of the three was about seventy-five pounds overweight. He asked me in a baritone voice, "Is there anyone who can help me with my obvious problem?" He patted himself on the stomach and laughed while he said it.

I immediately offered them a tour of the club. The older man introduced himself as Reverend Guy Sier. I led him and his two companions around the club.

After the tour, he said matter-of-factly, "I have no idea why we even came into your club today. We've passed this club hundreds of times on our way home from work and never once mentioned checking it out. Today when I turned in, my son asked what we were doing. I told him that I think God is telling me it is time to get myself into shape and lose some of this weight."

Somehow I knew God was in this apparently chance encounter. Reverend Guy Sier and I had an instant and unusual connection. I had toured thousands of prospective members over the years, but this was different. It was almost a spiritual encounter, like he was an angel sent from God.

He told me that he had spent the last forty years of his life working with destitute men on the streets and running a prison ministry at the state penitentiary. I shared with him what had happened to me over the last few years, while also going over how we would get him in shape.

He asked, "How much would it cost for me, my son, and our friend to join?" Before I could answer, he continued loudly, "They aren't too interested, but we are all going to join, and they can be my accountability partners. We'll stop in after work together. Since I'm paying for their membership, they don't get much say in the matter."

I said, "For the three of you, it would be $400 to join and $85 per month in dues."

He looked at me. "I just turned sixty-five, and I have this retirement program I have been paying into for years, and it has produced more money than I know what to do with. Would you allow me to pay a couple of years' membership in advance?"

I quickly agreed and figured out what the total would be. It was a little over $2,500, the exact amount of money I needed to cover payroll the next day.

As we were setting up their first workout appointment just before they left, I asked Rev. Sier if he would take a few minutes to mentor me in how to become a better Christian. In return, I would personally take him through his workouts and set him up on an eating plan that, if followed, would guarantee him great results.

His response was direct. "I will mentor you if and only if you do what I tell you to do. I am not, at my age, interested in wasting my time." I could tell he had little patience for pretenders, and I assured him that I would learn and do as he directed.

Givers or Takers

The next day, he and his friends showed up for their workout appointments. As promised, I took Rev. Sier through his first workout as he kiddingly blamed his wife for overfeeding him for the past forty years.

After he had completed his workout, I asked him if he could spare fifteen minutes to sit down with me and tell me more about God and his plan for my life. I thought we would get into some philosophical conversation about spiritual matters, but Guy caught me off guard by simply asking me if I tithed to a church or some worthwhile organization. I explained that because I was working such long hours, I wasn't attending any church; and to be honest, I had never been much of a giver.

He asked me how much money I was making. I told him $3,000 a month, and that didn't cover even half of what it cost to take care of my monthly bills or the millions of dollars I was in debt.

His response, as usual, was to the point: "If you're in that bad of shape financially, what will it matter if you give me 10 percent of your income? I will put it to good work at the men's mission downtown. The next time I come, just give me $300, and we will be square for the month." Then he added, "Son, you need to learn to become a giver, not just a taker."

He left, and I thought to myself, that wasn't exactly what I had in mind when I asked to be spiritually mentored. Then I thought, how could I give $300 when I could hardly feed my kids and keep our business open?

But I had promised to do what he said without question or exception. So the next morning, I placed three hundred-dollar bills in my right pocket. Sure enough, right at five o'clock, Rev. Sier walked through the door.

I went up to him and pulled the money out of my pocket. I felt like I was jumping off a fifty-foot cliff. It seemed foolish to me in light of my financial crisis.

I handed it over to him before I could talk myself out of it. He took it like it was no big deal and proceeded to the locker room.

Something happened to me in that moment. It was like something was broken off of me. It's hard to explain, but it was like letting go of all my problems and handing them over to God. I felt lighter. A fresh spirit of freedom came over me. I felt good about myself, something I had not experienced in a very long time.

At the beginning of every month, like clockwork, I would repeat the exercise of giving Rev. Sier the $300.

One day he said to me, "It looks like things are getting busy around here."

I told him business was getting amazingly good. He responded, "You need to start feeding the poor."

So together we came up with an idea to get our employees and members involved in a food drive for the homeless. We got local merchants to give gifts, literally thousands of dollars' worth, and put together an auction for the members. If they brought in cans of food, we would give them "funny money" which they could use to purchase nice Christmas presents at our club auction. Some members got so excited that they went out and bought hundreds of dollars' worth of food just to get enough funny money to buy a fifteen-dollar blender.

By the end of the food drive, we had raised in excess of twenty thousand food items. We threw one of the best Christmas parties in town. Our members and employees and their friends had a great time, but even better, there was a generous spirit in the club. Everyone felt good about what they had accomplished by collecting so much food, and the atmosphere among both employees and members was unequalled. It seems that people who feel good about themselves produce great results.

Rev. Guy Sier was never big on quoting scriptures on giving or, for that matter, on anything else. He was more a man of practicality. When he saw a need, he met it with whatever resources he could get his hands on. Never once did he mention to me that if I gave I would be blessed. For him, it was just living in a way that exhibited God's love.

He believed that giving your money was too easy and that it was important for a person to "get their hands dirty," to rub shoulders with the poor. One day he suggested that we build a workout facility for the guys down at the shelter. So I gathered a group of my employees and friends, and we went to work gutting out a room. Then our maintenance guys did the HVAC and electrical while the rest of us laid rubber flooring, painted the walls, and hung mirrors. Finally, we moved thousands of dollars of beautiful fitness equipment into the designated area. Within a week or so, we finished building a beautiful gym.

Many Saturday mornings we went down and taught the men different exercises, set them up on nutritional plans, and motivated them to follow the workout and nutritional program until the next Saturday, when we would have an accountability session with them. We discovered they were not that much different then we were, except they had made a wrong decision here or there or were struggling with addiction issues.

I owe a great debt of gratitude to Rev. Guy Sier for teaching me the value and joy of making giving an ongoing part of life. Over the years, my wife and I have adopted an attitude of generosity in all we do. In fact, it has become who we are. The gifts have become bigger as financial prosperity has rolled into our lives, but without exaggeration, the biggest gift we ever gave was that first $300. And the return on that has been ten thousand-fold and counting.

Law of Generosity

It would be pointless for me to recite the different gifts we have given, but I do want to review what God's word says about giving. Allow the Spirit of God to touch your heart as he has ours. Let him determine what you give and when you give it.

Over the years, people have often told us that we have a special gift of giving. I understand what they mean, but I am uncomfortable with the underlying assumption that I often sense in their words. They imply that they don't have that gift and are therefore exempt from giving.

God has not chosen some people to give and some to receive. We all give, and we all receive. The scriptures on giving are directed at everyone, not just certain people with a gift to give. I think we are all called to give extravagantly and to find joy in doing so.

Deuteronomy 28:1 says that if we obey God's laws, we will prosper. One part of God's law is to give 10 percent of our income to God as a tithe. It has nothing to do with God needing our money, but rather our need to understand that we are only stewards or managers of God's resources. Tithing eliminates the notion that our money is our money. From the air we breathe, to our gifts and talents, to the good health that enables us to work, all comes from God.

Yet, all he asks for is 10 percent. Actually, he demands it—at least if you believe the Bible is the infallible, inspired word of God. In Malachi 3:8-12, God asks Israel: "Should people cheat God? Yet you have cheated me! But you ask, 'What do you mean? When did we ever cheat you?' You have cheated me of the tithes and offerings due to me. You are under a curse, for your whole nation has been cheating me. Bring all the tithes into the storehouse so there will be enough food in my Temple. If you do," says the Lord of Heaven's Armies, "I will open the windows of heaven for you. I will pour out a blessing so great you won't have enough room to take it in! Try it! Put me to the test! Your crops will be abundant, for I will guard them from insects and disease. Your grapes will not fall from the vine before they are ripe," says the Lord of Heaven's Armies. "Then all nations will call you blessed, for your land will be such a delight."

This is a command. God asks us to prove him, even test him, on this. More than anything, God wants humility and faithfulness on our part, which are foundation blocks of our relationship with him.

I have been to churches where pastors, from the pulpit, have tried to explain this command away or even apologize on behalf of God when it comes to tithing. By doing so, they actually did a disservice to those of us listening. God doesn't need our money—he wants our hearts. As Jesus said, "Wherever your treasure is, there the desires of your heart will also be" (Luke 12:34). Why do you think Jesus asked the young ruler to give up all he had to follow him? Not because he wanted his money, but because he wanted his heart.

As we learn to give obediently, we go from being takers to being givers. This unleashes a principle I call the "Law of Generosity."

Earlier I discussed the Law of Attraction, which is the principle of faith. Learning to exercise vision and faith to attain success is relatively simple, but the success is limited, hard to achieve, and tends to "leak." You always find yourself straining and striving because you need more.

The Law of Generosity is the principle that generous people attract blessing. The more we give, the more we receive; the more we receive, the more we give. Generosity is not about manipulating God or leveraging some force of nature so that we can gain more for ourselves. Rather, generosity is a lifestyle of allowing the blessings or resources we have received to flow out from us to bless others.

It's easy to see how this works even with other people. When we are with someone generous, we usually find ourselves being generous back. When we are with stingy, selfish people, we tend to hold on more tightly to what is ours.

There are many verses in the Bible that promise us blessings if we give, but attempting to manipulate God through our giving, even subconsciously, is a dead end. At the end of Psalm 51, King David says: "You do not desire a sacrifice, or I would offer one. You do not want a burnt offering. The sacrifice you desire is a broken spirit. You will not reject a broken and repentant heart, O God."

David is saying, "First things first." First we give him our hearts. When God is the object of our desire (not just the things he gives us) his gifts and protection can flow more freely.

Ultimately, giving and getting should be a continuous cycle, like breathing in and out. It is the way of God. First he gave us life; then he gave his most precious possession of all, his son, so that he could have a truly loving relationship with us. He is the most generous of all. To be generous is to be like him.

As we give, our gift will be returned with an additional blessing on it. As long as we keep it flowing out, it will return enlarged. I've seen in my own life that we can't out-give God if we are giving from a pure and humble heart.

A generous heart is the subject of 2 Corinthians 9:6-11. "Remember this—a farmer who plants only a few seeds will get a small crop. But the one who plants generously will get a generous crop. You must each decide in your heart how much to give. And don't give reluctantly or in response to pressure. 'For God loves a person who gives cheerfully.' And God will generously provide all you need. Then you will always have everything you need and plenty left over to share with others.... For God is the one who provides seed for the farmer and then bread to eat. In the same way, he will provide and increase your resources and then produce a great harvest of generosity in you. Yes, you will be enriched in every way so that you can always be generous. And when we take your gifts to those who need them, they will thank God."

This concept flies in the face of human nature, at least at first. But once you get it deep into your spirit, you will become a magnet—good things will flow toward you instead of away from you.

Giving keeps us from becoming greedy. It keeps us from making money our god or falling in love with wealth. Money is a good thing if used properly and with the right mind and heart. But the blessing that we receive from God is a "hot potato"—if we keep it in our hands too long, we stop the flow of blessing.

Giving That Is Worth It

The Bible states that we can receive thirty-, sixty-, or even a hundred-fold return on our giving. I believe the lesson here is more than just giving and hoping we get a high multiplier. We should actually be intentional and careful to deposit our seed in fertile ground. We should make the most effective use possible of the resources God has entrusted to us.

This is where wisdom and giving intersect. When my wife and I first started giving back in the 80s, we fell in love with it. In our excitement, though, we gave to people and causes that had little or no return. Our hearts were right, but we lacked wisdom. So we wound up watching our money be used in ineffective and even foolish ways. Take time to find out if the ground is fertile before you sow your hard-earned money into it.

In general, the most fertile soil to sow into is the local church. Although we began giving to Rev. Guy Sier's ministry, Union Gospel Mission, God instructs us that the tithe should go to the local church so it can effectively do the work of God. If a church has a faithful and capable pastor, the tithe will cover the overhead of the church, support missionaries who are spreading the gospel, and enable the church to grow and flourish in good or bad economic conditions.

Many pastors are afraid of upsetting their congregations by preaching on tithing, and because of this they struggle along, barely surviving. I feel blessed that our leadership at The City Church in Seattle has been bold when it comes to teaching the importance of tithing. Even during this latest recession, our church—unlike many churches around the world—has not only survived, but flourished.

Our lead pastors, Judah and Chelsea Smith, have a vision to build a church of a hundred thousand people. It is inspiring for my family and I to be connected with a pastor and a group of people who have such a huge vision.

Giving toward a vision motivates you to become the best you can become. It encourages you to earn more and to give more because you see how your tithes and gifts have a multiplied effect. In business or in ministry, just as in nature, if something is not growing, it is dying.

Besides giving our tithe to our church, my wife and I have carefully picked out organizations around the world that we believe produce great fruit, both in quantity and quality. We give offerings, above our tithes, to missions and churches in Mexico, the Philippines, Africa, and the Dream Center in Los Angeles.

The Dream Center is very close to our hearts because it was started by one of our favorite pastors, Tommy Barnett, and it reaches out to young kids who are living on the streets and who are often mixed up in drug addiction and prostitution.

About eight years ago, our Arizona fitness company, Pure Fitness, built a beautiful gym in the Dream Center for youth who are overcoming alcohol and drug abuse. It is surprising how good a daily workout is for people struggling with addiction issues. As I described earlier, working out was one of the strategies God used to help me defeat drug-related problems.

I mentioned that Rev. Guy Sier and I started a food drive in one of our original clubs. This food drive became a tradition that has continued over the past twenty-plus years. It's worth pointing out that a businessperson can team up with other merchants and a church or charitable organization to do good.

From 2002-2010, our Arizona fitness company partnered with Tommy Barnett's church, major television stations, local merchants, and our seventy-five thousand members to help raise food during the holiday season. Our food drive would run from November until a week before Christmas. In less than forty-five days, we usually collected over three hundred thousand food items.

The Sunday before Christmas, Tommy Barnett would invite people from around the greater Phoenix area to church. Every family received a bicycle, a present for each child, and two hefty bags of food. Over thirty thousand people showed up to these special giving services. Many of our employees, including some who would never attend a church service, went with us to help hand out food. Countless times

I saw tears rolling down the faces of both giver and receiver. Nothing could be more moving!

My point in this illustration is that getting others involved in creative ways of giving teaches everyone how good it feels to be generous and to be a part of something bigger than us. When we join together in a positive activity like this, everyone wins.

My wife and I have developed a habit: when we encounter economic difficulty and that old spirit of fear raises its ugly head, and when everything inside screams at us to grab hold of our assets and not let go, we simply do the opposite. We pray together about giving a substantial gift to some charitable organization. When we exercise this kind of faith, two things usually happen. First, almost immediately, the fear that has taken hold of our hearts is defeated; and second, God gives us his supernatural power to face our obstacles, which often means new and very creative ideas to overcome our challenges.

Once, after giving sacrificially to a church plant in Las Vegas, Gina and I received a letter from the IRS informing us that we somehow overpaid our personal income taxes by $95,000 and that within six weeks we would receive a check for that amount.

Eight weeks later, we had not received the money, so I called our accountant to check into it for us. After a couple of days, he called me back and told me he had some bad news. Because it was such a large amount, the IRS was going to do a full-blown audit on us.

I thought, easy come, easy go. Even if they discovered that I owed them money somewhere else, it would be covered by the $95,000 they owed me.

Four weeks later, checks from the IRS started to arrive. They were from tax years dating as far back as twenty years, repaying money they discovered we had overpaid—with interest. We ended up receiving about twelve checks that totaled over $200,000.

To me, this was a miracle from God, because most of the time an auditor is not allowed to make adjustments on tax returns after seven years. Somehow, someone in the IRS decided to go all the way back and make these positive adjustments that benefited us during a very difficult time financially.

I remember my daughter Rachael, who is a strong believer in God's miracles, saying to me, "Dad, this is a good sign!"

After receiving this money, one business issue after another began to get solved. Before we knew it, we were out of the financial problems we had been facing. My wife kept copies of the checks we received from the government, just to prove it really happened!

More recently, we were again in a negative situation. My partner Eric Stearns and I decided to write a check to our friend Tommy Barnett. We took him out to lunch, and after lunch, I presented him with a large check.

He took it with tears in his eyes and said that this money could not have come at a better time. He told us general giving was down at his church because of the severe recession, and he and his staff didn't know how they were going to get by without making some major cuts in staffing.

As he was putting the check into his pocket, he stopped and said, "This isn't going to kill the golden goose, is it?"

If you don't remember the old story of the golden goose, it goes something like this. Once upon a time there was a farmer and his wife who owned a goose that every day laid a golden egg. This went on for years and brought the farmer and his wife great wealth. But one day, they schemed that if they killed the goose, they would find all the gold inside, without having to wait. So they killed it. But to their disappointment, there was no gold inside, and the now-dead goose could no longer lay golden eggs.

Pastor Barnett told us that over the years, he had seen businesspeople who were in financial trouble give money that should have been used to run their business, and in the end their business went under. From their point of view, God did not come through, so they turned their back on God.

I appreciated his concern and warning, especially since he truly needed the money, but I assured him that we had cash reserves and with God's continued help, we would be all right.

A Culture of Saving

It's interesting that the Jewish people, despite being displaced and persecuted often throughout their history, have not only survived, they have flourished. I think it is because they know the principles of accumulating wealth—principles that come straight from the Bible. Their culture emphasizes earning, saving, tithing, and generosity. In general, they are not only great merchants, they are well-educated and excel in nearly every field. In my point of view, much of the reason they have been mistreated over the years is people's jealousy and envy at their outstanding success and their wealth accumulation.

I think as Christians, we can learn from the Jewish people, especially since they read and adhere to the same principles that we do from the Old Testament.

I have heard people in certain Christian circles say that saving money is a form of greed or a lack of faith. I could not disagree more! Proverbs 21:31 in The Message paraphrase says, "Do your best, prepare for the worst—then trust God to bring victory."

This verse reminds me of what my mother taught me nearly fifty years ago when I first started making money in the strawberry fields. She often exhorted me to be excellent, to do my best, and to save as much as possible—preferably 50 percent but never less than 10 percent. This would allow my money to work for me through interest accumulation or wise investments, and I would have something in case of emergencies, which would happen from time to time. She warned me that it is unwise to grow dependent on anyone, especially the government or employers. She taught me that regardless of what I did to earn a living, I should try to build my own business so that I could not only make a wage, but receive the profits, too.

For being a mom who never worked outside the home, she understood the basics of capitalistic thinking very well, much like the majority of the Jewish people do. Maximize earnings by doing an excellent job, save, and create capital to invest in yourself. In this way your income can increase over the years, not because you work harder and longer in your old age, but because your savings, investments, or your own business work for you.

Most of the biggest givers I know saved a good portion of what they earned, used debt sparingly, and invested in themselves by starting a business centered around what they did best. Like I said earlier, my grandfather, with a sixth-grade education, learned how to become a quality carpenter, saved his money, and started his own home-building business. He was one of the most generous people I have known, both with his resources and his time. He was also a very conservative man with simple needs and desires. He risked money only on work that he did, because he could control the quality of it.

The Generosity Factor

About eight years ago, I went to Manila, Philippines to speak at a large conference on generosity. I gave a testimony on the importance of businesspeople keeping their marriage and family as their number one priority. To my surprise, many were moved by my own transparency about the struggles my wife and I had overcome.

One rather poor family came up after I spoke and asked me to pray for their family: mom, dad, and four children. As I was about to begin, the father put four one-hundred-dollar bills in my hand. He told me that this was their entire savings and that they wanted to use it as a seed offering for the healing of their marriage and family. The parents and children all had tears in their eyes as the father gave me their precious money. I tried to restrain them from giving me the gift, but they were emphatic that I take it. So we all gathered in a circle and prayed a faith-filled prayer for the healing of their marriage and their family issues. It was a very Spirit-filled moment for me, and I will never forget it.

Afterward, I felt bad for receiving their money. The last thing I wanted to do was be a burden on these people. I had even brought $10,000 that I intended to give away while I was there.

I spoke with a close friend and mentor of mine, Don Ostrom, who was on the trip with me. Don started a church in the Philippines fifty years earlier. Today, there are over seven hundred churches around the country that look to Don as a spiritual leader. He has great experience not only in the Philippines but in giving in general, since he has been a highly successful businessman for decades. He and his wife Marlene are two of the most godly, genuine people I have ever had the pleasure of knowing. I told him how guilty I felt and asked him if I did the right thing in accepting the family's gift.

He told me that their faithful gift and my sincere prayer most likely brought healing to their marriage. He said the biggest thing people in poverty need is to learn how to become faithful givers. Once they are set free from expecting others to take care of them, they will begin to grow confidently into financial freedom.

He went on to say that the biggest mistake good-hearted people make is thinking that giving to the underprivileged or poor is going to help them long-term. Once anyone—rich or poor—learns to give, God will open their hearts to new opportunities, and money will begin to flow toward them instead of away from them.

Then he mentioned that there were some faithful mountain pastors who travel hundreds of miles weekly to visit their congregations sprinkled throughout the jungles of the Philippines, and that for just $1,200 we could purchase motorcycles for them that would cut their traveling time significantly. That thought excited me. I ended up using the money I was given and much more to buy several motorcycles for these wonderful pastors.

Don and I, along with a couple of other business friends that were with us, rented a helicopter and traveled to some of these mountainous churches hidden away in the jungle. I was amazed by their love for God and their hospitality to us. Many had never seen a helicopter or a white man before. It was exciting and touching, and the whole adventure began with that faith-filled little family and their $400!

I've learned over the years that the "generosity factor" plays a primary role in achieving personal fulfillment and success—not only in business, but in our family, health, ministry, and walk with God. Giving must be a core part of our being, not just something we force ourselves to do once in a while. We need to become truly generous people.

This is something that is developed over time and by the grace of God. As you become truly generous, you find yourself alert to needs around you. You give freely because you know God will bring back to you more than you give.

True giving has a way of blessing both the giver and the receiver. As Jesus said, "You're far happier giving than getting" (Acts 20:35, The Message).

Generosity means giving out of love and faith, knowing that by giving we are blessing others and ourselves at the same time. Some people give just to meet people's needs, but they don't have faith that God will prosper them and meet their own needs. Others give selfishly, seeking the blessings of giving but without truly loving people or God. Both perspectives are incomplete.

With generosity motivated by love and faith, and with wisdom to discern where our money will most effectively help others, we can't go wrong!

Alms for the Poor

A spirit of generosity reflects the way God interacts with us. He loves us deeply, and therefore he gives us everything we need. God's nature of love is revealed through his actions of giving. In effect, giving is the essence of God.

God commands us to love our neighbor. The practical demonstration of our love often comes down to being generous with those in need. The Bible sometimes calls this giving alms, or gifts, to the poor.

However, our giving strategy must be carefully thought out. Our generosity is not just a way to make us feel less guilty about others' misfortune—we should truly desire to help those in need. Therefore, we should look for ways to not only meet immediate needs, but to inspire and empower people to achieve success themselves.

I believe that the original intent of the welfare system in America was good, and it originated from good people whose hearts were set on helping people in desperate need. But the end result of a welfare system that continuously gives to the disadvantaged through government funding has been disastrous. It actually steals from the poor—it erodes their dignity, confidence, and the self-reliance that helps build self-esteem. Through good but misguided intentions, we have created a culture where poverty is more secure than employment.

The answer is to help people get back on their feet through education, job training, advancement opportunities, and incentives to excel. We must teach people how to take care of themselves by giving them a hand up instead of a handout.

At the same time, we must teach them to become givers, no matter how small the gift is in the beginning. Everyone, from the poorest to the riches, must unlock the secret of becoming a giver instead of a taker.

I know some people have no other option than to receive government support, and I don't judge them for their circumstances or decisions. But I would rather clean urinals, toilets, and dirty ashtrays for the rest of my life and earn a paycheck than have someone give me a check every month for free. I think that most people, if they could experience the freedom and self-confidence produced by hard work tied to the right opportunity, would agree with me.

Pursued by Blessings

In summary, my thoughts always go back to Deuteronomy 28:1–2. "If you fully obey the Lord your God and carefully keep all his commands that I am giving you today, the Lord your God will set you high above all the nations of the world. You will experience all these blessings if you obey the Lord your God."

This passage says that as we are faithful to follow God, he is faithful to bless us. What I do not see here is a clause that says we have to be a doctor, attorney, star athlete, or genius businessman to be blessed. It simply says that if we obey God, we will be blessed.

Most reassuring of all, we don't have to rely on our own willpower to follow his commands. Actually, according to the Bible, we cannot be perfect on our own no matter how hard we try: we need God's grace and power, which are freely available and are sufficient to help us live as we should.

Always remember that we are blessed to be a blessing. Be intentional about developing a spirit of generosity. You will never regret giving.

08

Catching a God-Vision

When I became an owner in Family Fitness Center and began expanding the company, we had little cash, no credit history, and no debt. We grew to nearly $100 million in total revenue—only to lose everything.

With Hart's Athletic Club, it was worse than starting over. We had little cash, ruined credit and name, and over $30 million in debt, which we were struggling to pay off by selling our properties and assets.

We worked long days, sometimes seven days a week. We put our heads down in prayer and somehow got enough strength each day to face what felt like impossible odds. It was agonizingly slow.

One step at a time, through months of hard work, perseverance, and complete dependence on the Lord, we began to see profits. It wasn't much at first, but it grew; and once we started to post good profits, I could see a light at the end of the tunnel.

I knew that without God's help, we would not have made it this far. I promised God and myself that this time I would do things his way, not my way.

For years I had understood the power of creative thinking: that God gave us a brain unlike any other creature he created, a brain that could dream and then bring those dreams into reality. But now I realized that I had to make sure my visions were God-inspired, not generated by selfish ambitions or demonic powers. So I took time to carefully think and pray about what the Lord's vision was for our new life.

As I studied the Bible, I noticed something interesting. Often when people went through turning points in their lives, God had them change their names. Abram was changed to Abraham, Jacob to Israel, Simon to Peter, and Saul to Paul. The name change was to better reflect who they were in relationship to God and his specific purpose for them in life. It was a reminder to see themselves as God saw them.

Psychology supports the concept that how people see themselves determines much of their outward behavior. If we truly want to fulfill God's vision for our life, we must see ourselves differently, through God's eyes. Our identity must be firmly planted in who God says we are. No amount of positive confessions will help if our self-identity has not first been changed by God.

I wondered for a time if I should change my name—that is how committed I was to turning my life around. My name means "champion," so instead of changing it, I determined to be a champion for God by accomplishing his purpose for my life.

I took my family on our first vacation in some time and dedicated my mornings from five o'clock to nine o'clock to prayer, asking God to download His vision for my life. For ten days, I spent each morning writing out in detail what I believed God was saying to me.

The following is the vision statement that I wrote out on that vacation many years ago. I purposefully used the words "I am" to reject the person I had been in the past and the negative circumstances I was facing. At the time, little of it was true. But I believed it was God's will for my life.

For the next year, I took time daily to get quiet before the Lord, read this vision out loud, and pray. I must have read it hundreds of times.

Slowly, my identity was re-created. I understood how God saw me, what he wanted me to become, and what he wanted me to do. Today, nearly twenty-five years later, almost everything in my statement has materialized.

Vision Statement, 1988

I am a confident leader in all areas of my life, reinforced by God who gives me strength at all times. Since God is my strength, I am confident, comfortable, and at peace, regardless of the place, situation, or circumstances.

I derive most of my pleasure and satisfaction from my wonderful wife Gina and our children, Crystal, Rachael, Leslie, and Ian. I am their spiritual leader, educator, and protector. They are my number one priority at all times. I find creative ways to empower them and always instill in them security, confidence, and emotional stability. Each family member honors and respects one another. From this ongoing respect and honor they have for one another comes much joy and enthusiasm whenever we come together. I take the responsibility to nurture them with positive affirmations so that they grow individually into strong, mature, Christian adults. Regardless of how busy I am, I am never too busy to see that all of their needs are met while allowing them enough space to create their own strong and individual identity. My wife and children are in the process of becoming completely self-reliant except for their dependence on our Lord Jesus Christ.

I do not just believe in quality time spent with my family, but I believe quantity of time is as important. This is why I take every opportunity that presents itself to spend time with them. I purposely have developed individual relationships with my wife Gina and each child. I have discovered that prayer and communication are the keys to my successful relationships with them. I have also developed common areas of interest with each of them, so that we can enjoy one another's company to the maximum. I realize that life is short, especially the younger years with my children, so I concentrate on how to capture precious moments with them that we will forever cherish.

I am a God-fearing man. I realize that everything I am and everything I have is a result of God's blessings. I do believe that in most cases we reap what we sow; that is why I take sole responsibility for my circumstances. However, I realize that God is a sovereign God and that he may take or give regardless of my good or bad actions. Although I put much value on the days God gives me, I understand that these days are but a moment in eternity and in God's great purpose do not make that much difference, and therefore I do not take myself or my accomplishments that seriously. On the other hand, there is definite significance to my life on earth. I know that if I were the only one on earth, that Jesus would have still found it important enough to come down from heaven and die for my sins so that I would have the opportunity for eternal life with him. Because of this fact, I value my life on earth greatly.

God's greatest commandment for man was to love him more than anyone else. I believe, therefore, that my love for God is shown through my strict obedience toward his commandments. I understand that any form of immorality God despises and that he calls man to be holy and godly like himself. Although I know I will always fall short of God's glory, it is my ongoing desire to become more and more like my Lord Jesus Christ.

Because of how good God has been toward me, I will always give back to God and his people in the form of Christian service and monetary support that goes beyond tithing.

I am a mature Christian man who follows and adheres to the principles set forth in 1 Timothy describing what a good leader should be like. I feel comfortable in any leadership position within the church that accentuates my God-given spiritual gifts and talents. As a leader in the church, I go about my work in humility before God and man, knowing that a good leader has a servant's attitude at all times.

God was gracious to me many years ago when I had no idea what I would be or do in life. He blessed me with the perfect profession that fitted my innate abilities, that profession being the fitness business. Although I experience much joy in all areas of my life, the fitness business has always been a perfect fit. Because of this perfect fit, I have and will always excel far beyond others in this field. I believe God has destined me to be the very best. Getting people healthy is to me a very worthy quest in life and deserves my best efforts in bringing physical and mental fitness to as many people as will allow.

I am and will always be a picture of health unless God sees differently. Through God's power I have complete mastery over my body. I exercise regularly every major muscle group and eat and drink only what is nutritionally sound for my body. I exercise complete and relentless discipline over laziness and any form of physical or mental abuses. I am the epitome of physical fitness.

I practice good, sound, biblical principles when it comes to managing my financial resources. God has blessed me with the ability and know-how to make huge amounts of money. This money that God has blessed me with I take seriously and invest it wisely so that my wife and children are always secure financially, and so whatever businesses I am responsible for continue to flourish and my employees and business partners and families alike are secure.

I understand and accept and embrace all those people of authority over me, whether it be the president of the United States, an IRS collection agent, or a state attorney general representative. I always treat these people of authority with the utmost respect and care for the job they do, regardless of how they treat me. It is always my complete desire to follow all rules and regulations put before me with a good, positive attitude.

I rejoice about people's differences. I realize that God created all kinds of people; not only do they come in all kinds of colors and sizes, but in all sorts of varied personalities and gifting. I understand that God has given all people, because of their individual gifts and experiences, different perspectives on the same thing. These perspectives are neither negative nor positive, but just different. I have no problem ever with those who see things differently than I. I am secure with who I am, and although I care deeply about people's ideas and philosophies, my self-concept is never affected.

I have learned to develop strong and secure long-lasting relationships with people. I not only derive much pleasure from these relationships, but I am long-suffering and can endure much pain in order to preserve these treasured relationships.

I am positive through and through. I expect the best out of people and expect the best from myself. When I encounter people who are exhibiting negative emotions, actions, or ideas, I view it only as an opportunity as to how I can help make them positive. If at that time making that person or situation positive seems impossible, I simply move away from them or it, never once leaving with a negative thought, attitude, or action.

What has cemented my life together is my wife Gina. There is no one on earth who has given me more, from being the best mom to our children to the most supportive wife a man could ever dream of having. I treasure and honor our relationship. We put each other's needs first, and because of that, we have become best friends and have been successful at keeping that teenage romance alive throughout our marriage. I hope we will be soul mates forever.

Finding Your Vision

This vision statement was how God moved me at that particular point in my life. It is an example of the kind of vision each of us should have for our own life.

Our vision should be designed by God. His vision or destiny for our life is like a perfectly-fitted glove that was designed especially for us.

Note that God's vision for us is often specific to a time and set of circumstances. Over the years, I have created different vision statements dealing with aspects of my life that I was struggling with at the time. I would enlarge my vision statement with specific, descriptive, and even emotional language.

Remember, God gives us glimpses of our ultimate destiny, not the whole panorama. Once we accomplish a certain part of it, he may choose to take us in a completely different direction.

I warn you, however, to be slow to change until you know it is God moving in your life. I have watched many people get confused by obstacles that were meant to prove their faith and strengthen them for their next step. They thought God was changing their life direction. In order for us to become mature men and women of God, we must develop perseverance, determination, and long-suffering.

I can't stress enough the difference between a faith-filled prayer or confession and a weak, faithless one. In the first chapter of the book of James, the author describes the difference between prayers of faith and double-minded prayers that have absolutely no positive effect on our circumstances.

Again, be conscious of your thoughts and your self-talk. They can be your undoing. Combat negativity with either positive affirmations that surround your vision statements or power verses such as Psalms 34 or 91, which will strengthen you in times of weakness.

Remember, the greatest battle is not somewhere out there in the heavens above, but in your mind. Win the battle of your mind and capture the destiny that God has designed for you.

09

The Building of a Champion

My first company was about making money. My second company was about creating something worthwhile.

While Family Fitness Centers achieved a high level of financial success, the insides of the company were rotten. Excesses, conflicts, and a poor reputation defined us and ultimately ruled us. Finally, the company failed financially as well.

When we sold Hart's Athletic Clubs, the story was very different. We had a great reputation with our members and the community. We had six hundred employees, and they were proud to work for us. We were voted the best athletic club in Washington. Our profit margin was 35 percent, and we received the highest sale price ever paid for a group of clubs that size in the US. We won on all levels: economic, spiritual, and social.

The difference? For over a decade, we worked hard to build a different kind of company, one that was founded on wisdom, decency, and integrity. I remember asking myself often, if Jesus were to tour my clubs, would he have a smile on his face?

We were passionate about training and empowering people. We wanted to create men and women of valor. In the past, most of my key executives had moral and drug abuse issues. Over time, I led many of them to the Lord. They turned their lives around and became not only good at business, but good people. I was the best man at several of their weddings. They are now multimillionaires with successful marriages and families. To me, that is clearer proof of true success than any profit and loss statement.

Memories of the excesses in my first company still sadden me. I saw how God took his blessing off of it, and that instilled in me a healthy fear of God. When God takes his blessing and favor off of you, every decision you make is a wrong decision. You can have all the brains and capital in the world, but if you get off track spiritually, you will fail.

On the other hand, just because you are a good Christian and citizen doesn't mean you will automatically be successful in business. Many times while counseling people who are thinking of starting their own business, I've found that they haven't learned how to effectively and consistently take care of themselves or their families. Unless someone has learned the basics of becoming financially independent or self-reliant, their odds of success are so low that I discourage them from starting their own business.

As a result, I have been accused of being faithless and negative—but I have seen too many people get destroyed in the marketplace. It is a jungle, like it or not, and if you don't have basic economic and mental disciplines in place, you will get eaten alive. I have witnessed even savvy, experienced people lose everything because they took their eye off the ball for a minute or because they ran into a perfect storm that took them by surprise.

Starting your own business is a wonderful thing, but you must be prepared and have the stomach for it. The following subjects are short dissertations that are intended to help prepare you to earn more, save more, give more, and maybe even start your own business.

Please keep in mind that knowledge, no matter how good it is, is worthless unless executed effectively and habitually.

Pursuit of Excellence

Few, if any, successful people just fell into their success by chance. All of them have stories of grueling struggles that in time brought their talents to the limelight.

Author Malcolm Gladwell in his book *Outliers* analyzes and discusses personal and sociological factors that help produce success.

His analysis led to what he calls the "10,000-hour rule." From Bill Gates to The Beatles, highly successful people spend at least 10,000 hours perfecting their art. They are naturally gifted, of course, but their success is not instant or miraculous. It comes after a great deal of behind-the-scenes training.

As a high school student, Bill Gates would sneak out of his house nearly every night and go to the University of Washington, where he would program on the newest computers until the college students arrived. When he got to Harvard, he already knew what the best professors in the world were teaching.

The Beatles, who are known across the world for their "instant" success, had been playing music for years prior to their rise to fame. For over three years, they played seven nights a week in dingy nightclubs in Germany, perfecting their music.

I remember once, at the age of nine, my father sent me out to clean the garage. I had a negative attitude because it was a beautiful day and I wanted to be out in the street, playing ball. In my rotten mood, I was doing a rather crummy job cleaning up. About halfway through, I looked around and said to myself, "This is not a very good job!"

That realization didn't leave me feeling right about myself, so I started over. When I was finished, the garage sparkled, and I felt good about myself. I can't remember if my father commented on what an excellent job I had done, but what has stayed with me is the sense of satisfaction and fulfillment that comes from a job well done.

Years ago, my daughter Crystal showed me a school paper she had written and asked for my feedback. I read through it. Frankly, I was disappointed. I could tell she hadn't put as much effort into it as I would have expected. I pointed out some of the errors, reminded her the paper represented her, and asked if it was a true representation of who she was.

Big tears welled up in her eyes, and she admitted that she hadn't done her best. We worked on it together, and the finished product was something she could be proud of.

Crystal went on to graduate college with a degree in communications. She has beautiful writing skills and is an accomplished public speaker.

As parents and employers, we need to learn how to be both gentle and painfully honest. Ignoring mediocrity in the name of being nice doesn't do anyone a favor. If sooner or later you will have to deal with an issue in a person's life, you are better off doing it sooner. Most people want to be excellent, but they often need a leader's motivation, whether they appreciate it in the moment or not.

The great philosopher Aristotle said, "Excellence is an art won by training and habituation. We do not act rightly because we have virtue or excellence, but we rather have those because we have acted rightly. We are what we repeatedly do. Excellence, then, is not an act but a habit."

Decide to become an excellent person. Determine that everything you do, you will do in the best possible way. Excellence is not a once-in-a-while thing or a gift only a few people are lucky enough to have. It's a lifestyle, a habit, something you develop purposefully and over time.

The 10,000-hour rule helps you turn your gifting and passions into greatness if and only if you have a mind of excellence and you continue your quest to improve. Unthinking activity is sometimes worse than no activity at all because it becomes a habit, and we are usually prisoners of our habits, good or bad.

Mediocre, average, or even good people do not build excellent lives. When I look at God's creation or read God's specific instructions to King Solomon regarding the temple he was to build him, I see a God of excellence. He created us in his image, so we should be excellent.

Nothing can substitute for excellence. There was a time period when I travelled around the world, giving talks to churches on the subject of generosity. I left the day-to-day job of running my company "in God's hands"—which basically meant I hoped things would turn out right because my heart was right.

In the long run, that didn't work out too well. And it wasn't God's fault! I learned that if I was going to leave my business, even for a good cause, I had to do my part to make sure things got done. Specifically, that meant leaving competent people in charge.

Yes, that's just common sense. But I have talked to many Christians who, in effect, hide behind their good works or their financial gifts. They think that because they are tithing and obeying God, he will miraculously counteract their poor business decisions, lack of initiative, and lack of involvement.

When God does a miracle, he more often than not does it through us. He gives us creative ideas, opens up doors of opportunity, and guides our decisions even when we aren't aware of it. His blessings come in practical ways, so we must be ready to put in some sweat equity when the golden opportunity arrives. If we don't know the state of our business or aren't willing to work diligently, we may miss the very miracle we are waiting for.

When I evaluate new recruits for my business, excellence is one of my primary prerequisites. And again, I'm not looking for one-time excellence or even once-in-a-while excellence. Excellence must be a lifestyle.

Excellence is the surest path to promotion. As a kid picking strawberries, I became a field boss at fourteen years old. When I flipped burgers at Jack In The Box, I was asked to become a manager. As a college kid, my passion for fitness landed me a job offer and then a part-time position as fitness trainer at my first club. From there I worked my way up the management ladder and eventually became one of the owners. I believe that all these jobs were part of my destiny, and everything I did helped develop me for the next level.

It is important to realize that everything is a testing ground. Pass the test in an excellent way and graduate to the next thing the Lord has in store for you.

I have found that less than one person in a thousand always tries to do his or her best. One of my biggest pet peeves as a business owner is when employees say that if they get promoted, they will prove just how good they are. Or they say that once they get their dream job, then they will be motivated and truly shine. Prove how excellent and motivated you are first—then promotion will come!

Becoming an excellent person and producing excellent work increases your earning potential. You will receive constant praise, and because of this positive reinforcement, your confidence will grow. Your supervisors will look for ways to better use your talents. Set your mind on doing your very best. Bosses are looking for the person who always gives his best, and they can tell the difference between self-serving flatterers and truly excellent workers.

A mind-set of excellence has nothing to do with gifts and talents. Excellence will get everything out of you that you are capable of giving, which is always more than you expect.

For instance, I am not very good at administration, but if needed, I can do most of the administrative and accounting duties necessary for operating a fitness center. Is it in my major gift set? Probably not. But when we started our company with no money, I was able to keep the books until I had the resources to hire a professional.

I firmly believe that anyone who has a desire to own and operate his own business can and will have a large degree of success if they make excellence a habit.

Submission to Authority

I have an eighteen-month-old grandson. If anyone looks him in the eyes and says, "No," he has a meltdown: crying, screaming—the whole bit. As my daughter and I assure each other, he'll grow out of that. But even as adults, hearing the word "No" from an authority can provoke at least an internal meltdown.

A few months back, I was taking a pastor friend of mine out golfing at our golf club. One of the club staff, a young man about twenty years old, came up to me and asked politely if I would please tuck in my shirt.

My internal response was, "How dare you tell me to tuck my shirt in!" Thankfully, I have a reasonable amount of self-control, so I smiled and said, "Sure," while tucking in my shirt to his satisfaction.

Then my friend, who is eighty years old and has the sweetest disposition, whispered to me, "Don't you just hate people telling you what to do?"

My point is we are all born with some degree of rebellion in us—especially leaders. Many leaders have ruined themselves because they have not been able to conquer this rebellious tendency.

Everyone answers to someone. That means we must learn to submit our opinions, ideas, decisions, and actions to those in authority.

Think about it: even Jesus, when he came to earth and became a man, emptied himself of his authority and submitted completely to his heavenly Father. When Jesus was in the garden of Gethsemane, knowing what a painful death lay ahead of him, he prayed, "My Father! If it is possible, let this cup of suffering be taken away from me. Yet I want your will to be done, not mine" (Matthew 26:39).

No matter how high we climb on the ladder of life, we will still have to answer to authority in some arena. And in the end, we will all answer to God.

I have always taught my children that life is not fair, and that at one point or another, they will work for someone who treats them disrespectfully and unfairly. While quitting might be the easiest thing to do, if they can learn to work successfully even for a tyrant, then everyone else they work for in life will be a walk in the park.

The word "submission" in our culture has become almost a dirty word. I've lost countless highly talented people who have told me that unless I moved them to another club or fired their immediate supervisor, they were going to quit. They have tried to convince me that if they could work directly for me, everything would be perfect, and I would be able to develop them to the highest level within our company. I suppose that in many cases, I could have developed them faster or further than their supervisor could have—but there would have come a day when I would have had to say no to something, and they would have thrown a tantrum like my little grandson, then either quit or be fired. I saved us all time and trouble by telling them no from the start.

God commands us—he doesn't just ask us—to submit to our authorities, whether we agree with them or like them or not. Your ability to submit to authority is directly related to your level of humility. Proud people usually have a hard time with submission, especially rich, proud people. Because humility and respect for authority are not part of our basic nature, we must always be on guard and not allow rebellion to resurface.

I always think about how Jesus offered himself up to honor his Father's request, even though he could have taken out his accusers and torturers at any time. If we can see submission as a great strength instead of thinking that we are being weak or dishonored, we can begin to defeat this rebellion that lies so deep within our souls.

Even the most talented people—potential leaders in the marketplace and other spheres of influence—will ultimately experience failure after failure if they cannot overcome this defect in their sinful nature. The same tendency toward rebellion that you see in small children struggling against their parents' requests is still in us, and God asks that we overcome it through the power of the Holy Spirit.

If you find yourself in a job where you are constantly ridiculed and mistreated, you have the choice to quit. But before you do, ask God if there is something he is trying to teach you. Pray hard and long before you jump ship, because more times than not, God is using the negative circumstances to teach you what true humility and submission mean. Never speak disrespectfully about your employer—after all, he or she is giving you a paycheck.

Mentality of a Champion

A financially secure lifestyle begins with establishing proper habits that lead to monthly or even daily surplus. In the last twenty-five years, Americans especially have developed a culture of spending, and saving has become a foreign concept to many. I would venture to guess that if you asked, eight out of ten people under thirty years old couldn't give you an accurate definition of frugality.

This is not their fault as much as it is their parents' and teachers' fault. Over the years, our society has taught our children to become dependent on others, often the government. If something goes wrong financially, they receive unemployment benefits, welfare, disability, and the like. Recently, the government has given assistance to people who made bad choices in purchasing and financing their homes, thus giving them an escape from being financially responsible.

I don't mean to sound hardhearted, but as I mentioned earlier, we need to be concerned for the true, lasting welfare of people, not just their temporary comfort. Unaware, people are handing over their independence to a group of people who may or may not be trustworthy. In the process, they are losing invaluable qualities essential to a successful life and economy: things like resourcefulness, personal responsibility, work ethic, and creativity.

Not long ago, we watched rioting in the streets in Greece when the government reduced government workers' pay by 15 percent because the socialist Greek government was on the verge of bankruptcy. As I write this, here in the United States, some states are also hovering near bankruptcy, and government employees are picketing in the streets because they are being asked to take a small cut on government benefits that are attached to their compensation package.

It's easy to become judgmental toward these people, but when people grow up completely dependent on the government and then one day the government says, "Sorry, we are broke and you are on your own," they feel defrauded. This is all they know. The same thing happens on a smaller scale with parents who bail their children out of every financial crisis. Most governments and most parents have good hearts. They don't want to see those under their oversight suffer because of financial tragedy. But they inadvertently steal their personal resourcefulness and responsibility. In their desire to help, they create dependent societies and dependent children.

I remember an incident that took place a few years back, while I was spending a month personally managing one of my fitness clubs. It's something I do once in a while to evaluate our company's systems and procedures from the ground up instead of the top down. I find it to be a very valuable management tool.

I hired a really good recruit, a woman with a charismatic personality and a strong fitness background. She told me that she was recently divorced and had a young child, so we discussed her hours and strategized about how she would take care of her little girl while she worked full-time. I could tell she would be a fast learner, and I could teach her within three months how to make $4,000 to $5,000 per month selling memberships. We were both excited, and I looked forward to training her in a couple of days.

Two days later she showed up with a long face. She sadly informed me that she couldn't give up her government assistance because she was afraid of putting herself and her child at financial risk.

I tried my hardest to convince her that she would make twice as much working for us, and that in time she possibly could become a club manager and earn over $100,000 a year—but to no avail. She rejected my offer because she thought she was doing the most responsible thing for her little girl and herself. I understood her reasoning, but I strongly believe she made the wrong decision.

More recently, I lost a quality employee who had worked for me off and on over the last thirty years. She suffered from back pain, something I am very familiar with because it has been a major issue in my life from time to time. Because of her discomfort, we allowed her to take walks and in general made her working conditions as favorable as possible. She was well paid for her administrative duties and a valued employee.

One day she asked to meet with me. She told me she had been approved to go on full disability from the state. They would give her $2,850 per month, tax-free, and pay for her to go back to school at age sixty to become a paralegal. The government would pay her more than I could pay her after taxes and send her to school, all because her back ached.

I told her that was a deal too good to turn down and that there was no way I could match their offer. But in my mind, it was a lose-lose situation. She was losing her self-esteem, and taxpayers were paying the bill.

Don't get me wrong. There is an appropriate time for helping those in need. But it can—and has—become a slippery slope into worldwide financial crisis. Financial dependence of any kind is a trap and must be avoided.

Ultimately, God should be our financial source. Though there may be seasons when we depend on others or others depend on us, in general, God has given us enough gifts and talents to take good care of ourselves and our families.

We need to grasp the concept of producing more than we consume. This is a simple philosophy to understand, but it takes discipline and God's strength to execute.

It works like this: whatever you earn, first tithe 10 percent of what you make before taxes, then save 10 percent of your pay after taxes, and then put 10 percent toward consumer debt or other non-investment debt until you are free of debt, especially credit card debt. Then learn to live creatively on the remaining 65 percent or so of your income. Once your debt is paid, you can give the 10 percent away to a good charitable organization, add it to your savings, or spend it on luxuries. If you are just starting off on your new financial way of life, adding the extra 10 percent to your savings is the most prudent thing to do.

Working on the expense side of your financial plan is the first step toward a life of fiscal responsibility. Begin by creating two lists of expenses: necessities and luxuries. Get rid of all your sacred cows. It could be as big as the house you live in or as small as your Starbucks coffee. The question you must ask is, "How will I get my living expenses down to 65 percent of what I am making?

Unless you are totally committed to achieving financial freedom, this will be a horrible exercise that won't help anything and will cause great frustration, especially if you are married. Most fights between spouses center on financial matters. So prayerfully go through this exercise of deciding what is a luxury and what is a necessity. It can be an exciting adventure. You will be surprised by how much you can reduce your personal overhead once you set your mind to it.

Recently, some close friends of mine, an elderly couple who are very wealthy and also very generous, described to me what the average American family considered normal fifty or sixty years ago. The country had lived through two different but very painful periods: the Great Depression in the 30s and World War II in the 40s.

In general, people felt blessed to just be alive and well. Those who wanted to work were working, and there was a great sense of patriotism and mutual brotherhood. The majority lived in smaller houses, owned one car, one black-and-white TV, and one phone, and maybe ate out once a week at the local pizza place after one of their kids' ball games. Kids rode their bikes or walked wherever they needed to go (part of the reason childhood obesity wasn't the issue it is today).

Yet they didn't feel poor. They didn't think anyone owed them anything. If someone got sick or lost their job, there was a sense of community, and everyone naturally helped out. No one felt entitled to anything just because they lived in the United States.

Their contentment didn't mean they were complacent. People worked hard to improve their financial situation. They saved diligently toward the required 20 percent down payment for a new house. It was a process of sacrificing today for a better tomorrow.

I don't mean to idealize the past, because the country had its share of problems. But there was a significant difference in work ethic, savings ethic, and materialistic expectations.

I think we have lost a sense of simplicity and contentment that we would do well to recapture.

Financial Planning

Proverb 21:31, which I referred to earlier, summarizes how my wife and I run our personal and business finances: "Do your best, prepare for the worst—then trust God to bring victory" (The Message).

Financial planning should be designed around planning for the worst to happen. People in every generation throughout history have experienced some kind of financial crisis due to sickness, war, recession, or famine. My pastor once counted thirteen different famines that are referred to in the Bible. It is a fact of life that bad things happen, whether they are our fault or not.

This is the first reason we must develop a habit of consistently saving at least 10 percent, no matter what personal sacrifices we have to make. We must always be prepared for the worst to happen.

This is not my wisdom—it's God's wisdom. To live without savings is just plain foolishness. Under no circumstances should you draw on your savings to purchase luxury items: your savings should be used for wise investments, such as a house purchase, or for emergencies. I recommend having at least six months' worth of living expenses in savings.

The second reason for savings is capital accumulation. Begin to put your money to work for you. If you become a consistent, even obsessive, saver of at least 10 percent of your net income, with proper investments, you will in time make more money from your investments than you do from your job.

Invest for Success

Your first major investment should be to purchase your own home. Make sure your mortgage payment does not exceed 25 percent of your income after deducting tithe and savings. Interest on your house will be written off against your taxes, thereby reducing taxes and increasing your disposable income. Over most ten-year periods, your house will appreciate at 5–6 percent annually. It is by far your best investment, considering you have to pay rent anyway. Just don't purchase a house until all consumer debt is paid off.

Work within these guidelines even though many people will tell you they are too conservative. I have witnessed countless people over the years buy houses prematurely or buy outside these financial guidelines, only to become "house poor," with more money tied up in their house than they can afford.

Once you have mastered your trade or occupation, one the best investments you can make is to turn your occupation into your own business, assuming you have the desire and fortitude to do so. One of my objectives in writing this book is to help you analyze whether you should start your own business or not.

Many people who run their own businesses should not be doing so, while others who should be self-employed are not. It comes down to what you are called and gifted to do and what you enjoy doing.

I believe that in general, self-employed people have greater potential to achieve substantial income. They are not limited by anything but their own creativity and work ethic.

When I was a young man starting to make good money, my boss told me that for every dollar I had in my pocket, there were four people out there trying to steal it from me through one business scheme or another. My experience of being swindled out of $5,000 at age nineteen had burned me and burned me good, but I am by nature a risk-taker, and many times I have had to learn the hard way.

There is a huge difference between investing and speculating. Investing is putting money into something you know a lot about or have consulted an expert on. Speculating is taking a risk on something you aren't familiar with. There are honest professionals who devote their time to real estate development or stocks trading who make a good income speculating in fields they understand (although even the best get wiped out from time to time). But unless that field is your area of expertise, I suggest you stay away from speculation. It is my experience that if something sounds too good to be true, it probably is; especially if you know little or nothing about that area. For example, if I buy a fitness club in distress, it's investment; if you do, it's probably speculating.

On the other hand, I would encourage you to invest carefully into the stock market or into quality real estate that provides passive income. Over a ten-year period, the average yearly return on the stock market is usually 7–10 percent.

Note that the operative words here and with real estate investment are "over a ten-year period." That means that if you are going to invest in either, make sure you can get by without that money for ten years. It also means you must be willing to leave your money in place even during tough times. I own a fair amount of real estate. Currently the real estate market is terrible—probably 60 percent of what it used to be. But my holdings are paid off, and the last thing I want to do is sell now, at a loss.

The key with investing, of course, is to buy low and sell high. That sounds easier than it is. Most people buy high and sell low because they are ruled by the emotions of greed or fear when it comes to financial decisions. When the stock market is going up, they want to mortgage their homes to get in on all the easy money everyone is making. When the market plunges, they get scared and sell at the worst possible time. So, the majority of those who invest in real estate or stocks end up losing much of their money or just maintaining.

The question you must first ask yourself when investing is, "Can I afford to tie this money up for at least ten years?" The second is, "If real estate prices or stock prices plummet, do I have the courage and willpower to ride out the storm?" If the answer is no to either of these questions, you should keep your money in a high-yield bank account that is federally insured and do the research to make sure your bank is a profitable, well-run institution.

If you choose to invest your hard-earned and hard-saved money, hire wise people to help you. Call their references. Make sure they have spent at least ten thousand hours in their field and have become an expert. My stockbroker of twenty-five years makes good money from investing my money, but he is worth every cent I pay him. Many times he has counseled me to avoid purchasing particular stocks because he feels they are not a good company or the time is wrong. He primarily gets paid based on my stock transactions, so when he tells me not to buy or sell, he is costing himself money, at least for the moment. He knows that unless he produces an average of at least 10 percent profit annually I will fire him, so he is careful to make wise choices. He usually will not recommend a stock unless he, too, is purchasing it.

There are hundreds or even thousands of good books on budgeting, saving, and investing. I have read many of them—it is kind of a hobby of mine. I could write page after page discussing different kinds of investments and strategies. But the real focus should be on setting consistent, strict guidelines that you are committed to adhere to for life.

To review what I said earlier, get in the habit of first tithing to God his 10 percent, knowing he promises to bless, multiply, and protect the remaining 90 percent. Save and invest carefully at least 10 percent, use 10 percent to pay off all consumer debt (and make a decision to never pay interest on credit cards again), and learn to live comfortably on 65 percent or less of your income.

Keep in mind that man has an unlimited propensity toward desire. That means our desires can never be completely satisfied, so just learn to discipline them.

Don't spend your future! When creating your financial plan, do not base your budget on potential raises or increases in sales commissions. That will only set you up for disappointment and failure to live within your financial plan. View possible income increases as unexpected bonuses: then you will be psychologically, emotionally, and financially protected if they don't materialize.

Now let me discuss maximizing earnings. Aptitude, gifting, talents, hard work, and even genius are not enough unless tied to the right opportunity. More times than not, potentially great people tie their destinies to companies that use them up and then throw them away.

As the oldest son of five children, I watched my father chase his dream of great success throughout my childhood. He was highly talented and hardworking. I remember watching him speak before large audiences and being amazed at his ability to inspire and captivate their hearts.

He was promoted to general manager in a huge, billion-dollar company when he was in his twenties—one of the youngest managers they had ever had. He was a loyal, unquestioning company man. As he was promoted through the company, he moved our family from one place to another, wherever the company asked him to go.

I remember him leaving my mother with four children, all under the age of eight, to live in New York City to get trained for a higher-paying job. He was gone for nearly a year. The first thing he did when he came home was announce another move.

By the time I was eighteen, we had moved at least a dozen times. One of the most traumatic was just before my senior year in high school, which was very frustrating for me since I was in sports and was looking forward to graduating with my friends. My frequent childhood moves were the reason Gina and I determined to live in the same house no matter where my job took me.

My dad chased dreams that never quite materialized. His upward ascent stopped when he turned down a promotion because he refused to move his wife and children across the country to live in New York.

I saw my father slowly lose steam until he finally gave up his vision for success. Despite his talents and dedication, when he was fifty-four years old, he put in for early retirement and ended up selling insurance to support his family.

Don't get me wrong: we had a decent life, especially compared to many. But if he would have investigated where his talents would be best used and compensated both short- and long-term, he most likely could have found a company that provided better compensation and a better future with less sacrifice. Or, he could have gone into business for himself. He was every bit as talented as I was, but I think he chose the wrong vehicle.

When I was getting out of college, many of my friends were excited about landing great jobs with big companies. They were enamored by the companies' reputations, salaries, and benefits. I never interviewed with any of those companies. I knew the trap—I had lived it secondhand through my father.

My dream was to work hard, save my money, and own a company that would grow and prosper financially. I knew I had great potential. I just needed the right opportunity and the right vehicle to attach my dreams and ambitions to.

That is why I took the chance of taking a low salary, below minimum wage, plus 50 percent of profits that did not exist. At the time I could live on under $200 per month; I walked or rode my bike to work; and I worked twelve to sixteen hours a day, so I didn't have much opportunity to spend money.

It was my burning desire to create a company that would attract people like my father or myself who were talented, ambitious, and motivated to prosper. As I built my companies over the years, no matter how big we got, I always asked myself this question: "If I were young, talented, and driven to attain financial success, would I want to join our company, and would that be a good decision for me, both short-term and long-term?"

This question always helped me strategize on how to attract and retain the most excellent employees. I would give them tremendous opportunity if they had open-minded, positive attitudes—in other words, if they were easily coached. I believed that through our extensive training and personal development programs, I could take excellent, smart, driven employees and make them wealthy.

I am proud to say that over the years, I have helped many young recruits become millionaires. In the next chapter, which deals with the fundamentals of building a lasting, marketable company, I will go into more details about compensation packages and their power to inspire people to achieve great results.

Previously, I said you should always give your best to your current employer and never quit because of authority issues. But you only have one life, and you owe it to God to earn the most and make your time the most profitable for you and your family.

That does not mean negotiating for the most and producing the least. It means finding the invisible line where you produce value and you get an equal amount of value in return for your efforts, plus the possibility of a "blue sky" future through things like profit-sharing or ownership in the company. Look for a company that is profit-driven and will compensate you fairly based on how much you help drive those profits upward.

When negotiating with a current or potential employer, remember they are taking a risk, especially if it is one of the small businesses that make up 75 percent of American businesses. Unless they make a reasonable return on their risk, they will either not expand and therefore not create future opportunity, or worst yet, they will close up shop. Always look at both sides of the equation: what is fair for them and what is fair for you. It must be a win-win arrangement, or someone will end up a loser—usually that will be the employee, if the business owner wants to stay in business.

If you find the right opportunity, become excellent at what you do, and respect authority, you will advance from one leadership opportunity to another. All of us are potential leaders, or God would not have trusted us with the awesome responsibility to lead and develop our children. Learn your vocation excellently, and become the great leader God intended you be.

Your satisfaction will grow as you learn to lead others—and so will your paycheck. You will earn more, save more, and give more over time. Best of all, you will have learned how to produce more than you consume.

The Heart of a Champion

I believe God wants all of us to have the heart of a champion. The best definition I have found for "champion" is someone who gets the most out of their God-given talents and gifts.

In the parable of the talents (Matthew 25), one servant is given five talents, another is given two talents, and the third is given one talent. The servants with five and two talents both double their money; the one with one talent buries it, risking nothing because he is afraid his master will be angry if he loses it. The master rebukes the last servant because he lacked courage and saw his master through harsh cycs.

The moral of the story is that God, like the master in the parable, is pleased with those who use what they have been given. If we simply do our best with what we have been given, we are champions in God's eyes. Although God knows that we will fail at times, he expects us to keep getting up until we fulfill our purpose on earth.

Romans 8:37 states, "Yet in all these things we are more than conquerors through Him who loved us" (NKJV). In chapters 2 and 3 of the book of Revelation, Jesus commands us again and again to be overcomers and promises wonderful blessings for those who become champions through the power and authority of Jesus Christ. And again, one of the most famous verses in the Bible, Philippians 4:13, says, "I can do everything through Christ, who gives me strength."

There are many sins we must learn to defeat in order to live a victorious life, but I believe the greatest of these is the sin of fear. Fear keeps us tied to the ground, defeated before we even start.

I truly believe that "attitude is everything." Fear can be camouflaged in many ways, and sometimes we have so effectively covered up ours fears we are not even aware of them. Yet our attitudes reveal our inner motivations. Our self-talk and our attitudes about daily life are a clue as to whether we are burying fears that will steal our dreams in the end.

We must ask ourselves: "Am I positive through and through? Am I enthusiastic 100 percent of the time? Am I optimistic about my desired outcomes? Am I filled with joy and thrilled that I get to participate in God's plan for humanity, or has fear gotten me down in some way? Such attitudes reveal a healthy self-confidence, especially when that confidence is based on God's promises.

On the more negative side, we should ask ourselves: Am I overcritical of others? Am I pessimistic about future outcomes, claiming to just be realistic? Do I frequently use sarcasm to cover up my insecurities? Do I feel victimized by my circumstances, seeing myself as uneducated, brought up in poverty, or of the wrong race? Am I petrified to step out of my comfort zone, like making a speech in front of a crowd of people? Am I afraid to invest my money in a wise, well-thought-out idea because I might fail? Do I isolate myself from others because I am afraid of rejection? Do I feel depressed and out of energy, or am I uptight and tense most of the time?"

These are signs that fear has gotten a hold of us. We must defeat it if we want to fulfill our God-given assignment and experience maximum joy here on earth. God could not be any clearer than he is in 2 Timothy 1:7. "For God has not given us a spirit of fear, but of power and of love and of a sound mind."

Everyone deals with certain fears, but most people hate to talk about or even acknowledge them. So they play the cover-up game their whole life, and as a result they sacrifice their dreams and ambitions. As painful as it is, we must face our fears.

When I was fifty-seven, while in Hawaii with our extended family and friends, my sixteen-year-old son Ian and his friends asked me if I wanted to jump off a rock cliff with them. It was forty or fifty feet down into the ocean. I said, "No sweat, let's go!"

I had done a lot of high diving and jumping as a kid, so I thought it would be easy. We got to the top of the cliff, and one boy after another jumped, until it was my turn. They were far below in the water, screaming for me to jump. But as I came to the edge of the cliff, suddenly my heart began to race, and an invisible barrier of fear, impenetrable as a brick wall, loomed in front of me.

Because we had to aggressively leap out to clear the cliff and land in the water, any hesitation could be fatal. It shouldn't have been that hard, but the height amplified my fear and made it nearly impossible. If it weren't for my reluctance to embarrass myself in front of my son and his friends, I probably wouldn't have jumped. But my fear of humiliation overcame my fear of a violent death. Thank God, I cleared the cliff and fell safely but hard into the ocean, only slightly jarring my neck.

The fear was real! Where it came from didn't matter. I had to either defeat it or be defeated by it. I doubt I will ever jump off that cliff again—it probably wasn't the wisest idea in the first place—but that same fear is the culprit that destroys or at least limits many of our Holy Spirit-inspired visions.

I've faced my share of fears. I remember as a kid that I would rather be kicked in the face in a fight (which I got into often) than get up in front of my classmates and give a speech. Once my father almost begged me to give a speech in front of a club of businesspeople that he was the president of, named The Optimists. I turned him down and stood by while a friend of mine delivered the speech that I was too afraid to give. To this day, I remember the shame of being so shy and insecure. Over the years, I have delivered well over a thousand speeches and training classes, and I think I do it rather well. But I still feel those familiar fears dance around inside me prior to beginning a speech.

Everyone is different. Friends have told me that getting in a fistfight would scare them half to death, while for me, even at sixty years of age, it wouldn't bother me in the least. I might even enjoy it, much as I hate to admit it. Whatever fear you are facing is real, but it must be defeated in order to become a champion.

Many people think they are the only ones who struggle with fear. In a way, that is their biggest problem. They don't admit their fears, even to themselves, and therefore they don't deal with them.

They mistakenly think that if they are doing what they are supposed to be doing and living in God's will, they will be comfortable the whole time. The presence of fear doesn't mean we are weak or on the wrong path. Often, fear is simply an indicator that we are out of our comfort zone. There is nothing wrong with that, as long as we are still within our grace zone, which is what we were created to accomplish.

I recently read in the Seattle Times about an interview with Ichiro, who plays baseball with the Seattle Mariners and is possibly the greatest hitter of all time. Ichiro is from Japan, and in 2009 he returned to Japan to play in the World Baseball Classic. His team had won eight games to advance to the championship game against South Korea. Ichiro had had a terrible series so far, hitting .167 with only three runs batted in for the entire series. When he came to bat, the game was tied 3-3 in extra innings. There were two outs and runners on first and third.

In the interview, Ichiro describes his state of mind. "I was having such a poor tournament that honestly, as I approached the plate, I said to myself, 'Please, just walk me.'" He continues, "It was simply to spare my pride.... If I made an out, everything I had accomplished to that point, 262 hits [the MLB season record, in 2004], 3,000 hits [America and Japan combined, reached in 2008] would be rendered irrelevant. My entire career would be defined by that one at-bat. I've always prided myself in not reveling in past accomplishments and focusing on future achievement, instead. That's been my career motto, yet here I was fretting about how this at-bat might eradicate my past accomplishments. It was such a contradiction to my very being."

His interviewer asked, "So you were encountering an unfamiliar you for the first time?"

Ichiro replied, "Yes. Such thoughts simply didn't make sense to me and I couldn't recognize where they were coming from. But then, suddenly, just as quickly, everything changed. The instant the catcher crouched down to begin my at-bat, all those frivolous thoughts just evaporated. I had no choice but to face reality and with that, my mind then shouted, 'Hey, bring it on. Don't even think about walking me, pal.' Now, I was determined to get it done."

Ichiro proceeded to deliver one of the most celebrated hits in Japanese baseball history, a two-run single over the pitcher's right shoulder. It made the difference in Japan's 5-3 victory, and unmistakably defines Ichiro in Japan today. (Source: Brad Lefton, "Ichiro Reveals Himself in TV Interview: Ordinary and Extraordinary," Seattle Times, Feb. 20, 2011, seattletimes.com)

My previous pastor, the late Wendell Smith, used to say, "We have a very big God, and we are opposed by an itty-bitty devil." That's a good perspective. People tend to look at things the other way around: they exaggerate what they fear, and they forget how big God is.

Yes, fear can protect us from making serious mistakes. But there is a level or spirit of fear that takes us over and makes us freeze up like a deer in headlights.

I use fear to motivate me to get creative. When finances are tight, instead of lying in bed, wondering what in the world I'm going to do to meet payroll, I harness the fear. It's a conscious decision. I feel the fear coming and decide to let it inspire me, not petrify me. I pray for God's power to overcome it.

The source of fear is not as important as whether we deal with it and defeat it, rather than allowing it to capture our hearts or limit our accomplishments.

Fear is usually an indicator that we are on the verge of breaking through to the next level of our God-given destiny. Our battle cry must become, like Ichiro, "Bring it on!" Maybe we will never play our "game" in front of millions of people like Ichiro, but God's plan for our life is every bit as important.

Most of us are familiar with the story of how David, a young shepherd with no military training or experience, killed the giant Goliath. Through Goliath's intimidation, the enemy nation of the Philistines had humiliated God's people for forty straight days. King Saul, a physically imposing man in his own right, had offered anyone who could slay the giant large amounts of money, no taxes for life, and his daughter in marriage. But there were no takers.

Then along came David with a few rocks and a sling, offering his services in man-to-man combat with the giant. Where did this undersized kid find the courage to face a nine foot six, four hundred-pound warrior giant wearing over two hundred pounds of armament?

Why did the fear of dying not deter David like it did the king and the thousands of soldiers gathered on the battlefield?

The answer is simple: David knew who he was. Samuel the prophet had anointed him the future king of Israel, and David believed in God's anointing and destiny over his life. Whatever fears he might have felt were not strong enough to overcome the belief that God would be with him on the battlefield and help him defeat Goliath. The million-to-one odds were irrelevant.

I'm sure David realized he couldn't be king if he died on the battlefield, so he didn't fear death. Rather than run from the danger in an attempt to preserve his destiny, he gained courage to face the danger by focusing on his destiny. David knew God didn't want to see his people melt into a puddle of weakness before their enemy, and the king within him rose up and motivated him to do something about it.

David had successfully faced real dangers before, including killing lions and bears intent on devouring his sheep. There was no fanfare when he succeeded. He was probably alone at the time. But because he had courageously faced past trials and tests, he was now prepared for a greater challenge.

In the same way, God uses each battle to prepare us for the next. Every victory is another stage in fulfilling our destiny. This is how God makes us into champions.

If our belief in God's destiny for us and his commitment to never forsake us possesses every molecule of our minds, hearts, and bodies, we cannot be defeated. Remember, it was God who said through the Apostle Paul that we are "more than conquerors."

Were you born to be a champion? Absolutely!

The Body of a Champion

Besides God and my family, fitness has been the love of my life for nearly as long as I can remember. At twelve years old, I would go out into our unheated garage in near-freezing weather, bundled in heavy sweatshirts to keep warm, and work out for hours, hoping to someday have big muscles. I recall waking up one morning unable to move my arms because I had done hundreds of arm curls the night before. I read every magazine on fitness and body building I could get my hands on.

In my youth, big muscles helped with two of my problems. First, they enabled a naturally undersized kid to play hard-hitting sports like football. Fifty extra pounds of muscle acquired through strenuous workouts made a big difference. Secondly, they helped me overcome an inferiority complex I struggled with due to my reading disabilities. Having big muscles, being tough, and being a good athlete helped balance out the playing field for someone who struggled in the classroom. I remember my father offhandedly remarking that I should spend more time working on the muscle between my ears.

Even during my hippie years I would work out. I think I was the only hippie with eighteen-inch arms. I remember my mom once asking, "Neil, what are those bumps all over your body?" Back than it was rare to see someone with muscles that size.

My love affair with fitness deepened when I used it as a tool to help me overcome alcohol and drug addictions. A natural chemical called beta-endorphin is released when you work out. It is a pain reliever and stress reliever that has no negative side effects, and it gives you a natural kind of high.

If someone is trying to overcome food, alcohol, or drug addictions, this chemical can be a significant aid. I believe that some people, especially hyperactive people like myself, can find a state of prolonged relaxation if they learn to exercise and eat properly.

Much scientific research supports the power of exercise and nutritional programs to heal or ameliorate all sorts of diseases, especially diabetes and heart-related issues. It is my opinion that many, if not most, alcoholics suffer with blood sugar issues that drive them to drink excess alcohol in order to feel right mentally. I think the same is true with many who suffer from acute obesity problems, which itself is linked to diabetes.

Some segments and ethnic groups in America now suffer from a diabetes rate as high as 50 percent. Besides the pain and suffering involved, this disease cuts people's lifespan by an average of eight years, according to some studies.

I don't mean to sound like a prophet of doom, but we may be seeing just the tip of the iceberg. The potential long-term results of a culture of poor nutrition and lack of exercise are frightening: our nation already faces health care problems, but that could multiply dramatically if we don't make widespread changes in our lifestyle.

Contrary to most people's reaction to this sort of talk, the changes aren't difficult. Many health issues can be eradicated by following some simple guidelines for proper exercise and nutrition. The average person in America could increase his or her lifespan by several years and add quality to those years. We all want that!

Of course, exercise and nutrition cannot guarantee an illness- or accident-free life. Some people are born with genetic predispositions to certain illnesses, and we all face the possibility of accidental injury or death. But these things affect a minority, which means most of us are completely in charge of our health. For those who have a propensity toward illness or who might suffer unexpected injury, a healthy lifestyle will delay or lessen the effects of many of those things or help them avoid them altogether.

Each person's body is unique and responds to various food groupings and exercise differently. It is imperative that we learn what works best for us in the area of fitness. Our bodies, minds, and spirits are connected, and for us to be healthy, they must work in synergy. We need prayer and worship for the spirit, the word of God for our minds and hearts, and proper exercise and nutrition for our bodies.

Unless we gain control of our bodies, we will not fulfill our destiny here on earth. Poor health or premature death will limit what God wants us to accomplish.

I feel very qualified to present principles about achieving a quality lifestyle of total fitness. Through my own workouts and continuing education over the course of forty-five years, I have clocked in over fifty thousand hours dedicated to this one subject matter. I have worked closely with thousands of people to reach their fitness goals, and I have seen what works and what doesn't.

There are probably people who will take exception to some of my beliefs surrounding exercise and nutrition. But I stand by them because I have not only studied this subject intellectually, I have personally tried out just about every type of nutritional and exercise program known to man. I believe that the principles I give here are wise instruction for building the body of a champion.

The Apostle Paul says in 1 Timothy 4:8, "Physical training is good, but training for godliness is much better, promising benefits in this life and in the life to come." Even though fitness is important, it should not become an obsession. That is something that people like me must continuously fight against. The majority of people don't have this problem—they just want to stay healthy enough to lead a disease-free, pain-free, active life.

Proper, ongoing nutrition makes up most of a person's good health. Many people are addicted to destructive food types that are harming their bodies, whether they are aware of it or not. Anything with white, refined sugar or white, processed flour is a killer and should be eliminated or at least limited to very infrequent use. This means that all those things that taste so good, like ice cream, cookies, candy, soda, most breakfast cereals, and the like, are highly toxic foods, if you can even call them "foods" at all.

Learn to study labels while shopping. Anything that contains sugar, fructose, corn syrup, or ingredients you can't pronounce is probably bad for you; even worse, these things are often addicting. Almost all soft drink products, like Coke, Diet Coke, and Pepsi, are very harmful to your health. They have a high concentration of sugar, caffeine, and other, even more harmful poisons. Some artificial sweeteners are so detrimental to your health that they are outlawed in certain countries.

Also try to eliminate deep-fried foods from your diet. Many people know these products are bad for them, yet they continue to use them. Why? For the same reason people do anything they know is bad for their body—they are most likely addicted to them. It's a socially accepted addiction, but an addiction nonetheless.

The abuse of alcohol, tobacco, and caffeine fall into the same dangerous-to-your-health category.

Some people have a gift for moderation, but in my experience, most do not. For years, I went to a church that frowned on drinking alcohol or using tobacco; yet nearly every Sunday after church, there was a potluck where church members would gorge themselves on huge quantities of poisonous food. Many times these were the same people who were asking for prayer to heal their bodies.

God tells us that our bodies are a living temple for the Holy Spirit (1 Corinthians 6:19). If we are physically sick, it is difficult to be spiritually or mentally acute. One of the qualities the Holy Spirit brings us is the power of self-control. We must first acknowledge that we are, in fact, sinning when we purposely ingest large amounts of poison. Then we must ask him for his power to be set free from these addictions.

You will be amazed at how much better you feel once you eliminate these excesses of poisons from your body. And amazingly, much of the extra weight will melt away.

On the positive side of the nutritional element, we must learn to eat moderate amounts of quality food from all the food groups. Proteins include lean meat, chicken, fish, and fowl. Complex carbohydrates are found in things like whole-wheat breads, potatoes, rice, beans, and vegetables. Use quality simple carbohydrates like fruits sparingly. If you are hungry, eat as much raw vegetables as you want. Quality fats are needed, but for the most part these will be found in your proteins, especially nuts. Drink about a hundred ounces of water daily to help your kidneys and other vital organs in the elimination process.

It is a greater challenge for people to eat properly than to abstain from alcohol or tobacco because we must eat to survive. Every time we eat, we must practice self-discipline. We must be able to say, "No," or at least, "I've had enough," to things like cookies and ice cream that make our mouth water but that we know are bad for us.

As you free yourself from food addictions, it will become easier and easier to resist these poisonous substances. If you have the discipline to go on a three-day, water-only fast, you will overcome in three days almost all your cravings for the harmful substances you have been putting into your body. After you break your fast, avoid completely these harmful foods for a full year. This will give your body a chance to heal itself. After a year of sobriety from harmful food substances, you may experiment with trying to lead a life of moderation. I think you will feel so good you might not even want to risk returning to old habits of poor nutrition.

I recommend two excellent books that will shed a lot of light on the science behind fasting and the diseases associated with ingesting poisonous substances like sugar: *The Miracle of Fasting* by Paul Bragg and *Sugar Blues* by William Dufty. These books were ahead of their time when they were written years ago, and scientific research continues to support their assertions and principles.

A lot has been written about how often and what time of day we should eat in order to burn the most calories. The simple fact is that all of us have a particular metabolic rate, which is the speed at which our body burns calories. This metabolic rate can be drastically changed, a subject I will review later on, but if we ingest calories at a faster rate than our metabolism can burn them, we will gain weight regardless of what time of day we take in the calories.

Eating small meals or healthy snacks throughout the day can reduce the cravings for candy bars and other harmful things. These cravings are usually a physical response to a variation in blood sugar levels. Eating sweets momentarily satisfies the body's needs, but an hour or two later, the cravings resurface. By the end of the day, you have taken in more calories than you burned, and your weight increases.

Generally speaking, lean proteins and complex carbohydrates are released into the bloodstream slowly and will not cause drastic variations in blood sugar levels. Keeping your levels relatively stable reduces the cravings for sweets, which makes it easier to keep your calorie count down.

Experiment to find what foods and times work best for you. Some people can go twelve hours between meals without problem; others can barely make it two hours.

A pound of body fat is equal to about 3,500 calories. If your daily metabolic rate is 2,000 calories per day and you only consume 1,500 calories, you create a 500-calorie deficit. Within a week, you will lose one pound. It's as easy—or as hard—as that.

If you are gaining weight, you are eating too many calories for your current metabolic rate. If you want to lose weight, then you need to eat less, increase your metabolic rate, or both. Barring other health issues or extenuating circumstances, this formula for gaining or losing weight will work.

Exercise yields two benefits with regard to weight loss and weight control. First, a high-intensity, thirty-minute workout that mixes weight training and cardiovascular training will burn approximately five hundred calories. Second—and even better—over time, this type of exercise replaces body fat with lean muscle mass, which increases your daily metabolic rate. If you work out on a strenuous cross-training program three times per week for thirty minutes, exercising every major muscle group (stomach, shoulders, back, chest, arms, and legs), in less than three months, your normal metabolic rate will increase by about five hundred calories per day.

So by exercising just one and a half hours per week, within three months you will be burning about five thousand more calories per week than you were burning prior to exercising. Assuming you don't increase your food intake, you should lose about a pound and a half per week, or six pounds per month. And if you simultaneously reduce your calorie intake, you will lose even more.

It's such a small investment in time—just one and a half hours per week of active fitness training—but it will bring dramatic results. Two-thirds of Americans are overweight, and they could solve this self-induced problem in a matter of months without even cutting back on their total caloric intake. People would feel better, look better, have more active lifestyles, and avoid many of the illnesses that accompany obesity.

It is true that the older people get, the slower their metabolism becomes, and therefore the easier it is to gain weight. This is not directly due to age, however, but rather to a lessening in lean muscle fiber due to a lack of physical activity. As long as a person can exercise major muscles, especially their legs, they can slowly build up muscle, which increases their resting metabolic rate. Even as we age, we will look better and feel better if we include moderate exercise in our weekly routine and reduce or eliminate harmful foods and substances. This will prolong our life and, just as importantly, improve the quality of those years.

Depending on your fitness level, it is smart to start slow and easy with your workouts. It took most people a lifetime to get out of shape, so there should be no rush to get back in shape.

I remember years ago when I quit smoking, I decided that every time I felt an urge to smoke, I would go out running. In the beginning, I could hardly run a quarter of a mile without gasping for air. But as time passed and I kept to my plan, I found myself running up to fifty miles per week at a rather fast pace. I never smoked again because doing something positive to my body felt so much better than doing something destructive.

If you are very deconditioned or overweight, walking with two- or three-pound weights in each hand is a great way to get started. Even if you only have the physical capacity for five or ten minutes when you begin, you will be surprised how quickly your body responds. Within a month of walking a few times per week, you will be able to increase walking time to thirty minutes and beyond.

The keys are consistency and not pushing yourself into a painful place that will cause injury or make you psychologically averse to your exercise routine.

Fix in your mind that exercising and practicing good nutrition are going to become a way of life. Many people will go on crash weight-loss and exercise programs so they can lose fifty pounds. They practice great discipline and achieve their goal, but immediately regain the weight—and then some. Their mistake is viewing exercise and diet as temporary disruptions to their everyday life. Then they make it so uncomfortable that their fitness program acts like aversion therapy to incorporating ongoing exercise and nutrition into their lives.

My motto is easy does it, a little at a time. If the first month you only manage to walk three times a week and don't lose any weight, at least you are doing something positive for your body. In time, the exercise will become enjoyable. And as you get stronger, you will automatically increase the distance and time you walk. You will have the courage to add more and more physical activity into your workout regimen. My wife loves to walk and hike, and many times we will walk and talk together, and before we know it we have walked ten miles and burned about fifteen hundred calories. (She's not counting of course, but I can't help myself.)

I believe the safest, most time-efficient, and most effective type of exercise is high-intensity resistance training, often referred to as cross-training. It is not advisable to enter into this kind of training until you are at least moderately in shape. These programs have varying degrees of intensity. They are challenging but produce excellent results.

The overall concept is to use light weights, exercise multiple muscle groups with each exercise, and move rapidly through the routines in order to keep your pulse rate increased throughout a twenty- to forty-minute workout. Over time, increase the weight you are using and decrease the time it takes you to go through your workout. It's also important to follow a different workout for each of the three days a week you work out, which creates muscle confusion (that is, exercising the same muscles differently) and yields the best results.

These workouts burn calories, increase your metabolic rate, increase muscle, and improve cardiovascular health. They also relieve stress and increase your energy throughout your day. Just about every quality fitness center or athletic club in America offers these types of organized workout routines. If you are averse to working out in the gym, look up cross-training online and find predesigned workouts that you can do on your own.

As an example, here is one of my favorite workouts that I've designed. I've used it off and on through the years, and it produces great results. The goal is to complete four cycles in less than thirty minutes. You most likely won't be able to complete the entire routine to start with, but it gets easier.

The workout cycle consists of:
- 13 pull-ups
- 25 dead lifts with a 135-pound barbell
- 25 push-ups
- 25 eighteen-inch box or bench jumps
- 15 135-pound bench presses
- 13 one-arm 35-pound dumbbell clean-and-jerk presses, with each arm
- 25 leg lift sweeps

Repeat this cycle four times, as quickly as possible. This workout is not for the faint of heart, but it will produce tremendous muscular and cardiovascular results in a short time.

After working in the fitness business for nearly forty years, I have witnessed thousands of deconditioned people completely change their lives. Looking at them, you would never know that they had struggled with weight problems or fitness-related issues.

It begins with choosing to make a positive change in your life. I believe it is God's will that you be physically fit, so ask him to give you the strength to make the necessary changes in your lifestyle, especially in how you eat and in incorporating a moderate amount of exercise into your life.

Start off slow and easy, then pick up steam as your workouts begin to become enjoyable. In the beginning they might be a little painful, both psychologically and physically, but hang in there. You will soon start to look forward to them. Within a few short months, you are sure to see positive results.

Good luck!

10

Building a Company That Lasts through Organized Effort

There was no spectacular moment of breakthrough for Hart's Athletic Clubs and no shortcut to success. We worked hard and followed simple principles, month after month, year after year. It paid off.

I don't believe our success had anything to do with luck. For one thing, this was the second time in my life I had built a multimillion-dollar company, and it wouldn't be the last. Rather, the success was due to a combination of things: God's grace, finding my calling, walking in integrity, making wise decisions, patience, and of course, hard work.

If you've read this far, you are serious about finding personal and financial success. That's why I wrote this book—especially the next few chapters. The hardest-earned and most valuable secrets I've learned are summed up in the following pages. I also describe in detail the PSROPS system I developed that has consistently propelled my companies past the competition.

Are You Built for Business?

Do you believe you have a vision from God to build a great company? Do you have the courage and wisdom to risk all of your financial capital and good credit? Do you have enough money to live on for at least the first year while you are getting your business off the ground and becoming profitable? Have you made a habit of godly stewardship? Are you willing to pour all of your energy and time into your company's infant stages—for at least five years? Are you sure you have the gifts, talents, and skills to build your dream company? Have you put in ten thousand hours mastering the basics of your field of expertise? Does your spouse support you completely in your endeavor? (In other words, if the business were to fail, would your marriage survive?) Are you and your family prepared for the possible negative outcome of losing everything?

Finally, do you have the courage and internal fortitude to go forward no matter what fears or obstacles arise? Once you start, there is no turning back. Most first-time business builders must risk all of their money and credit and often tie up their most valuable asset, their house, as collateral for a business loan. Do you have the stomach for this, knowing that most start-up businesses fail within a year of opening?

I'm not trying to be negative—just realistic. There is no shame in not owning your own business, just as there is no shame in not climbing Mt. Everest. Nor do you have to start a business to prosper. I know many people who never started or owned their own business, yet they are satisfied, fulfilled, and prosperous. In my own companies over the years, I've had dozens of employees become millionaires and many more earn six-digit incomes.

Starting a new business and succeeding at it is the most difficult thing I know of. But if you have a courageous heart and can answer yes to all of the above questions, you are ready to get started.

I have been in business for forty years, and as I've shared in this book, I have made millions, lost it all, and made it back again. The road has not been easy. But it has been exciting and fulfilling to walk out the destiny God created for me, a destiny I could never have imagined in the strawberry fields of Oregon.

If you are called to own a business, it will be more exciting and fulfilling than you can imagine. You will face challenges that seem terrifying, but you must see beyond them and not stop until you accomplish your vision.

Who Are You?

Begin by creating a company mission statement that defines your company. What does your business do? Where is it going? There are many books dedicated to helping people create mission statements—some are good; most are not.

The key to your mission statement is to make it real. It must come from your heart and clearly define your company's identity, the service it provides, and whom it serves.

I have met with countless people who were starting new businesses but could not clearly explain what their company was going to do or how it was going to make money. If you cannot define your vision to someone and get them excited about it in sixty seconds, it will most likely never get off the ground.

Another common mistake is creating a mission statement that sounds great but is all ephemeral fancy. The bottom line is that your mission statement must address your bottom line! How is it going to become profitable, and when?

Your business strategy will dovetail with your mission statement. If your mission statement is right, you will be able to operate with perfect synergy, connection, and harmony between the mission statement and the strategy.

Ask yourself practical questions. What is your specific plan to bring your product to market? Why will consumers want to buy your product over established competitors? Will you offer more for less? Will you attack the marketplace strictly by having the lowest price and the best value for your low price, or will you create a new product that will create a new demand?

Proper pricing is one of the most essential elements to successfully selling your product. If the price is too low, it doesn't matter how much you sell—you can't make a profit. If it is too high, the product becomes uncompetitive and therefore unsalable. It is critical that you study your competitors and figure out realistically how you will compete with them for your market's customers.

Study your potential customers' demographics. Who are they? How old are they? What level of household or individual income can afford your product? What is the expected use by the particular population for your product? How much of the population that uses your product or a similar one can you expect to capture? Will that number be enough to show a profit, and can you capture them quickly enough to post a profit before your capital runs out?

How many other competitors will you be competing with? Will you be able to survive if your biggest competitor decides, for instance, to build across the street from you and lower his prices to try to drive you out of business? What would be your strategy to survive and prosper in this and other worst-case scenarios? Remember Proverbs 21:31 when strategizing to build your business: "Do your best, prepare for the worst—then trust God to bring victory" (The Message).

Begin with the End

Begin with the end in mind. Specifically, project a level of profit and a realistic timeline to attain it. This is most effectively accomplished by creating financial projections, or pro formas, that detail realistic costs to create your product and bring it to market. The types of expenses will vary from one business to another, but projected costs must be lower than projected income.

Entrepreneurs usually get themselves into trouble because they underestimate their expenses and overestimate their revenues, leaving them with losses. Do yourself a favor: overestimate your costs by 10 percent and underestimate your revenue by 10 percent, then see what your projections look like. It pays to be realistic, even pessimistic, when making these projections. If you outperform your projected profit level, you gain credibility with your team and investors; even more importantly, you gain a new level of confidence and energy to keep moving forward. If you underperform, you lose credibility and confidence when you need it the most. That can spell disaster, regardless of how good your product or service is.

It is better not to begin building a business than to go all in financially, only to find out after it's too late that your idea was not well thought-out. Count the cost before you start.

Jesus talks about this principle in Luke 14:28–30. "But don't begin until you count the cost. For who would begin construction of a building without first calculating the cost to see if there is enough money to finish it? Otherwise, you might complete only the foundation before running out of money, and then everyone would laugh at you. They would say, 'There's the person who started that building and couldn't afford to finish it!'"

It takes a lot of faith to build a business, but it also takes knowledge, understanding, and wisdom. Too many faith-filled people, full of enthusiasm and excitement, end up with crushed dreams and shipwrecked faith because they fail in business and then blame it on God. I have seen it more times than I care to remember.

My objective in writing this book is to help point the way to personal and financial freedom. Once again, that doesn't mean you have to go out and start your own business. Regardless of whether you are an employee, an executive, or an entrepreneur, you can achieve a high level of financial stability and success.

I am a big proponent of developing your own business, and I strongly believe that many people—more than we think—can build and run a profitable company. But I just as strongly believe that for some it could be the most disastrous action they could take. Just as not everyone was cut out to be a professional athlete or a pastor, not everyone was designed by God to own a business.

Whatever course you take, embrace it with confidence, wisdom, and hard work. The following principles will help you develop a winning attitude and strategy in every endeavor.

PSROPS

For over thirty years now, I have used a specific formula to build and continually evaluate our different businesses. I believe it can be an effective tool in any business. Its acronym is "PSROPS," which stands for Personality, Service, Results, Obligation, Promotion, and Sales.

I came up with the PSROPS concept while eating breakfast alone in a Denny's restaurant in 1976. I was twenty-five years old and had recently begun managing the Lynnwood club, my first club. As I thought about how to improve our profitability, I jotted these six words down on a napkin. I had no idea at the time how important they would become.

In business, in order to do an in-depth and accurate analysis, you must know what each function is supposed to look like and how it affects other company systems. That is what the PSROPS system provides: a way to look at each piece of the company both on its own and in relationship to the rest of the company.

Since all the parts of a business are interconnected, they can be analyzed separately, fixed if necessary, and then put back together. In that way, a business is like the human body. A surgeon can open the body up to examine the lungs, heart, liver, or other vital organs; fix dysfunctional areas as necessary; then put the body back together again. But if a dysfunctional organ is not fixed, it will have a negative effect on the entire body, potentially causing death.

The PSROPS system will also help you identify obstacles to running your business and enable you to properly prioritize your actions in light of that. We often think we're doing important things when we are really wasting our time on low-priority items, while other, more important task remain undone.

Step 1: Personality

Personality refers to people. Specifically, it encompasses everything that has to do with building a championship team. It includes personnel, leadership, attitude, aptitude (business-related gifting and talents), payroll expenditures, and support people such as outside accounting and attorney firms.

Your team will be a direct reflection of you. It is your responsibility to identify who you need, the position they will play on your team, and what their job description entails, including laying out clear, concise objectives and rules of engagement.

Your priorities for hiring should be based first on character requirements. It doesn't matter how talented people are: if they have character flaws, they will end up hurting your business more than helping it. When I train my managers, I emphasize that we are running a company that develops leaders, not a rehabilitation center. Do thorough background research: check references and past work experience. Develop a quality interview process with specific questions that uncover whether they have the level of integrity and honesty you expect.

At the same time, realize that character is only the first step. It is not reason enough to hire someone. Talent is essential—there is no substitute for it.

Probably the greatest college basketball coach ever was John Wooden of the UCLA Bruins, who won 151 games in a row and 8 national championships. When he was asked what the most important part of developing a championship team is, he answered without hesitation, "Great players."

The interviewer asked again, "Really, coach, what is the most important aspect in winning all the games you have won?"

Again he answered simply but emphatically, "Great players!" Yet he was known to be the best teacher, educator, motivator, and disciplinarian that ever coached.

Most of my experience has been in developing young people in the fitness business. We look first for character, then for love for fitness and people. We say we want people who are PhDs: poor, hungry, and driven! If we don't feel they have the aptitude to be a high performer, we normally won't take a chance on hiring them.

They also need to have what we call OMPA: Open-Minded, Positive Attitudes. They must be coachable. If they have a problem taking orders or following directions, hopefully we won't hire them in the first place; but if we make a mistake and hire them, we will wash them out quickly if they have any kind of problem with authority. We simply invest too much time, money, and energy into training them. We don't want a rebel upsetting the overall Personality of the company.

Attitude is everything! In the fitness business, attitude is the difference between members achieving their desired fitness results or quitting in frustration. Degrees in fitness or nutrition are pointless if a personal trainer can't inspire members to follow the programs he or she teaches. So we look for positive, energetic, enthusiastic, humble people with servant attitudes.

Each business is different and calls for a unique skill set, but cheerful, uplifting, helpful employees add a positive flavor to any atmosphere. In an office environment such as an accounting office, an attorney office, or a dentist office, I believe positive employee attitudes will increase your profits by at least 10 percent. In public-facing retail businesses, a winning, can-do, helpful attitude can improve your profits by 50 percent.

Attitude is the biggest difference-maker in any business that interacts with the public. Greet people with a wide smile. Immediately learn new customers' names, and use them in conversation with them. Find something about people to compliment them on. Go the extra mile to serve them enthusiastically. Concentrate on satisfying their needs as if they were the only customers you will see today. These small things will endear customers to you forever, and they will go out of their way to help you build your business.

The hiring guidelines I have laid out will work in most businesses, because there are certain indispensable qualities you look for in candidates for your team. It's like the difference between building a football team and a baseball team: the specific skill sets are different, but you will find in all excellent athletes the same underlying attitudes, work ethic, and "hustle."

The more specialized and high-paying the job is, the more care you should take in the hiring process. Get the right people in the right jobs: people with outstanding character who put themselves second to the good of the team and who produce quantifiable results. Remember, it's a lot easier to hire someone than to fire someone. Take your time and make wise choices.

Successful companies create budgets that include all expense categories, and they have the discipline to work within them. Payroll is usually the single largest and most important expense for a company. The budget should reflect that. If payroll is not carefully controlled, it will lead to the company running at a loss.

When creating your payroll budget, ask yourself what level of skill and experience you need in your employees to effectively compete in the marketplace. Our philosophy, especially in sales and personal training, was to hire relatively inexperienced staff. That way we didn't have to "teach old dogs new tricks," or retrain them with our DNA. We minimized our risk by starting them out on a lower pay grade; but if they were capable and hard workers, within a year they could be earning up to $100,000 a year. It was a win-win strategy.

We found that in our business, investing large amounts of money and time into training young people produced the best return on the dollar. We created certification schools for trainers, salespeople, and managers (who were most of our work force) that produced the best-trained employees in our industry. Usually our employees earned 20–50 percent more than our competitors' employees received. Those that rose to district manager level (managing multiple locations or clubs) could make as much as $200,000 per year. Many accomplished this while still in their twenties. If they were truly rising stars, we would eventually make them minority partners. If or when we sold the company, they could become millionaires.

We realized that if we could offer customers the best service, at or near the lowest price, while paying our employees significantly more than our competitors did, then we would eventually dominate our marketplace. It is important to understand that we were only able to charge less because we sold more, and we were only able to pay more because we taught our employees to be more productive than their counterparts in our competitors' companies.

Many employees that we hired from other companies ended up quitting or getting fired because they thought that they had to work too hard and that we expected too much from them. The advantage of training young people with little or no experience was that we could work them to the bone and pay them like kings, and everyone—employees, company management, and our customers—felt they were getting the best end of the deal. And since our employees were happy and making great money, it was difficult for our competitors to hire our best employees away from us.

Again, let me use a sports analogy to illustrate how different compensation philosophies can work within the same business. The famous New York Yankees run a payroll that exceeds $250 million a year, while the Oakland Athletics' payroll is often below $30 million. While the Yankees have created the most valuable sports franchise in the world, the Oakland A's also operate a successful and profitable baseball club and have increased their franchise value significantly over the years.

The point is to figure out a payroll philosophy that will operate within your preset budget and produce a profit. In essence, you must somehow get employees to produce more than you pay them (regardless of how much that is) so the company makes a profit from their employment. I'm not talking about paying them less than they deserve, but about motivating employees to produce more than they consume.

If they are not producing at acceptable, profit-creating levels, it is your responsibility to cut them loose. You aren't doing them or yourself a favor by keeping them around if they are not getting their job done. None of us can hire and develop winners all the time, and if people are trying hard but still struggling, it usually means they are in the wrong profession.

I should mention that when it comes to hiring accountants and lawyers, I strongly believe in never cutting corners. One of my mistakes in my early years in business was getting cut-rate or dishonest advice in these areas. Take the time to research and find people who are honest, professional, experienced, and smart. It will save you a lot of time and money in the long run. I have taken companies through very complex sales over the last twenty-five years, and because of the professionalism of my accountants and lawyers, I've never been audited by the IRS on any of these sales.

A proverb I always keep in the forefront of my brain is, "The blessing of the Lord makes a person rich, and he adds no sorrow with it" (Proverbs 10:22). I don't like loss or sorrow, especially if it could be avoided. That's where it pays to hire the best.

Like many entrepreneurs, I am not very detail-oriented: so it's imperative that I surround myself with people who will fill in the blanks. I have lost hundreds of thousands of dollars on one or two words being out of place in hundred-page documents. Sometimes companies hire attorneys just to put this kind of trap into contracts, and even a well-seasoned businessperson wouldn't spot the pitfall.

Invest in attorneys and accountants that understand you and your business. Even though you are hiring a top-paid and hopefully savvy attorney or accountant, ultimately it is still your responsibility to train them thoroughly on your business. They often work with many businesses, and what means one thing in one business means something entirely different in another.

Excellent leaders gather a team that accentuates their strengths and compensates for their weaknesses. They cast vision and create strategy, but they also gather diverse types of people with diverse gifts and perspectives, people that can execute the strategies even better than the leader.

On the other hand, weak leaders surround themselves with people that have the same talents, perceptions, opinions, and attitudes as themselves. They often believe that if a key executive disagrees with the leader's strategies or plans, that executive is negative and should be removed from the team. This is the surest way to create blind spots that will ultimately take down the leader and the company.

Having a diverse team does—and should—lead to robust dialogue. That means intense discussion, passionate arguments, and strong emotion. It takes patience and self-control to get a group of people with contrary perspectives and ideas to share passionately but respectfully until the best possible plan is created.

Many people think that unity means everyone being agreeable. Unity is really being open-minded enough to get an honest contribution from each individual so you can have the best perspective as a group.

A great leader strives to create one mind, one voice, and one language among everyone who work for him. Let your leaders voice ideas and concerns. Decide on the best solution. Then leave difference behind in the boardroom and stand united in your course of action.

If respect and honor are core values, and if the welfare of the company and its mission and goals—not individual aspirations—are always paramount, an incredible "super-mind" is created that is the blending of the best of everyone's ideas. The famous author Napoleon Hill referred to this as creating a mastermind group: a unit of people working in synergy toward the same goal.

Step 2: Service

We must be obsessed with delivering a service or product that exceeds our customers' expectations. The customers' perception is most important in building a successful business. They must feel they received more value in service or product than they paid for. As you do this on an ongoing basis, your business will prosper.

In our industry, we receive direct feedback through members who cancel their memberships. If we ask and listen to why a member is choosing to no longer use our club to accomplish their fitness needs, we can improve.

For example, here are the reasons why people have quit using our athletic clubs, in order of importance to them. First is the cleanliness of the club facilities. Next is the friendliness and helpfulness of the staff: from an enthusiastic greeting as the member walks through the door, to helpfulness on the exercise floor, to a "Have a great day!" as they leave. Third is providing state-of-the-art fitness equipment for all ages and types of members, from relatively passive equipment to free-weight barbells and dumbbells for the serious weight lifters. In some instances, we have spent over a million dollars on equipment with the latest conveniences, such as TV and iPod hookups on cardiovascular equipment. Equally important as offering the best equipment is providing specialized classes, such as yoga, stepping, low- and high- impact classes, aggressive cross-fitness training, and group boot camp classes.

If our competitors provide services or equipment that is better than ours, in time we will lose members. If we do not have a finger on our members' pulse, sooner or later we will lose business—probably sooner. And if we don't correct things quickly, we will find ourselves out of business. That is the beauty of the free marketplace system: it forces you to improve or perish.

Many companies make the mistake of trying to dictate what their customers want instead of listening carefully to their concerns and complaints. Actually the chronic complainer, if listened to with no ego, will help you build a successful business faster than hundreds of customers who do nothing but sing your praises. It is human nature to move away from those who complain and gravitate toward those who are positive, but it is wise to get in the habit of getting feedback from your most critical customers regularly. If you can please the most difficult person, you will satisfy everyone else, too.

In America, I believe customers miss great service. Nearly everywhere you go, you find self-service. Even grocery stores are replacing checkers with computers to avoid paying for labor. The self-service philosophy is efficient and saves on payroll costs, but it is also impersonal and mechanical. In my opinion, it opens up a great opportunity for competitors in all businesses to invest in quality, trained, service-oriented people who will provide a human service. For many customers, that is more valuable than incremental cost savings. I am convinced that customers will pay more for the positive human touch.

My greatest pet peeve is calling the so-called service department of a large company and being shuffled from one recording to another, then placed on hold for five minutes, then talking to someone in another country whom I can hardly understand, only to be told I must write or email details about my request—and then never hearing back from them once I do write them.

I'm sure this is done to weed out weak complaints or needs so that the company doesn't have to deal with them individually. But when I get bounced around like this, they lose me as a customer. People don't want to deal with phone trees and automated systems— they would rather talk to someone who is real, intelligent, pleasant, and able to immediately solve problems.

If I am treated with respect and dignity when I call about an issue that needs resolved, I will continue to be a customer and even refer others.

One of my favorite companies is Apple. Besides producing wonderful products, they surround the experience in awesome service, from the moment they make the sale all the way through the life of the product. I can walk into an Apple Store any time and be greeted by a smiling, knowledgeable, customer representative who usually solves my problem within ten minutes.

Starbucks increased the cost of a cup of coffee by almost 300 percent twenty years ago by delivering not only a great cup of coffee, but also the greatest service experience ever offered in the marketplace. No matter how complicated of a concoction you order, their baristas nearly always get it right; and if you are not happy with your drink, they remake it with a smile and often even give you a free drink. Twenty years ago, if you would have asked ten strangers on the street if they would ever consider paying four dollars for a cup of coffee, all ten would have looked at you like you were nuts. Yet at six o'clock this morning, when I was getting my coffee at Starbucks, there was a line twenty people long. The cashier called nearly everyone by name and even knew his or her favorite drink. If people came through the line that she didn't know, she would ask them their name so next time she could greet them personally.

The department store Nordstrom has thrived for years through fantastic service. People know they will pay more for clothes at Nordstrom than they would for the same outfit at other stores down the street; but because Nordstrom has basically a no-questions-asked return policy, customers feel safe shopping there for themselves and when buying gifts for friends. They know they or their friends won't be hassled if they return their purchase. Does this return policy get taken advantage of sometimes? Sure—but overall, their great customer service reputation has more than covered for the occasional dishonest customer.

In a competitive marketplace, cost control is imperative—but so is continuous customer feedback. Your customers will tell you if you are delivering a service and product that is worth more to them than what they are paying.

Step 3: Results

Results is where the rubber meets the road. Ask yourself and your clients if you have under-promised and over-delivered. If the answer is yes, your customers will not only continue to buy your product or service, but they will tell their friends, and your business will flourish.

In the fitness business, we can be rather quantitative in measuring our results. Most of our customers have specific fitness goals: they want to lose x amount of weight or body fat, trim x amount of inches off their waist, and improve their MOU (a measurement of cardiovascular fitness under stress), all in the shortest period of time possible. If we are successful in fulfilling their desired fitness goals in the allotted time frame, we will capture them as members for the rest of their life. As a bonus, they will recommend our club to their friends. You can't buy that kind of advertising!

Every business should determine exactly what they are trying to accomplish for their customers and be able to concretely measure those results. Maybe it is running a small restaurant that specializes in giving customers great food at a low price and getting them in and out on their thirty-minute lunch break. The management knows that if they accomplish this, they will make a good profit. I've seen restaurants put stopwatches on the table and promise that the food will be free if it takes longer than a certain amount of time. This puts positive pressure on the staff to fulfill the promise of fast, quality service.

On the opposite end of the spectrum is the restaurant that hires a renowned chef to create the best food with the best presentation in the city. The waiters are world-class: they can describe in detail how the meal is prepared, the ingredients in each course, and which type of wine will accentuate the meal. The dining experience might take over three hours, and every course of the dinner is timed to bring maximum enjoyment. The price for this experience would shock some people, who might say that no service or food is worth that kind of money. Yet the upscale restaurant keeps to its vision and strategy of delivering the best dining experience because there is a demand for it.

Business owners must ask themselves if they can deliver the results they promise on a consistent basis and whether they can make a profit doing so. If the answer to both questions is yes, then in the long run, the business will likely flourish.

Step 4: Obligation

Obligation is simply a restatement of the ancient biblical law of sowing and reaping. As I have purposefully repeated, if a person or company consistently provides better service or a more valuable product than what customers pay for, in time they will be successful.

This is an absolute law that cannot be circumvented over the long term. As 2 Corinthians 9:6 says, "He who sows sparingly will also reap sparingly, and he who sows bountifully will also reap bountifully" (NKJV).

Many people fall into the trap of thinking they can get away with tricking the public by producing an inferior product and overcharging for it. If market conditions are right, they might get away with that, sometimes for a long time. However, sooner or later, businesses that defraud or mislead will end up paying for it. God's spiritual law of sowing and reaping is every bit as absolute as the law of gravity. The only difference is that the cause-and-effect relationship is not as immediately visible.

It is human nature to look for shortcuts in business to accomplish financial goals. Unfortunately, that often means cutting the wrong corners and making decisions that short-circuit long-term goals. Capitalism is built on weeding out those who disregard this law of first giving and then receiving. The marketplace is self-governing.

One of the major problems young businesses get themselves into is under-capitalization. Since they have to show positive cash flow quickly in order to stay in business, they take too many shortcuts and produce an inferior product.

I have operated from an under-capitalized position many times. I started one business with nearly no money and another one while hugely in debt. Yet I was able to survive and flourish. Why? Because I didn't compromise my service, even on a very limited budget. I was able to do that for several reasons: I knew my business intimately; I was trained and had reached personal excellence in my particular field; and I was able to keep my costs down by doing the work of several different employees.

That translates to a lot of hard work, something every new business will require. When we began Hart's in 1987, besides managing that first club, I did all the janitorial work, maintenance, sales, and advertising, and I even handled the accounting for a short time until I could afford a professional. Meanwhile, my wife ran customer service and sold memberships. Instead of running the club on a normal payroll of $50,000 per month, we ran it on just $10,000. We saved $40,000 per month until our revenue increased enough so we could replace ourselves with quality employees.

The greatest lesson my father taught me was how to be a hard worker, and I am blessed to have a wife who shares that work ethic. In many ways her workload was even greater than mine, because she not only always worked long and hard at the club when the situation called for it, but she invested thousands of hours into our children and household affairs. God's grace and our hard work were the difference between making it and going under.

I admit that during some of those seasons where our capital was low, we found ways to "reap before we sowed," like raising cash by selling prepaid memberships at a discount to make payroll or pay the rent. It was not immoral or illegal, but it certainly was not ideal. You pay a high price if you continually get before you give. Our knowledge of this law kept us from making this behavior a habit, and as soon as we could afford to eliminate it, we did.

Don't fall into the trap of overextending yourself, then cutting corners on quality just to make ends meet. Plan ahead and maintain sufficient cash flow to continually provide an excellent service or product.

Delivering quality is the pivotal point of the PSROPS system. If we provide sub-par products and services, customers will eventually feel cheated, and in the end we will lose them. But if we exceed their expectations, they will feel grateful and more loyal than ever.

If a business goes beyond what is expected, customers experience what psychologists call "cognitive dissonance." That means they feel indebted to us and have an emotional need to return the favor. Customer respond to this emotional imbalance by coming back; if the good service persists, they tell others about it. They develop a sense of loyalty to the business and become walking, talking billboards. The bigger the difference between the cost of our service or product and its value to our customers, the easier it is to create customers like this.

At first we might think that when we provide more than people expect, we are wasting resources or giving away more than we can afford. But in reality, we are buying the loyalty of our customers, and our investment will be more than repaid over time.

Step Five: Promotion

Promotion refers to the intentional branding and marketing of our service or product. As I've said already, the best form of advertising and promotion is our customers' positive words about our business. Most small businesses live or die by the customer reputation they create.

I used to stand in line for an hour to get into a hole-in-the-wall Italian restaurant in downtown San Francisco called Little Joe's. The slogan printed on the T-shirts they sold said, "Rain or shine, there is a line at Little Joe's." People actually enjoyed the wait—it created a feeling of camaraderie and anticipation. Despite the beat-up appearance of the place, the food was delicious, the price reasonable, and the atmosphere electric.

The owner acted as the host and seated each customer with a friendly attitude. His apron was always dirty and food-stained, but somehow that just added to the atmosphere. He worked hard to make sure everyone was served quickly and had a pleasant experience.

One night, I saw a beautiful, black Mercedes-Benz pull up in front of his restaurant. A woman who appeared to be his wife moved over to the passenger seat, and he jetted away in his luxurious car. I am sure he had built a multimillion-dollar business.

He likely spent little or no money on advertising, and yet he produced a huge profit. Why? He knew how to leverage customer-based marketing, which is simply word of mouth. This is the best way to build a long-lasting, successful business.

Don't misunderstand me: I believe in advertising and promotion. But it should accentuate or add fuel to an already successful business. In our clubs, we provide an awesome product and service and then shout it from the mountaintops through strategically chosen media.

Advertising should never replace what made you successful in the first place: customer satisfaction. Marketing is the easiest and quickest way to grow, but if it is not matched with customer satisfaction, company growth will last only as long as your advertising campaigns. So build expectations with great ads, then work even harder to exceed those expectations once customers walk in the door.

Most of the companies I've operated have spent 5–10 percent of revenue on promotion. If our clubs do $20 million in sales a year, we budget around $150,000 a month for advertising.

Our long-term goal is always to buy the market's mind through consistent advertising campaigns. The advertising not only brings in immediate customers, it also keeps our name in the forefront of people's minds. When customers who live near our clubs think, "I need to lose some weight and get in shape!" we want them to automatically think of our club.

For example, when people go into a store looking for a soft drink, they usually think of Coke or Pepsi products first. There are other brands that probably taste just as good and cost less, but because advertising has programmed their mind subconsciously, they won't give the less-known brands a chance.

This is called branding. To be most effective, you must maintain a good product, and your advertising must be strategic and consistent.

We are disciplined in our strategies to penetrate and dominate the marketplace. Even if we find ourselves in a tough economic climate, we keep spending on advertising. It is tempting to eliminate marketing to save money, but we have discovered that the first thing our competitors cut when things get tight is advertising and promotion. So, the economic downturn becomes an opportunity to pick up market share. Additionally, advertising is usually cheaper in a depressed market. We can get up to twice the coverage we did when rates were higher, and we no longer have ads from our competitors running next to ours.

The marketplace is always changing, so marketing that worked last year will not necessarily work this year. A good example is newspaper advertising. We used to take out large newspaper ads on Mondays and Wednesdays. The ads always got immediate results: phone calls would come into our clubs nonstop, especially if we ran a trial membership offering six weeks for ten dollars. But today, if we ran the same ad, with the same offer, in the same newspaper, we would get little response. These ads cost up to $12,000, and it would be a waste of money.

It's not easy to change old habits. Our brand and our marketing strategy can become institutionalized and antiquated more quickly than we like to think. I often challenge myself to think like a twenty-something-year-old. What is new? What is working? Where are the customers, and what do they want?

One of the hottest forms of advertising today is social media. Honestly, I don't really understand it. So, I decided to hire someone to spend four hours a week teaching me how to navigate social media. At nearly sixty years of age, I am going through the painful process of learning to "tweet."

I love advertising, and over the last forty years I have done much of the marketing myself. In my early years, I was considered a marketing genius. I say that honestly, not arrogantly—especially since I now find myself working hard to get up to speed with a new generation.

As any businessperson can attest, advertising is fickle. Sometimes it's like taking a wheelbarrow of money over to a fireplace and burning it. Advertising is at best an educated guess, and because of that it can be very frustrating.

I will mention a few methods of advertising that I believe will work best in most businesses today. Again, because of how quickly the marketplace changes, what works now might not work in a year or two. You must stay on top of your advertising dollar. Study the results of your different advertising expenditures to find what works and what doesn't, then adapt quickly.

One of the most valuable forms of advertising is your website. Invest in an attractive and informative website that captures your audience. It is worth the money to ensure that your website communicates effectively why you are different and better than your competitor. Remember, the average customer is bouncing from your site to your competitor's site, and in many instances, the customer will make the decision to buy based on what your website communicates and how it communicates it.

Hire someone smart and creative, someone you can communicate the intricacies of your business to. It's like hiring an architect to help design your dream home: if you pick the right one, he or she will make your ideas even better than what you saw in your head. But if the web designer is unqualified or arrogant, the result can completely miss the mark. You might end up staring at a huge bill for a website that is nothing like what you wanted. So be careful with your choice, and work closely with the designer.

Social media is a relatively new but incredibly effective form of media that is revolutionizing advertising by the minute. It operates beyond the reach of your website, helping bring web traffic to you through online links. Social media includes things like Facebook, blogs, and Twitter.

As I write this book, people are saying the man who ruled Egypt for thirty years was brought down by one intelligent person who understood the synergetic effects of properly timed and placed social media. They say he struck such a chord among the young people of Egypt that, within three weeks, an entire nation revolted. That is unbelievable power. It is word-of-mouth advertising on steroids.

Other forms of media that we use to varying degrees include television, radio, billboards, direct mail, door hangers, web ads, door-to-door sales, phone solicitation, and lead boxes in restaurants and retail stores around town.

Your advertising strategy will depend on the nature of your business, your market, and your overall budget. Think and pray about what I believe to be the ultimate question in promoting your business: "How can I differentiate myself from my competitors?"

Most businesspeople fall into the trap of following the rest of the sheep. I will give you two examples that worked in our businesses in the hope of sparking your imagination, which is your most valuable asset in creating a profitable business.

The first example is a television advertising campaign Hart's Athletic Clubs ran in the early 90s. When we finally had the budget to advertise on TV, I asked my partner to be the spokesman for our company. At first he looked at me kind of funny, because I was the one who worked out fanatically, was in good shape, and was much younger. He was about fifty pounds overweight and pretty deconditioned.

But I felt like I would come across as the stereotypical athletic guy with big muscles. Even though I could present a wholesome image of what fitness is, I thought it better to do the opposite.

We ran an ad featuring my partner working out in our athletic club, sweating away, then looking up and saying something like, "Even though I'm the owner of these clubs, I'm no different than you. I struggle with losing weight, but if I can do it, so can you!"

The viewing audience fell in love with him because they could relate. The response was almost magical: phones rang off the hook, and over time he became a household name. He and I would walk through the shopping market together, and people would say to him, "How are the workout and diet going?"

He would reply, "I'm trying my best!" And people would walk away feeling encouraged because he was like them.

Some of my friends and associates criticized my choice of making him the star instead of me, since I better represented our product. That was true, but my goal was to differentiate our company from our competitors. I believe these commercials, as offbeat as they might have appeared, were an important reason why we not only penetrated the market, but ended up dominating the fitness industry in our region.

The second example is a charitable foundation that my most recent company, Pure Fitness of Arizona, helped start to fight childhood obesity. (In a later chapter, I'll discuss the roller coaster ride that was Pure Fitness.) Our clubs worked hand-in-hand with this foundation. We ran free, twelve-week sessions for groups of extremely overweight kids. We provided the space, equipment, and instructors, as well as spending hundreds of thousands of dollars. Probably a thousand kids went through this program.

The results were amazing. Some kids lost up to fifty pounds in a twelve-week period. Their lives were changed dramatically; some may have been saved from premature death.

Both children and parents gave touching testimonies on how we changed their lives. Some spoke about how they had lost overweight friends due to premature heart issues and diabetes. Their stories brought all of us to tears. When a twelve-year-old girl who was made fun of at school for her weight loses fifty pounds and thanks you, with tears streaming down her face, for changing her life—that's priceless.

Our employees and members were excited about the project. We received great word-of-mouth advertising from our members, and a major TV station came out and ran a positive news story on our company. The goodwill this program created in the community and with our staff and members was incalculable.

People have asked me if we created the program because we had a heart for kids or because we wanted the good publicity. The answer is both. We saw a need that we could fill, and we realized it was an opportunity to differentiate ourselves from our competitors. It was a win-win strategy.

The program cost us a huge amount of money to get off the ground, but we believed in time, it would bring a hundredfold return on our investment by creating for us that magical branding that sets us above our competitors. It's an example of why generosity is good business.

Step 6: Sales

I have spent much of my career training salespeople. In the fitness industry, professional salesmanship is imperative. We have developed comprehensive sales presentations that team members memorize. We train our team to overcome objections from prospective members, which are usually related to why they cannot get started on their fitness goals today.

Our surveys have shown that if we do not give prospective members a quality presentation when they come in to inquire about a membership, less than 10 percent will buy. On the other hand, if we educate them thoroughly on the benefits of adopting a lifestyle of fitness, we can improve sales to over 70 percent. And keep in mind that we are "selling" fitness, which faces greater inherent sales resistance than things like coffee, food, and alcohol.

Over the years, many of our competitors have—to their demise—completely cut salespeople out of their strategy, hoping to save money. Others have used unprofessional, ill-equipped salespeople—and that also fails. It is important to determine what level of salespeople you need to sell your product or service effectively.

Sales can usually be broken down into four distinct steps. If you follow this outline, you can teach sales to just about anyone, regardless of the business you are in.

1. Establish rapport. Learn how to get customers to like you and trust you. Connect with them on an emotional level.

2. Find the need. This is accomplished with artfully posed questions that help customers become transparent about what they want. Once you think you have established their need, repeat it back to them to confirm that you understand what they are looking for. For example, you might say: "If I could get you the dress in red, and in your size, am I right in assuming you will want it"?

3. Fulfill the need. Once you identify the need, satisfy it immediately! Present the service or product they have indicated they want, describe the terms or price, and do anything else conducive to closing the sale.

4. Close the sale confidently and quickly. Sales is often momentum-based; people have a tendency toward procrastination that you should overcome by reminding them of the reasons to buy today. Then write up the order and get paid.

The art of sales often gets a bad rap due to salespeople who don't know the first thing about proper salesmanship and who come across as high-pressure con artists. Quality salespeople sell almost effortlessly. They make the transaction between the seller and buyer a truly positive experience. They win and keep the buyer's trust. Often, they get dozens of quality referrals over the years from that customer.

20/80 Formula to Prioritization

Most leaders have a good work ethic. But many fail to accomplish what is most important because though they work hard, they don't work smart. The PSROPS system helps business leaders step back from everything that is happening to them and around them in order to see the big picture. It helps them focus on areas that need additional emphasis so they can effectively prioritize their time.

The 20/80 formula to prioritization means that if you identify and do with excellence the top 20 percent of things you should do, you will accomplish at least 80 percent of your job. That's normally enough to run an excellent business.

This takes meditation, analysis, and practice. Great business leaders must continuously have their priorities in place with respect to God, family, and business. Because these priorities can be so interwoven, leaders can be confused at times and end up doing low-priority things when they think they are doing high-priority ones.

The secret to leading a balanced life is learning when to become unbalanced. That's an important paradox to grasp if you are running your own business. There will be seasons when you must focus more on certain areas while spending less time on others. This temporary imbalance is necessary to maintain long-term balance.

The notion that leading a balanced life means every day spending the first hour in prayer and Bible reading, eating a wonderful breakfast with the family, seeing the kids off to school, working eight hours, catching a workout after work, coming home for a family dinner at six o'clock, then going to a church service or a sporting event, and finally tucking the kids into bed—not to mention dedicating both Saturday and Sunday to the family—is an unreal expectation.

I am not saying that it is impossible to simultaneously have a quality prayer life, family life, and business life. But what is rare—if not impossible—is accomplishing this goal by dedicating the same amount of time to each priority every day.

For example, if a husband and wife who own their own business lose their key manager responsible for day-to-day operations, they will need to make adjustments in their family expectations until a replacement can be found. If the husband, trying to be a supportive spouse and father, still eats breakfast and dinner with his family every day, attends all the kids' games, and spends weekends at home, but the business falls apart, what does he gain? The business failure will cause more financial and emotional chaos than working twenty extra hours a week for a season. The same is true if it is the wife who has to dedicate more time to the business at the expense of other areas.

A wise businessperson can see around corners. He or she can see problems before they happen, make necessary adjustments immediately, and avoid letting the situation deteriorate to a point where the problem completely disrupts the business and consequently damages his or her personal life.

This skill develops over time. Learn to become a realistic thinker—maybe even a bit paranoid. Develop the courage to confront developing situations immediately with maximum wisdom. Don't wait until small issues grow into large ones.

Avoid the mistake of doing only what falls within your area of gifting. It's always easier to focus on the things that we are passionate about, things that come naturally to us, or things that we are confident we can do well. But smart leaders are concerned about every area, not just the ones they are gifted in.

Delegating responsibility to exceptional, trustworthy people is important, as I have already said—but that doesn't absolve us of all responsibility in those areas. Stay informed about what they are doing. Learn enough about these areas to manage the people you put in charge.

For instance, if as a business owner you are strong in sales and marketing but weak in administration, you should employ the best executive administrator possible, someone who can handle the accounting and other general administrative duties. But your responsibility in administrative areas doesn't end there. Though you may have little interest or expertise in those areas—or more accurately, *because* you have little interest or expertise in those areas—you can't just check out. Stay involved. This part of your business is the most susceptible to weakness or failure.

This is particularly true at the beginning. Once you have surrounded yourself with trustworthy, excellent people who respect your leadership and who can execute your strategy, you can focus more of your time on your strengths.

When it comes to priorities, a good exercise that a business leader should get in the habit of doing every morning, preferably after a time of prayer and meditation, is what I call mind-dumping. Here's how it works.

Go through each point of the PSROPS system and make lists of what needs to be done, in no particular order of priority. Write down everything, big or small, that is worrying you or that you know needs to be dealt with at some point. Don't limit yourself just to business issues—personal, family, and spiritual issues are often intertwined with business decisions.

Simply listing out your goals and fears will bring instant clarity to some decisions. But your goal at this stage is mainly to get everything swirling around in your mind out on the table so you can evaluate it as objectively as possible.

Next, number the items in your list in order of importance. Only you can determine priorities, and your order of priorities will shift frequently, based on your circumstances.

This process is what separates hardworking, successful executives from hardworking, unsuccessful ones. We all have the same twenty-four hours in the day. Most of us need to sleep approximately eight hours, leaving sixteen hours for business, family, church, and so on. We know God wants us to be champions in every area, so the key is to use those hours effectively.

The great part about proper prioritization is that if you are able to identify the top 20 percent of things you need to do and execute them with excellence, you will never need to do the remaining 80 percent. I should warn you that in the beginning, the items on the top 20 percent list will probably be things you hate to do, don't care about, or fear. This is an exercise in both wisdom and discipline, so be prepared to face some obstacles within yourself.

Within a month or so, you will be amazed at how much more smoothly your life runs and how much time and energy you have left at the end of your day for your spouse and children.

Hustle

From an early age, my mom and dad encouraged me to succeed. I grew up confident that if I did my best at whatever I put my hand to, I couldn't fail. I remember my father teaching me about enthusiasm and hustle. He said this attitude, coupled with initiative, would help make up for deficiencies in any area.

When I was eight, I wanted to play baseball. I was short, skinny, and inexperienced—not a likely athlete, at least at first glance. My dad told me that no matter what position my coach assigned me, I should field that position the best I could with a winning attitude.

The smallest or least-talented kids always had to play right field, and that was where they sent me. When I told my father, he said to run as fast as I could out to my position, to play with the same intensity and determination as if I were in my dream position, and after each inning, to sprint off the field and beat the pitcher to the dugout. Because I was small for my age, he taught me how to bunt for base hits and how to squat down in my batting stance to draw a walk. He always said a walk is as good as a hit. He convinced me that sooner or later, my coach would appreciate my hustle and enthusiasm and gain confidence in me.

He was right. As time passed, I grew in size and ability and became a top-notch ball player. I was a leader in most of the teams I played for.

Eventually, my dream of becoming a professional baseball player faded away because I didn't have the talent necessary to play at a professional level. But the attitude of enthusiasm and the habit of hustle never left me. Many times in business, it has been the difference between winning and losing.

Multiply Excellence

A big question small business owners face is when and how to expand their business. I've seen many business leaders fail because they tried to grow too soon, too fast, or the wrong way.

My first advice to business owners is, start small. There's nothing wrong with that. Get very good at what you do. Then, if God has given you the ability and if you have the desire, you are ready to grow.

In other words, before you try to take over the world, perfect your prototype. If your vision is to own and operate a hundred coffee shops, clothing stores, or fitness centers, or if it's to build a billion-dollar software company, work out the kinks while you are small. If you learn to be profitable on a small scale, you will be able to expand with confidence. If you aren't profitable now, you will only duplicate failure if you try to expand.

When I got into the fitness business, my dream was to run the best, most profitable fitness center on the West Coast. I soon discovered I had a lot more talent for business than I did for sports, and in less than two years, we were making more money from that one club than most operators made from four clubs. I had also trained myself out of a job. I had raised up managers to take my place, and there was nothing left for me to do. It made sense to expand.

That's how I have started nearly every company I have owned since. I build up one club and then expand from there.

Training a Team

A key phrase in what I wrote above is, "I trained myself out of a job." Many small business owners, even the successful ones, are terrible trainers. I have heard countless owners complain in frustration, "I can't find anyone who will do a good job!" Or, "This new generation just doesn't get responsibility!" They usually finish up with, "If you want a job done well, you have to do it yourself!"

Not only is this untrue, it puts a ceiling on your company's growth, creates unneeded stress for you, and keeps people who ultimately will be more qualified than you from rising to the surface.

Imagine a professional football coach teaching his players how to be a winning team. Months before the season starts, he gathers the team together and lays out his overall philosophy. Then he convinces his players to buy into his belief system. This is a continuous process of programming his team to believe like he does. The deeper he can drive his belief system into his players, the easier it will be for them to think and act as a cohesive unit.

Then he lays out his goals for the team. These must be optimistic, yet grounded in reality. For a coach to proclaim that his team is going to turn last season's 0-16 record into a 16-0 winning season this year may be impossible for his players to buy into, even if the coach really believes they can do it. He is better off creating a goal that his team can intellectually and emotionally take hold of, even if it is below what he wants to accomplish. So maybe his goal should simply be coaching his team to a winning record.

The most motivating thing a coach can do is get his team to start winning. The coach only has to show some progress for his team to begin to have faith in him and his ideas. In the business world, by the way, winning is being profitable and teaching your employees to increase their paychecks.

Once the coach's philosophy and objectives have been clearly laid out, he hands out his playbook. This is his strategy on how they will win. For each play, all players must understand their specific role and how that relates to the rest of the team. This is commonly called the Xs and the Os, referring to the play diagrams on a chalkboard.

Once the team learns the plays on an intellectual level, they head to the field to feel their way through the strategy on a practical level. This goes on hour after hour, day after day.

Finally, after months of intense training, they face off against opposing teams. That's where the training pays off, as talent and teamwork determine their wins and losses for the season.

Imagine a team heading onto the field without an understanding of the team's goals, without knowing any plays, and without having worked together on the field. It would be disaster.

It's normal in any sport to invest months of work and great amounts of money into training. Why do we think it would be different in business?

Many business owners either don't have the patience or don't know how to train effectively. Part of determining whether you should expand your business is finding out if you are capable of reproducing yourself in your managers and staff.

If your company is profitable and you think it's time to expand, try going on an extended vacation—at least a month—and leave your business in the hands of your most capable manager. Don't call or check in, and don't allow him or her to call you unless it's a true emergency. When you get back, if everything is operating as well or better than when you were there, you are ready to expand. But if your business is in chaos, do yourself a favor and stay small, at least for now.

You may have reached your limits in business. There is no condemnation if that is the case. Honestly, most small businesses should not try to dominate their market or become a nationwide chain. Either they aren't capable of it, aren't ready for it, can't afford it, or maybe just don't want it.

You can create a prosperous, fulfilling life by running a small business or, for that matter, working for someone else. That is much better than chasing after something God has not called you to or gifted you for.

On the other hand, maybe your business fell into chaos because you had the wrong people in place. Or maybe you had the right people, but you hadn't trained them properly.

If you have a burning desire to grow, and if you know you can get the right people, put them in the right place, and train them to complete their jobs excellently, then the following discussion will help.

Fifty percent of good training happens during the hiring process. The business owner or manager must clearly and concisely outline the rules for new employees. Is punctuality important? What do they need to learn? By when? How should they dress and talk? These are just a few of the areas that may need to be addressed.

Explain that when you want them to do something, you will ask them politely, and then you expect obedience. At most, all you want from them in response are questions of clarification—not debate or contradiction. You don't expect to tell them more than once to do something they have been adequately trained on, and you expect them to do it with a positive attitude, with no grumbling. Any behavior that does not coincide with their agreed-upon job description will be met with a strong rebuke or reprimand. Encourage them to respond to correction by changing their behavior, and not to take it as a personal attack.

Look for a solid commitment that for the first few months, regardless of their experience or age, they will trust you and depend on you, learning from you until you see that they have successfully made their job description a habit. You will gradually move them into a relationship of independence. At that point, you will expect them to perform their duties on their own.

Emphasize from the beginning that a dependent relationship is not the end goal. Once they master their job, they will have the freedom to succeed or fail on their own.

They must not grow comfortable with you giving directions, praising, and reprimanding them continually. Don't fall into the trap of creating a parent-toddler relationship that keeps your employees from taking initiative and forces you to always think for them.

Personally, I am not intimidated when zealous applicants tell me during the interview process that they want to learn as much as they can so they can start their own fitness center. This just tells me that they are burning with ambition. If they have an open-minded, positive attitude and are trainable, we can show them how to create more wealth for themselves by working for us than by running their own club. Later in this book, I will explain how to keep your stars working for you once you have developed them.

Make sure you explain your expectations, their job description, the compensation plan, and a realistic time frame to achieve their financial goals, and then ask for a firm commitment. Once they agree, it's time to begin strategic training.

I believe teaching people how to perform their job well is the greatest motivator there is. It encourages both the subordinates and the teacher. There is no greater joy than mentoring people to fulfill the greatness that lies within them.

My formula for teaching is: *tell, show, do,* and *redirect.*

The first step, telling, is best accomplished through a written, comprehensive manual on how best to perform their job. The manual should include tests that help evaluate their learning progress. You or one of your managers must also be able to effectively teach them this information orally. That means clear, inspirational communication. Teachers all have their own style, but they must be engaging, and students must be excited about learning the material. If the information is taught properly, students will learn 30–40 percent of what they need to know.

The second step is showing them how to do their job correctly. Most people learn faster by demonstration than by classroom education, or telling. However, the combination of explaining it to them coupled with seeing the procedure carried out correctly seems to trigger a switch in their brains. The demonstration part of the education should continue until both the employees and the instructor are sure the subject or procedure is clear.

The third step in the training process is for the trainees to do the task. The teacher must let them do the job with little or no input, regardless of how good or bad they do. Once they have completed the task, the teacher should communicate the parts they did well on and then give positive yet honest feedback on how to do better.

The fourth step is to redirect students by repeating the process of tell, show, and do until they can not only perform the task with excellence, but have made it a habit.

Business owners should see employees as extensions of themselves. Any variance in the level of efficiency between owner and employees will cost in bottom-line profits.

Train employees in the processes you follow to achieve goals, but don't make processes more important than goals. An excellent manager knows when to step in and manage the process and when to let go and manage the result. Even within processes and systems, I promote initiative, innovation, and creative thought. My favorite expression is "figure it out."

In the long run, micro-management will kill creativity and initiative in our employees. It is imperative for the business owner or manager to soon move his or her employees out of the dependent part of the training process and into a place where their creativity can flourish.

You have to understand the individual. Some people are comfortable being told exactly what to do; others need more freedom. While the majority of people need the process managed, very creative people will be frustrated. You are better off giving these people freedom to invent new methods, as long as the results are the same or better than your preferred process. The more creativity necessary, the less we should manage the process.

Let me give you an example. I have two very creative children that find it nearly impossible to color inside the lines. But if they are allowed to work freely, they can design and create at a genius level.

Some time ago, when my son Ian was just eighteen, I asked him to do some video work for me for our new website. I wanted seven unique, three-minute commercials that illustrated the group classes we offered, such as yoga, dance, and high-intensity cross-training classes. I wanted him to not just show how the class looked, but to capture the feeling of each one.

As I was explaining in detail everything I had in mind, I could tell my son was shutting down. I asked him what was wrong, and he responded, "Dad, with all due respect, don't I know a lot more about creating video than you do?" And then he added the real killer. "When was the last time I turned in anything that was less than excellent?"

He was right, so I gave him free rein on the project. His videos turned out better than the professional thirty-second commercials we had paid thousands of dollars for.

I firmly believe that our employees are our greatest resource. They can bring creativity and effective execution to our dreams, igniting them with positivity and contagious enthusiasm. Or, they can destroy our dreams through negativity, dishonesty, carelessness, or a poor work ethic.

Keeping Your Best Employees

Your success will come down to whether you can execute your dream through other people. Although strategies, systems, and technology are important ingredients in creating and growing a profitable business, the most important thing is being able to develop high-quality managers or executives that can carry out your vision naturally.

But it's not enough to train them. You have to keep them. Otherwise you will waste tremendous amounts of time and money on training people who will end up working for your competitors.

It's devastating to watch an employee that you mentored go across the street with a handful of your other key employees to compete with you. It might even destroy your business. You can be mad as a hornet and complain about his or her disloyalty, but it doesn't change the fact that a once-loyal disciple is now trying to crush you.

This happens all the time, in every type of business. Usually, the owners play the victims. In reality, they were the dumb ones. They failed to out-strategize their most outstanding employees by creating a road map for success for them.

If talented, ambitious employees know they could create their own successful business and reap great financial benefits, should they remain in a dead-end or poor-paying job simply out of loyalty? I believe they would be disloyal to themselves to live that way.

On the other hand, they might not be cut out to own and run a business. Creating a fair compensation system will not only keep you from losing valued employees, it will keep them from being driven by desperation or greed into a situation that will ultimately destroy them.

So the question becomes, how do you protect yourself and your employees from this sort of falling-out? The answer is to maintain a "value-for-value" relationship with your employees. This means rewarding your employees according to their level of value to the company. Employees who demonstrate hard work, sacrifice, skill, loyalty, positive attitudes, and good leadership add value to your company and should be compensated accordingly.

The best way to determine if you are providing value for value is simply asking yourself what you would want if your positions were reversed. Fair is fair: what is fair for you must be fair for them, or it's not fair at all.

The more talented, productive, and ambitious a star employee is, the more you will have to compensate him or her. That's not a bad thing. Good workers more than pay for themselves through the profit and value they add to the company. Don't focus on how little you can get away with paying in salaries. Instead, work on getting the right people in the right place, then pay them generously and demand a high level of productivity.

Incidentally, if I had to choose, I would rather employee be productive than loyal. That might sound backwards, and of course I'd rather have both—but if I have employee who are motivated and productive, I can find ways to get them to be loyal, even if they are a little hard to get along with. I have always wanted tigers fighting for me rather than kittens, so if I get scratched or clawed once in a while, I am okay with that. In business, thin skin isn't good for your health.

Salary isn't the only thing that keeps people on your team. Winning helps, too. People love playing for a winning team, and the psychological effect can outweigh financial compensation. You see it often in sports: a player will take a lower salary just to be part of a winning team. Developing a business with great momentum not only adds value to the company, it also drives down the costs of compensation. The reverse is true as well: if you have a losing team, it will cost you more to attract champion players.

Another key in retaining key employees is to develop a mentoring relationship with them. This is almost a father-son relationship, where you truly desire their success even more than your own. Mutual honor and respect will usually help you negotiate with them over the years as their importance to you and the organization increases.

When the time is right, you should include key employees in a profit-sharing plan that pays above the going rate for their job position. This should happen when you determine, after studying their individual performance, that it would cost you more to replace them than to have them share in the profits.

It is always better that you initiate the increase in their compensation rather than them coming to you. They will feel honored, and it will usually cost you less in compensation than if they had initiated the negotiation.

If you always act first, they will see you through the eyes of generosity. Many of my key employees say that it is better for me to initiate their compensation plans than for them to do it, indicating that I give them more than what they feel they could have successfully negotiated themselves.

When I have star employees that have proven their worth over years of performance, usually individuals who could start their own business if they decided to, I will often approach them about becoming my partner. I would rather it be me that gives them the opportunity to succeed, not an outside investor or a competitor.

This means that not only will they be paid above industry standards for their position and share in profits, they will share in ownership as well. When the company sells, they will get a significant share.

If you have built a winning company with a good reputation, treated your employees with dignity, and compensated them generously over the years, they usually jump at the offer of being a partner.

Let me stress that these are individuals who have worked their way up the company ladder and have produced outstanding results in every position. These people are few and far between.

The partnership agreement is a two-way street. It is good for them and for the company. We usually give them a reduced buy-in for their partnership share: they mainly pay for their ownership in sweat equity. On the other hand, we have them sign a partnership agreement that says, among other things, that they will not compete with us within a fifty-mile radius of our clubs nor use any of our trade secrets and systems. There is a provision that allows us to buy them out if we so choose at a fair price, paid to them over an extended time (so that we don't face the double negative of losing a key person and having to pay out a large amount of money).

Again, the partnership is based on a value-for-value relationship that benefits both parties equally and is designed to keep a winning team together for a long time.

Over the years, I have developed a reputation for connecting young, hungry, talented people who are willing to put in a lot of hard work with opportunities for great financial profit, especially after we sell our companies. When word gets out that you could become a millionaire if you work your tail off and produce great results, it is amazing how many quality recruits come knocking.

When it comes to my main partners, I have the greatest dream team that I could ask for. Our bond has been forged over decades of working together, going through probably more bad times than good. Many of them started as entry-level employees twenty years ago. Through hard work, creative genius, and loyalty, they have been promoted to partners. Together we have built several successful companies. We are more than business partners—we are friends and family. We have gone through war together, and we would do anything for each other.

Eric Stearns has been with me since 1991. He is a man of integrity and great ability. He is not afraid to stand up to me, but at the same time is tremendously loyal. He is my right-hand man, a close friend and confidante, and a very capable executive leader.

Michele Sharar has also worked with me since 1991. She is a woman of integrity who is everything I am not in the administrative area—I would be finished without her! She has been our CFO since Hart's Athletic Clubs.

Willie Schober is my brother. He is seventeen years younger than I and has worked with me since 1991 as well. He is a great executor and administrator, a hard worker, and dedicated. His gifts are a great asset to me.

Leon Doris came to work with me in 1984 when he was only nineteen. I taught him the business, and he helped develop four successful fitness chains. He has a great work ethic, is responsible, is an excellent salesman, and is committed to me and to the cause.

Commodore Mann has been with me since 1991. He has a military background, and his strength and staunch loyalty have meant a lot to me. He works with consumer affairs, legal issues, and training.

I can't say it strongly enough—you need a dream team. It would be laughable for me to take all the credit for what our companies have achieved. It was the result of a team effort: everyone doing their part, everyone putting the good of the company first, everyone staying loyal to one another through good times and bad.

Whether you call it breakthrough, momentum, or the tipping point, we have somehow been able to capture the magic in every company I have run, in different places and different economic environments. It is a complicated recipe requiring just the right amount of vision, faith, prayer, giving, obedience, discipline, hard work, excellence, determination, perseverance, love, gifting, and most importantly, God's power.

Theorists, sociologists, and analysts can theorize all they want, but my partners and I have actually created successful companies. What I am most proud of, though, is that we kept our honor and integrity along the way.

Unfortunately, in the middle of all the success, I nearly lost what was most valuable of all: my family. That is the subject of the next chapter.

11
Love Never Fails

In twelve years, we went from being broke for over $30 million to building a company worth many millions of dollars. Starting with one broken-down club in Everett, we penetrated and even dominated the marketplace in the greater Seattle area. Our company profit margins were four times the industry average, and we had the reputation of being a well-organized company whose first interest was to serve its members. In 1998 we were voted the best fitness club in Washington. We had captured an incredible momentum, and our hearts were set on taking our company national.

I was only forty-six years old, and I still had a lot of enthusiasm and drive to continue to expand. But like the weather, the atmosphere of a company can change in unforeseen ways. I soon found myself facing very difficult decisions.

My partner had slowly become obsessed with how we were, from his point of view, overpaying our club managers. Most of them were making over $150,000 a year in salaries, commissions, and profit sharing. He frequently pointed out that that was about twice the national average.

I always responded that we were making four times the profit that most clubs were making. Most of their income came from profit sharing, which was the result of years of pouring their hearts and souls into developing our very profitable clubs.

He believed we could replace these experienced managers with young, aggressive managers that we could pay half as much. On top of this, his educated and talented daughter had just graduated from a prestigious law school, and he wanted her to take over his job. He instructed me to interact directly with her instead of him. His next step was going to be to have me train his son to do my job, and then he and I could step back and let his kids run the company.

His plan had some major flaws. As talented as his daughter was, she had no experience running a fitness business. She didn't understand how the sales and marketing side of the company interacted with the administrative and legal side. His son needed at least five years of training to understand sales and marketing. Even if he had what it took to do the job, promoting my partner's young son over key executives who had invested years of dedication and hard work would have destroyed their motivation.

I had spent as much as twenty years developing these exceptional club managers. Our relationship was more than just employer-employee. In many cases, I was instrumental in introducing them to the Lord. I had been the best man for some of them at their weddings. Together we had shed much blood on the battlefield of business. They were my courageous men and women of honor and valor.

Now, my partner wanted me to cut their pay in half and break all the promises I had made to them through the years we had struggled to build this wonderful company.

The situation was further complicated by a change in our relationship with my friend and consultant, Ray Wilson. Ray was the person that years before had offered to be a consultant for Family Fitness Centers. In my youthful arrogance, I had turned him down. When I started Hart's Athletic Clubs, though, I was determined to hire the best possible team.

Ray was an experienced and very successful businessman who, besides consulting, was running a group of over sixty fitness centers in California. He decided to sell his clubs to a well-funded company that intended to expand into our Seattle marketplace. He would become an advisor and board member to their company. That created a potential conflict of interest with our company. He was a man of integrity, so he encouraged us to sell our clubs before our profits could be affected by their expansion into our marketplace.

I had made a crucial mistake twelve years earlier when I started our company. I didn't have the majority interest in the company and a reasonable buy-sell agreement that I could exercise to buy my partner out in adverse conditions.

He was a good partner, but he didn't understand the dynamics of running the whole company. I hired him when I ran Family Fitness Centers, and after a number of years, I invited him to be my partner. If I would have owned at least 51 percent of Hart's, I believe he would have come to his senses, or at least just submitted to my control. Instead, he dug in his heels. Meanwhile the new competition was threatening expansion, and my consultant was pushing for us to sell.

I looked at the situation from every angle, trying to figure out how we could overcome the internal and external attacks. Inside, though, I knew it was over. A quiet voice that I have learned to listen to—some might call it intuition, but I believe it is God—told me it was time to sell.

The thought broke my heart. This company represented so much more to me than just a source of income. I was emotionally attached to it: it was part of my identity, and it represented my creative energy.

Now, I knew God was saying, "It's over."

It was a difficult conclusion, but eventually I put aside my emotions and donned warrior's armor. I decided to get the most money possible for the company and generously compensate my key people for their hard work and loyalty.

I knew it would be hard for my partner to sell as well. I told him that I felt we were going in different directions, then I asked him for his approval to sell our company and what a bottom-line number for the sale would be.

After contemplating it, he gave me a number. We agreed that if I could get at least what he wanted, we would proceed with the sale. We also committed that we would carve out over $2 million for our key executives if I could get him the amount he wanted for his stock. I knew his word was good, even though it would be hard for him to sell.

Another company, 24-Hour Fitness, had been offering to buy us out for some time. Within weeks, I was able to negotiate a price for our company that far exceeded what my partner and I had agreed on.

I began the process of selling something more valuable to me than money. It felt like my heart was being ripped out. In the fall of 1998, after six months of intense negotiations and due diligence, the company sold for every dollar we had been promised. My partner and I also retained ownership in our buildings, and the rent supplied us with an ongoing cash flow after the sale.

Thinking back, it was more bitter than sweet. If I would have exercised wiser judgment along the way, we might not have had to sell. But we were millionaires now and to all outward appearances, very successful.

Church Involvement

While we were building this successful company, we were also very active in our church. In 1987 we had joined a church that was just getting started, led by a young pastor and his wife. There were about twenty of us that met in an elementary school. In time, the church grew to around three hundred.

My wife and I had come from a Catholic background that didn't really promote Bible study. This church emphasized not only reading and studying the Bible, but also weekly Scripture memorization. For thirteen years, renewing our mind through the word of God was the primary focus of our church life.

We were a small church, so everyone helped out. Many Sunday mornings I would get up at five in the morning, go pick up the worship equipment, take it to the school where we had our service, and set it up in time for the worship group to practice before service started at ten thirty. Then I would hold a Bible study for adults or a Sunday school class for kids. I was usually assigned the rowdy seventh- and eighth-graders. Church would end at twelve thirty, and we would finish storing the worship equipment by two in the afternoon.

Gina and I would be back at church at six for Awana, a children's program that taught Bible stories, gave prizes for Bible memorization, and held other activities. We usually ran a kids' gym program that was divided into four age groups, with games and events designed for each group.

We would get home around eight thirty at night, exhausted but satisfied, knowing that we had invested our time and energy in a good cause. Best of all, we had spent the whole day with our kids in a wholesome environment.

Looking back on it, I don't know how we did it, especially after attending multiple soccer games on Saturdays. But we were both dedicated to raising good kids and helping them avoid some of the issues we had gone through growing up.

Within five or six years, Gina and I began running the youth group. We did our best to do fun things with the kids, such as games and retreats. We also organized service projects several times a year, including taking as many as thirty kids to downtown Seattle to sleep over at the Union Gospel mission for destitute families. Along with our company maintenance team, we also renovated several rooms at the mission with new carpeting, paint, furniture, and even fresh flowers. I think the kids got more joy and positive memories out of the service projects than any other activity we did. There is something about going out of your way to help people in need that brings life to your soul.

I also served as an elder on the church board. I probably wasn't mature enough to be an elder, even though I was a good leader and had a sincere heart for the Lord. But we were a small church, and the talent pool wasn't very deep.

What Money Can't Buy

Though I envisioned achieving financial freedom and building a great company, those were not my most treasured dreams. More than anything, my wife and I wanted something money couldn't buy: a successful family. And though we had had our share of rocky moments, by the time we sold our clubs, we had a fairly stable marriage and four children we loved with all our hearts.

Gina and I have several important things in common: we love God, value family more than anything, are committed to financial freedom, and are driven to be excellent. (We also share a fiery temperament and independent nature, which can be both good and bad.)

For the most part, though, we are complete opposites. And though it might be true that opposites attract, that doesn't mean they live together easily.

My wife is very nurturing. She seeks security, especially for our family. She is not a risk taker and desires financial stability over wealth. She is driven toward perfection, but she goes about it in a non-linear way that I don't relate to. Our younger children, Leslie and Ian, are a lot like her in their artistic, abstract ways of achieving excellence.

On the other hand, I am very driven—maybe borderline obsessive-compulsive. I am strategic and sequentially organized, and I follow a strict schedule. Sometimes days go by where I couldn't even tell you what the weather was like because I am so obsessed with executing some plan of action.

An Impatient Decision

When we sold Hart's Athletic Clubs in 1998, Gina and I had achieved our goal of financial freedom. From Gina's point of view, it made sense for us to take it easy for a while and enjoy our newly acquired financial freedom. She would have liked me to retire, or at least to switch to a less stressful career.

But I was at the peak of my game. For the first time in my life, I had capital and credit to expand rapidly, and I had a team of people who were loyal and capable. I loved what I was doing, and at forty-six, I couldn't imagine retiring or changing careers. I also knew that our family's extensive financial commitments required an ongoing income.

There was another reason I felt I could not sit still. When we sold Hart's, I signed a non-competition agreement with the purchasing company stating that I would not compete with any of their clubs for three years. There was just one major area in the western United States that the purchasing company had not expanded to: Arizona. If I could get at least one location there before they did, I could build and grow as needed to capture that fitness market.

I believed I had heard from God, and I knew I needed to move quickly. Gina was adamantly opposed to the idea of starting a new business fifteen hundred miles from home. She knew the time commitment involved in a startup, and she argued that we had four small children that needed their father close to home. The idea of risking all our money and having her husband gone five days a week bordered on insanity.

But I had made up my mind, and to Gina's dismay and frustration, we bought our first club within a month of selling our previous company. We had four new locations within four months. Of my team from the previous company, ten families moved to Arizona, including my top five people, who also became my partners. I bought a condo where I stayed during the workweek. Everyone was excited to conquer a new territory and re-create what we had experienced in Seattle.

The first year was hell. We were trying to establish our brand in an unfamiliar marketplace, and we lost over a million dollars. I had never experienced anything like this before, since I had started my prior companies with little money or credit and built them up slowly.

When I would return from Arizona on the weekends after working sixteen-hour days all week, my wife was anything but loving and sympathetic. She was either completely distant or openly hostile.

Our marriage turned into a war. I can't put into words the pain I felt, caught between doing what I felt was best for our family and business and yet watching my marriage disintegrate.

Things continued this way for a year and a half. I remember crying out to God with tears in my eyes, asking for his help to bring love, understanding, and peace back to our marriage. I loved my wife, and I knew she loved me. But we had gone from occasionally struggling in our marriage to somehow hating each other even in the middle of our love. The only thing that kept us together that long was our love for God and our love for our four children. Neither of us are quitters, and we wanted desperately to protect our children from the pain of a divorce.

I began to feel distant and disconnected not only from Gina, but from my kids, my pastor, and my church friends. They said that I had made an error in judgment by expanding to Arizona, and they couldn't understand why I needed to continue my furious pace so far from home.

I was not leading a secret life of sin. Nor was I motivated by greed—by this time we had given millions of dollars to further God's kingdom. I was simply following a deep passion inside my soul to do what I believed God had created me to do.

In retrospect, I am convinced that my biggest error was impatience, which is something I have always had an issue with. If I had waited and given God a chance to change Gina's heart, I believe she would have given me her blessing to go to Arizona. But I thought more of myself and my plans than I did of my wife's feelings, and as a result, a conflict began that nearly destroyed our most precious possession: our family.

Divorcing the Family

For the first time, I began to seriously contemplate divorce. I knew God hated divorce, and I remembered Jesus's strong words about marriage and divorce. But the emotional pain had become unbearable.

In November of 2000, I left Gina and the kids. The memory of the night I broke the news to my children will never leave me. Over the years, we had often gathered as a family in our living room to discuss family issues. It was not only a time for Gina and I to give direction to our kids, it was a bonding time that usually ended with each of us praying for one another.

This night could not have been further from those happy memories. We sat in front of our beautiful fireplace in our dream home on the lake, and I announced to my children that their mother and I were getting a divorce.

My children's reaction is forever burned into my memory. My words instantly and completely broke their hearts. My second daughter, seventeen-year-old Rachael, rolled up into a ball, big tears streaming down her cheeks. My youngest daughter, thirteen-year-old Leslie, just stared, as if someone had hit her with a stun gun. My oldest daughter, Crystal, who was our family peacemaker and usually had loving advice for all of us, had nothing to say. My eight-year-old son asked the most penetrating question: "Dad, why are you divorcing the family?"

I didn't have much else to say. Finally, I got up and left, leaving my family in shock and indescribable pain.

I was angry with God and my wife. I had lost faith that all things were possible through the power of Jesus Christ. The pain I had inflicted on my wife and children went deep into my soul, too. I had no answers. I was leaving behind my most precious dream of all. Everything I had fought for was for the betterment of my family. It was like throwing a bucket of black paint on a beautiful painting.

Although I am a warrior at heart, I am also very sensitive. Walking away from God and my family nearly devastated me. But I viewed divorce as my only option to survive emotionally.

Some of the pain was covered up, at least superficially, when I ran into an old girlfriend that I hadn't seen in twenty-eight years. She had been divorced for ten years. We renewed our friendship, and I willingly fell into an adulterous relationship.

In my mind, I rationalized my immoral behavior. I had made up my mind that I was getting divorced, and I had lost faith in God because he hadn't helped me solve my marriage problems. I told myself that life must go on, with or without the approval of God, my wife, or my children.

I detest hypocrisy, so I met again with my wife and kids, this time to tell them that I was seeing someone. I said it was better for them to hear it from me than from someone else.

Now my three youngest kids went from being hurt to deeply hating their disloyal father. My daughter Rachael, always my star pupil in the Sunday school classes I taught, summed it up in a letter to me. She basically said, "Dear Dad, I will always love you, but everything you have taught me was total hypocrisy. I no longer respect you and am not interested in any future relationship with you. Please do me a favor and don't try to contact me. Love, Rachael."

I would pick up my son Ian at school every other Friday, and he would reluctantly stay with me over the weekend. One Friday while waiting for him, I saw my youngest daughter Leslie out of the corner of my eye. I hadn't seen her in months. As our eyes met, she quickly spun around and ran in the other direction. That instantly brought tears to my eyes. Ian soon got into my car, barely saying hello, clearly wanting to scream out, "Take me home and away from you." Instead, he courageously endured the time he had to spend with his father.

I began to think that my wife was sabotaging my relationship with my children. My pain turned into greater hostility and anger toward her. From my point of view, she had destroyed my life. I had lost everything I had worked so hard for and everything that was important to me: God, my wife, my kids, my church involvement, and my good reputation.

One of the paradoxes of life is that money is the most important thing in the world if you don't have it, but the least important thing once you have it. Even though I was a millionaire, I felt like the poorest person on earth.

Tenacious Love

Every other week, I would meet with my oldest daughter, Crystal, at Seattle Pacific University, where she was a freshman. We would have coffee and visit for a couple of hours. Sooner or later, the discussion always turned to her desire to see her mom and me reconcile.

I would emphatically state that there was zero chance of that happening and that the sooner she gave up this dream of reconciliation, the better off we would all be. She would always describe the positive changes her mother had made, and I would roll my eyes in disbelief.

Crystal has always been a powerful negotiator, especially with me, because even in horrible circumstances like this, she radiated only love toward me, not condemnation. She has always seen the best in her dad, even when there wasn't much good to see.

She told me time after time how Gina had gotten all the kids together and insisted that she would not allow any of them to say anything negative about their father, that she had accepted responsibility for a failed marriage, and that she wanted them to believe and pray for reconciliation.

Crystal told me that her sisters' biggest stumbling block to forgiving me was my disloyalty to their mother by having a girlfriend. She said that her mom's response to their complaints was that she had forced me out of the house, and that prior to that, I was a very loyal husband.

In the beginning, I completely blew my daughter off. I told her I just wanted to maintain our relationship through this painful ordeal.

She would always reassure me of her love for me and say that regardless of the outcome, we would remain close. She would conclude by saying no one, not even me, would dissuade her from believing that soon we would be restored as a family.

I would shake my head in disbelief, and we would part. In my mind, my marriage was over.

During this time, Gina, who is even more strong-willed than I am (which is really saying something), had decided that she was going to believe for the restoration of our marriage. Over a period of months, Gina and her good friend Diana Capato prayed and fasted together for our marriage. Sometimes they prayed for four or five hours at a time. During this period, Gina lost twenty-five pounds, and she wasn't overweight to begin with.

She found the Bible I had left behind when I moved out. I had spent hundreds of hours reading that Bible, making detailed notes and highlighting passages that I believed God was speaking to me. Gina declared to God that I believed in his word, and she prayed that God would reactivate his truths and rekindle my love for him. She put family pictures in my Bible and visualized that once again our family was one. Her prayers were faith-filled and powerful.

Her mind was made up. If anyone told her to be a realist and get on with her life, or if they didn't speak faith for our marriage, she matter-of-factly dismissed them from her life.

Toward the end of that year, Gina began to attend a new, Spirit-filled church called The City Church. It was a church whose hallmark was faith that God could do miracles in even the most impossible situations. After one service, she went down to the front and, with desperate tears, asked the pastors to pray for our marriage. These men of God, filled with the Spirit of God, prayed for healing for our family.

At one point, the church held a prayer conference with worldwide evangelist Marilyn Hickey. The speaker asked people to come to the front if they were praying for a need to be answered in a specific way and time. Gina grabbed Ian's hand, looked him in the eyes, and told him she was praying that I would be back in our home no later than April 30, just one month from then. Hand-in-hand, they walked forward and received prayer for the full reconciliation of our family.

Fire the Lawyer

Months before, Gina and I had both hired high-powered, costly attorneys to represent us in the divorce. The experience was bizarre. I have used attorneys my whole business career, so I know quite a bit about their role and about the legal system in general. But the divorce negotiations were a cat-and-mouse game that made no sense to me at all.

I was offering Gina and the family a much larger settlement than the law required. I wanted them to be taken care of for the rest of their lives. I didn't want Gina to ever have to work or worry about money. I figured I was still young and could earn more than enough to live out my life.

My attorney thought I was crazy for offering so much. Gina's lawyer thought that somehow I must be cheating her.

It became clear that her attorney's goal was to shut down our newly-formed company in Arizona and destroy me. At our monthly meetings, I would tell Gina and her attorney that that would just destroy us both financially. Then my attorney would end up insulting Gina and her attorney, and Gina's attorney would counter by calling me a thief and accusing me of hiding assets. We always left the meetings upset and more confused than ever.

My lawyer assured me that things would work out. He said that Gina's attorney used to work for him, and that over some long lunches he would sort things out with her. These meetings resulted in nothing but hurt feelings, distrust, and thousands of dollars spent in attorney fees.

I was at the point of saying, "Just take it all!" This was the closest I ever felt to hell. It was like two devils ripping the hearts and souls out of us both.

Then my attorney called me with some really bad news. He said Gina had just fired her attorney, and she would need to hire another one so we could start the painful process all over again.

What I didn't know was that Gina had had a showdown with her attorney when she demanded Gina put a freeze on all of our business and personal accounts. Gina knew we were losing money in Arizona, and if I couldn't fund payroll with personal money, the business would close. She understood that that would have a domino effect on our entire financial estate because of all of our personal guarantees.

Gina told her attorney that her husband was not deceptive and would never cheat anyone, especially her and the kids. To top it off, she told her that she was believing for total reconciliation.

Gina's lawyer thought she was the most stupid, naive person on the planet. So Gina fired her.

Saving Neil Schober

Something very unusual started to happen to me. Out of the blue, I began to think about returning home.

That scared me. Emotionally, I couldn't handle the thought of returning to an environment of conflict and hatred. When I would remember the pain, the thoughts of going home would dissipate.

One day, during one of my talks with Crystal, she told me excitedly that she had had a "born again" experience with Jesus. I remember thinking that she already had the qualities of God operating in her more than just about anyone I knew, but I told her I applauded her enthusiasm and her decision to dedicate her life completely to God. I remembered my encounter with God in college, and though I was far from the faith that I had lived for years, I was secretly jealous of her renewed passion and desire to follow God.

Then she asked a penetrating question: "Dad, do you still believe in God?"

I answered weakly, "Yes, but I'm still trying to figure some things out."

She asked, "When was the last time you went to church?"

I told her I hadn't been to church since I left the family.

She looked at me. "Would you do me a big favor?"

I said hesitantly, "Maybe, depending on the favor."

She replied, with tears in her eyes, "Just go to this new church all of us are going to in Kirkland. I know you will love it."

Her request was so sincere that I couldn't reject it. I said yes—though I qualified it by saying I didn't want to go to a service that her mom was at. She told me that they always went to the eleven thirty service and that there was an earlier service, at nine o'clock.

That Sunday morning I woke up dreading even the thought of going to church, especially a church I had never been to before. But, I had given my word to Crystal, and I had never broken my word or lied to her.

To my surprise, I walked in an hour late. I had forgotten that daylight saving time began that Sunday. It was a very big church, and an usher walked me all the way down to the second row from the stage. I had planned on finding a spot in the back somewhere, but because I was late, I was stuck front and center, not ten feet from where the pastor was preaching.

The pastor captured my attention right away. He was speaking on marriage and family, and he disclosed some of the personal struggles he and his family had experienced. His words of faith moved me to tears. He asked if there was anyone who wanted prayer.

I stood to my feet and answered his call, tears flowing from my eyes. Two pastors accompanied me into another room for council and prayer. Their names were Fred Kropp and Aaron Haskins. I started to introduce myself, and they told me that they knew who I was and that they had been praying for my family and me. They said Gina had explained our situation to them. At the time, they had asked her if they could call me, but she warned them not to because it would only drive me further away. She was right, of course. But now I had come on my own, looking for help.

These men of God embraced me with love, not condemnation. What closed the deal for me was when they told me that whether I proceeded with the divorce or not, they would welcome me into their church, no strings attached. I had never experienced that kind of unconditional love, even in the church, in my whole life.

As I got back into my car, I remember thinking, "What just happened?" When I arrived at church I had no intention of going forward for prayer, and I knew I didn't want to be reconciled to my wife. I drove away dazed.

The Road Home

Suddenly, for the first time in a very long time, I could feel God's presence in my life, his almost irresistible Spirit reaching out to me. I don't mean to sound spooky, but it felt like something invisible had shifted, and now all of God's forces were working together to bring our family back together.

One Monday morning a couple of weeks later, while I was down in Arizona, I woke up and, without much contemplation, called my wife and asked her if she would consider reconciliation. Before she had time to answer, I added that we would have to have a different, more loving marriage.

She immediately assured me that our marriage would not resemble the past at all and that she was willing to try to work things out. We agreed to go on a long walk the next Saturday to talk about it.

When Saturday came, we walked and talked for nearly ten miles. It was the beginning of something new. We asked each other for forgiveness for the pain we had inflicted on one another over the years. We made a commitment to love each other and make our marriage work.

Later, I called the woman I had been seeing and told her that Gina and I were going to try to restore our marriage. She understood, and we never saw each other after that.

In May of 2000, six months after walking out on my family, I came back home.

The only way I can explain the miracles that took place over the next few months and years is to quote Romans 8:28. "And we know that God causes everything to work together for the good of those who love God and are called according to his purpose for them."

The process of reconciliation started when my wife humbled herself before God and cried out to him in desperate faith to save our marriage. I had given up completely on our marriage and my dream of creating a wonderful, loving family. Without her unwavering faith, I know that my life and my children' lives would have been forever affected by our divorce.

I have an undying appreciation for my wife: she refused to react to the pain I caused her, and she put the preservation of our family first. Though we were both to blame in the deterioration of our marriage, I needed the most grace from God and my wife.

My children were excited that I had returned home, but there was still a lot of mistrust. They rightfully believed that I had been disloyal to the family, especially their mother. And though it sounds immature, my feelings were hurt that three of my kids had completely disowned me for six months and didn't give me credit that maybe part of the reason I left had to do with their mother's treatment of me.

For a time, we all struggled with inner turmoil and conflicting emotions of love and hate, faith and distrust. I am sure they were wondering when mom and dad would get in a fight, and dad would leave again, this time for good.

Gina asked me if I would pray with her daily, and I agreed. We had always prayed, but normally not with one another. This was a key to pulling our family out of the dark hole it had been cast into. Not a day went by for many years without the two of us praying with each other. If I was in Arizona, we prayed every morning by phone.

Sometimes this was a painful process, because even prayer can get off track when a husband and wife start asking God to fix their spouse. Believe it or not, Gina and I are quite capable of breaking into a fight while we pray together.

But something divine happened as we focused on God together. As we drew closer to him, we drew closer to each other.

Loving Differences

One thing that Gina and I had going for us was that we genuinely loved each other. What we didn't have going for us was that 90 percent of the time, we saw things from completely opposite points of view. And, as I've said, we both have very strong wills.

Just because we had reconciled and committed to praying daily didn't mean that we miraculously had new personalities and perspectives. Even today, we can both look at the sky, and one of us will say, "It's going to rain"; and the other will say, "It's going to clear up."

We probably have some pride issues that still need to be dealt with, but after being with Gina for over thirty-three years, I have concluded that we simply see things differently, and that is okay.

Like I said earlier, I am a full-on, triple type-A personality. I love to tackle life and take on risk. Once I make my mind up, I don't hesitate—some might call me reckless. My wife is the direct opposite. And yet, what attracted me to her were those qualities that I didn't possess, like nurturing, which has made her absolutely the best mom and grandmother. I love her ability to create a family atmosphere. Nearly every week there is someone or something that she brings us together to celebrate. Birthday celebrations usually last an entire week at our house. And on every holiday or vacation, we spend time with each other. Nor have I ever worried about her fidelity.

As strong leaders, we must learn that if our spouse sees things differently or doesn't get their pompoms out and start cheering for our wonderful vision, it doesn't mean he or she is a negative person. Our spouse simply has a different—and equally important—point of view.

It's hard for me to admit, but just about every time my wife has dug in her heels and fought me on a business decision—even when she couldn't explain why she disagreed but simply said, "It doesn't feel right"—she has turned out to be right.

Because I am a hardhead, I have usually gone forward anyway. And then somehow, I turn the wrong decision into some kind of success, though I have to work four times harder than if I would have slowed down and approached the situation from a different angle.

The Bible says, "As iron sharpens iron, so a friend sharpens a friend" (Proverbs 27:17). It would be terrible if Gina were a weak person, because I would have dominated her—to the detriment of our family. We balance each other. Because she is able to stand up to me when needed, she has protected me from many wrong decisions that would have harmed our home and business.

The revelation that has taken me most of my married life to learn is found in Ephesians 5:29. "In the same way, husbands ought to love their wives as they love their own bodies. For a man who loves his wife actually shows love for himself. No one hates his own body but feeds and cares for it, just as Christ cares for the church."

It's a change of perspective, a paradigm shift—from seeing yourself and your spouse as two distinct people to seeing yourselves as one. As the Bible says, "A man leaves his father and mother and is joined to his wife, and the two are united into one" (Genesis 2:24).

In other words, the perspectives, gifts, and insights of your spouse become yours. Once we grasp that, we no longer need to resist differences or be insecure about ourselves. The greater the differences between us, the more powerful we can be as a couple. It's good that opposites attract, as long as we learn to value and celebrate each other's unique qualities instead of fighting them.

It's been nine years since I returned home, never to leave again. My wife and I can still disagree on just about anything, but the negative energy generated from our disagreements has been reduced dramatically because we understand that we are, in a spiritual sense, one person.

Another thing that has helped was the advice of a close pastor friend and his wife to simply make a strong commitment to each other and to God to never fight. It is surprising how many stupid eruptions can be avoided by just making this commitment and living by it.

The late Pastor Wendell Smith used to say that in school, an A is great, but a C is still a passing grade. I've met couples that never fight, and they are probably getting an A+ in marriage. While Gina and I have to work harder than some couples might, I'm happy to say we are getting at least a C in our marriage. And with God's grace, we are working to pull that grade up even more!

A Dream Come True

I get very emotional when I look back over the years and see what God has done in our family, not only in restoring our marriage, but in blessing us with four incredible children.

Crystal has been married for five years to a true man of God, Mark. They have blessed my wife and me with two beautiful grandsons, Roman and Boston, and a brand-new granddaughter, Adele. They are both pastors and oversee our church's college ministry as well as one of our church campuses, located near the University of Washington. They love God with all their hearts and are wonderful parents.

Rachael is married to an amazing man named Jason. They run the foundation I referred to earlier, the Future Generation Project, that fights childhood obesity. They are also part of the leadership team at The City Church. They have a wonderful, fight-free relationship and are truly each other's greatest fans.

Leslie is amazingly creative; she is a student at the Art Institute in Seattle and the display coordinator at a large clothing store. She is very involved leading and mentoring groups of brand-new Christian girls.

Ian graduated high school as a National Honors Society Student and is studying at our church's intern program. He is also on staff at The City Church, where he functions as an artistic director. He is creative, high-energy, and driven, and whatever he does will succeed.

Best of all, each of my children love God with all their hearts, have great self-esteem mixed with authentic humility, and are very active serving God and people. Instead of being damaged by the near divorce, they somehow were strengthened by it.

None of us take family lightly anymore. We know how valuable it is, and we know how fragile it is, too. In our own way, we all protect it. We look forward to the family vacations we take together, including an annual two-week trip to Hawaii. Each of us, including our sons-in-law and grandchildren, have distinct and strong personalities; but we have an unusual love for each other. Maybe it was forever burned into our imagination what could have happened if things hadn't worked out for Gina and me.

I am forever thankful for a faithful wife who didn't give up on our marriage and family when she had every reason to. Our children love her with all their hearts and respect her for what a fighter she is. She is the glue that holds us together, and we are blessed to have her.

The Ultimate Contradiction

The Bible describes authentic love in 1 Corinthians 13:1-8.

If I could speak all the languages of earth and of angels, but didn't love others, I would only be a noisy gong or a clanging cymbal. If I had the gift of prophecy, and if I understood all of God's secret plans and possessed all knowledge, and if I had such faith that I could move mountains, but didn't love others, I would be nothing. If I gave everything I have to the poor and even sacrificed my body, I could boast about it; but if I didn't love others, I would have gained nothing.

Love is patient and kind. Love is not jealous or boastful or proud or rude. It does not demand its own way. It is not irritable, and it keeps no record of being wronged. It does not rejoice about injustice but rejoices whenever the truth wins out. Love never gives up, never loses faith, is always hopeful, and endures through every circumstance.

Prophecy and speaking in unknown languages and special knowledge will become useless. But love will last forever!

Love is the epitome of the Christian walk. It sums up all the character traits that we associate with godliness: patience, humility, gentleness, and more.

At first glance, love and business savvy appear contradictory. I've seen what it takes to build a company, and successful business leaders usually don't display the qualities described in 1 Corinthians 13, at least not naturally. Being courageous, pragmatic, iron-willed visionaries usually means they are confrontational, absorbed with their goal, hard-driving, and willing to sacrifice people to attain their vision.

The qualities that make leaders successful in business can destroy them in the end. That's because naturally great leaders are often weak in the areas that are necessary to be loyal spouses, good parents, and in general nice human beings. At the end of their life, they are often left alone with a list of empty accomplishments and, of course, their money—which is almost a curse because they are so lonely and depressed.

I've heard it said that for every strength or gift, we receive a corresponding weakness, and that in the end the game of life is evened up for all. Some of us are naturally gifted to become great business people, but those same gifts will be our undoing if we fail to focus on becoming spiritual people who walk in God's love. Other people, often those who have to work harder to be good at business, seem to easily walk in the love that Paul describes in 1 Corinthians 13.

The Bible teaches that all things are possible through the power of Jesus Christ, but it doesn't say all things are easy. It is hard for the typical, high-powered businessman to attain this kind of love, but it is the only thing that will bring him or her overall happiness, far beyond achievements and riches.

How can business leaders to whom love doesn't come naturally acquire it? Simply trying harder is not enough. That only results in frustration. Most of us tend to lean on our natural gifting because that is what is easiest for us. There's nothing wrong with embracing the gifts God has given us, but we must live on a higher plane than that.

The secret, quite simply, is Jesus. I don't mean to sound hyper-spiritual, but Jesus is not only the prime example of love, he is the source of true character transformation. The Bible teaches that as we come to know Jesus more, we will be transformed into his image (2 Corinthians 3:18).

This happens supernaturally, through the Holy Spirit. The Spirit guides, encourages, empowers, comforts, and teaches us how to become supernatural humans.

God is the initiator, and we are the responders. While we can't fix ourselves on our own, we also can't expect everything to improve in our lives without our active participation in the process.

One of the most effective ways to experience character transformation is through studying the Bible. Read and meditate on passages like Galatians 5:22–23, which says, "But the Holy Spirit produces this kind of fruit in our lives: love, joy, peace, patience, kindness, goodness, faithfulness, gentleness, and self-control. There is no law against these things!"

Change often won't happen overnight, but as you come to know Jesus better, you will be surprised at the wisdom and strength you discover. It is a journey worth embarking upon—your true success depends on it.

12

The Perfect Storm

It was a beautiful September day in Arizona last year: barely 100 degrees, a cloudless blue sky as far as I could see, with a gentle breeze that took the edge off the heat. After three months of humid, 110-degree days, this milder weather was more than welcome.

I was leaving our Tempe club and driving thirty miles to our Scottsdale club for my evening workout. As I was getting into my car, I noticed a dark cloud forming on the eastern horizon, over the Superstitious Mountains. By the time I reached the freeway a few miles to the east, the entire sky was filled with ominous, dark clouds, and a strong wind had picked up. The dust from the severely parched land was blowing across the freeway, and huge raindrops had begun to fall.

Within twenty minutes of leaving Tempe, heavy rain mixed with dirt pelted my windshield. It was only four in the afternoon, yet it was almost completely dark. Traffic was barely crawling. I looked at the temperature gauge on my mirror and it read sixty degrees—the temperature had fallen forty degrees in less than twenty-five minutes. Never had I seen weather change so dramatically in such a short period of time.

As I neared my destination, I decided to call ahead to see what the weather was like up there. My receptionist warned me frantically, almost hysterically, to stay away. She screamed something about giant hailstones the size of golf balls and baseballs being thrown from the sky.

I tried to calm her down, then finally asked to talk to our manager. He confirmed that huge hailstones were crashing down on everything, breaking out sunroofs and windshields and putting deep dents in cars outside the club.

I heeded their warning and headed instead to my condo in central Scottsdale. As soon as much of the storm passed, my curiosity got the best of me, and I jumped back into my car and headed up to our club.

What I saw was almost beyond description, especially since an hour or so earlier it had been one hundred degrees with clear blue skies, and even now it was no cooler than sixty degrees. A freak hailstorm had knocked down trees and destroyed property everywhere. Every car I saw, from old clunkers to Bentleys and Maseratis, was dented up beyond belief. Nothing had been spared from the storm's destruction.

I don't know how ice balls of that size could fall when the weather had been perfect just hours before. All I can say is that conditions were just right—it was the perfect storm.

Caught in the Storm

Recently, a perfect storm hit our business and the US economy in general. Like the hailstorm, it seemed to come out of nowhere, leaving a trail of destruction.

At the time, things couldn't have been better. My family and marriage were healthy. I had recently sold a group of fitness centers in Washington for a nice profit and paid off most of our debt. We had money in the bank, we owned a significant amount of real estate that was appreciating at about 25 percent a year, and income was flowing in from a variety of properties we owned. Our fitness business in Arizona was flourishing. I had a fantastic team of partners who were handling the day-to-day operations, freeing me up to give more time to other areas.

My wife and I had recently returned from speaking at leadership conferences and churches in the Philippines and Mexico. I had spoken on the topic "How to Overcome the Fiery Trials of Life." I thought it was a good message for people who were facing negative economic conditions.

We had just given a large monetary gift to the missionary work in Mexico, enough to build a church building for them. Gina and I have come to sincerely enjoy giving significant gifts, above our tithes, especially after large sales. It is our way of thanking God for his generosity and protection over our lives.

Life was good. We were finally doing things right, and after years of hard work to overcome personal and business issues, we were sailing on smooth water.

The perfect storm began one September day in 2007. I was at our cabin up in the mountains of Washington. This was our home away from home—a beautiful house on the tenth hole of a golf course, with a breathtaking view of mountains in the distance and a lake and river down below.

It was a clear, sun-sparkling day. I was playing a round of golf with my dear friend Don Ostrom, pastor of the business ministry at my church, and Paul Chase, pastor of a large church in Manila, Philippines. We had a wonderful time laughing at each other's miserable golf game and just enjoying our friendship.

As we approached the eighteenth green, I took out my nine iron, then swung nice and easy. Suddenly, I became terribly dizzy and disoriented. My friends helped me sit down in the golf cart. Sweat was pouring out of me, and it felt like my head was going to explode. My friends got me off the golf course and into the car, but I still didn't feel right.

I was in extremely good health: I worked out nearly every day, my body fat was below 10 percent, and I saw a naturopathic doctor regularly. His blood tests had showed that I was in good health overall, so I had no idea what could be wrong with me. I was a little embarrassed, too. Paul prayed for me for nearly an hour as Don drove us down the mountains and dropped me off at our house, where my wife was waiting.

After about an hour, Gina talked me into going to the Swedish Emergency Clinic down the street. I don't like hospitals, so it took a lot of convincing. She has more wisdom than I do.

The doctors thoroughly tested me. They said something a little out of the ordinary showed up on the brain scan, but that I did not need to worry, because it was probably nothing. They warned me to come back if it happened again.

The symptoms went away, and I shrugged it off as having an extreme reaction to low blood sugar. I have struggled most my life with blood sugar issues, and I've experienced dizziness before when I have gone long periods without eating. A few days later, my partner Eric Stearns and I even played what we call "gladiator tennis," which is playing in one-hundred-degree heat until one of us drops. It's great competition, good for the cardio, and burns a massive amount of calories. We played nearly two hours, and I had no negative effects afterward. I was healthy, as far as I knew.

Three days after that, I was on my couch watching the evening news after work. I tried to stand up, and suddenly I felt like someone hit me on the back of the neck with a baseball bat. I fell back onto the couch. I was instantly sopping wet with sweat and had an excruciating pain in my right temple. After sitting there for about an hour, trying to get my equilibrium back, I took a handful of aspirin to ease the pain and went to bed, hoping to sleep off whatever was bothering me.

My sleep was restless most of the night, and finally I pulled myself out of bed around seven o'clock, two hours later than normal. Something didn't feel right. I walked into the kitchen and grabbed a bottle of water out of the refrigerator. To my surprise, it was lukewarm. I thought maybe my brother-in-law and roommate, Gerald, had restocked the refrigerator with water before he left for work.

I reached into the microwave to get my tea. Oddly, it felt lukewarm as well. I switched the cup of tea from my left hand to my right hand, and instantly I knew something was wrong—the tea was burning hot. Then I realized I was having trouble swallowing. I picked up my phone, called my wife, and told her I thought I was having a stroke. She immediately called my partner Eric, and in minutes we were on our way to the hospital.

After hours of testing, they informed me that I had suffered a major stroke, a vertebral artery dissection. The doctors told me I was lucky to be alive and able to walk. I soon felt better, though for a while I had trouble swallowing and couldn't feel hot and cold sensations. I was out of the hospital in just two days, and to Gina's dismay, back to work the next Monday.

Teaching, which was most of my job, was difficult at first since I would sometimes choke on my saliva and begin coughing uncontrollably. I tried not to show any weakness, because the fitness business is mostly made up of young, aggressive, physical people; and like young lions, sometimes they can't help but try to take out the older lion.

This was just the beginning of the storm. Next my partner Eric developed severe stomach pain and nausea. Within a month, he had lost over twenty pounds. He went to every type of doctor imaginable, but they couldn't figure out what was wrong. Soon he was incapacitated, unable to get out of bed for more than a couple of hours per day. He felt like he was dying.

I told him to take a month off to try and get better. That was highly unusual for him—I don't think he had missed a day of work in twenty years. He was the president of our company, so all of his responsibilities now fell on me.

Around that time, an ex-partner filed a lawsuit against me, claiming I had cheated her out of millions of dollars and accusing me of discrimination based on sexual orientation. I described this situation in detail earlier. It was a very serious and costly lawsuit that put in question my integrity, character, and reputation.

Then without warning, a fitness company that I had sold clubs to ten years prior and that was leasing two of my buildings for about $85,000 per month abandoned the rented buildings and opened up new locations down the street, leaving me with broken-down, aged athletic clubs. They continued to legally pay the leases until they expired, which was just a few months longer. We were left with no rental income, large mortgage payments, no members, and unleasable space, at least in the current condition.

Then I was notified that a club we had recently sold to a wealthy, high-powered attorney was in financial trouble. The new owner was threatening to sue me for misrepresenting the economic facts surrounding the sale when he bought the club. In reality, he didn't know how to run a fitness center and had run the membership down so far that he was receiving only half the revenue that the club had been earning when we sold it to him. My partner Michele Sharar and I were still guarantors on the building lease, which had a liability of about $2.5 million in lease payments.

On a side note: never sell a business to anyone who does not know how to operate it, even if it is an all-cash transaction. It will only cause you heartache and suffering, and in the end they will blame you for their misfortune.

Finally, the hailstones hit. Arizona and eventually many other regions were struck with a recession that seemed to come out of nowhere.

Real estate prices had doubled in the previous three years due to a large increase in population and to banks lowering their requirements for mortgage loans. Mortgage lenders began offering people deals that they couldn't refuse to remortgage their houses. Some of my managers, who less than five years earlier had moved into homes with little or no money down, refinanced their homes and pulled out sometimes in excess of a hundred thousand dollars. Some spent the money on new cars, boats, and expensive trips, while the ambitious ones turned around and bought rentals, believing that in another three years, they would double their money.

Then everything turned upside down. First the banking crisis hit. Then the stock market tanked, devaluing all of our securities by 50 percent or more. Then came panic in the marketplace like I have never witnessed in all my years in business. In some regions where we had clubs, real estate values plummeted over 50 percent and real unemployment climbed to 20 percent.

In less than three months, our company lost over 25 percent of its paying members, or about 15,000 members. New member sales decreased by 50 percent and personal training revenue in some clubs decreased by 75 percent. My employees were paid mostly on a commission basis, so paychecks decreased by an average of 50 percent.

Within a short time, our company went from being very profitable and worth a lot of money to teetering on the edge of bankruptcy.

As if that weren't enough, the bank holding the mortgage on our Everett building notified me that they were not going to renew our $2.5 million mortgage. That was unexpected and uncalled-for, since we had never been late or failed to make payment over a ten-year period of time, and the building was appraised at more than $5 million.

Then the same bank tried to refuse to term out a $4 million tenant improvement line of credit, and they demanded we pay back a personal line of credit that in the past they had always renewed—even though we were current on all our loans and operating within the covenants that we had agreed upon.

On one hand, they told us again and again how much they valued us because, unlike many customers, we always performed on our loans; but on the other hand, they demanded that we make payments that would capsize the boat. This was all done with smiles, but it was by far the most vicious game I had participated in in years.

Controlled Panic

Day after day brought only more bad news. "Controlled panic" is how I can best describe it. It was as if everyone had been hit with a stun gun. For years we had taught our employees to be positive regardless of the circumstances, so everyone walked around with plastic smiles, pretending everything was okay, even though they knew in their hearts that it wasn't. We were a small business losing almost $200,000 per month. It was gut-wrenching. Something had to change quickly.

A spirit of fear overtook me like I had never felt before. It was worse than when I went broke twenty-five years earlier. Unlike when I was younger and more naive, I now knew just how bad things could really get. And at the age of fifty-seven, I knew that if we went broke, I most likely wouldn't have the time or the strength to rebound.

My mind grew cloudy with fear, my positive personality evaporated, and my nervous system was shot.

I remember one day my youngest daughter, Leslie, asking me, "Why are you so uptight all the time?" I'm embarrassed to admit that it took every bit of self-control I had not to bite her head off. I'm glad I kept quiet, because she has a sensitive heart, and careless words could have destroyed the trust between us for years to come. Maybe it was just the proverbial straw that broke the camel's back, but her words reduced me to almost hysterical tears when I was alone later that night.

For the life of me, I couldn't figure it out intellectually. I got caught up in the "why" game. I asked God many times, "Do I deserve this? Is this a case of sowing and reaping?" I thought back over my past mistakes. I knew I had asked for forgiveness, and with God's help I had seen major changes in my life.

Like King David, I asked God to search my heart to see if there was any wickedness in me that I was blind to. I reminded God that I had been loyal to him for many years in my tithes and offerings. I pointed out how I had gone out of my way to help others find the saving grace of Jesus Christ. I recited back to God all of the promises that he had made to me through the Bible about safeguarding my life. I knew in the deepest part of my soul that God was not a liar, and his word would not fail.

Strawberry Fields Forever

One night, I was reading the book of Psalms late into the night, crying out to God as King David had. I circled the phrase "cry out" every time I read it in the Psalms. I saw that David really didn't have a very easy go of it, even though God proclaimed that he was "a man after my own heart."

Then, in my tears and brokenness, God began to speak to my heart. He said something like this: "Neil, you had more courage when you were nine years old and had to face the bullies in the strawberry fields then you have now. You know everything my word says about faith, but you have lost your ability to practice it. You are consumed with doubt and fear. These things are not from me. Stop your crying and whining and get up!"

Not exactly comforting words! But they were what I needed to hear. It was like God dumped a bucket of cold water over me, and it brought me to my senses. I had been so caught up in self-pity that I couldn't take any positive steps to get out of my problems.

I have always believed that God knows when to exercise tough love. He is more concerned with our development into men or women of God than our immediate comfort. This was one of those instances.

In my mind's eye, he took me back to the strawberry fields of my childhood. I hadn't thought about those experiences in years. I relived the terror I felt when the bullies beat me up. I remembered how I faced my fears and ended up becoming the best worker of them all.

Something clicked. I realized God had prepared me for this battle fifty years earlier. Banks weren't a bigger obstacle than bullies! Here I was with decades of experience, a relationship with God, and a lot of Bible training, and yet I was more paralyzed than I had been in the strawberry fields so long ago.

I remember thinking, "I can do this!" I felt hope rise in my heart for the first time in a long time. Courage and a competitive thrill rang out deep in my spirit. The lessons I had learned picking berries—courage, excellence, diligence, savings, hard work—crystallized in my mind. I remembered the sage advice my mother had taught me in those years.

I didn't know how or even if I would win the battle in front of me, but I was sure of one thing: I was going to give it my very best. That horrible spirit of fear no longer had hold of my heart.

That was a turning point. In the two years prior, nothing had changed. But the next nine months were miraculous. There is no other word to describe it.

We had about $4 million in savings once we used up the entire line of credit attached to our house. This became our war chest, and we would use it as need arose.

My CFO and partner, Michele Sharar, and I began to think critically and creatively about how to reduce expenses without further eroding our revenue. There were no sacred cows. Everything and everyone was under our microscope. Our battle cry was "More for less!" As we turned over every possible rock, we discovered huge savings.

First, we reviewed the services we outsourced, especially our collections and payroll companies. Our collections company collected a million dollars a month in dues receivables, which was about half of our revenue, and our payroll company processed nearly a million dollars in payroll per month.

We were up front with both companies. We told them we were under water and needed them to get creative with us, or both of us would lose. To our amazement, they couldn't have been more helpful.

We discovered that there was a lot of duplication of efforts between our collection company and us, so we streamlined our processes. We had a good bottom-line option with them—we could bring the collections in-house. That was the last thing we wanted to do, though, since our entire executive team was already working more than twelve hours a day. Eventually, we renegotiated our contract with them, saving us $35,000 per month.

At the same time, we increased overall collections by about $10,000 per month, mainly through my brother Willy's diligent work to increase our company's efficiency. These two changes increased our cash flow by $45,000 per month, and we had just begun.

We ended up switching to a new payroll company, which saved another $15,000 per month. The new company provided a better overall service as well.

We saved another $10,000 a month on smaller expenditures: things like the amount of collection letters that we sent out, company cell phones, and copy machine use.

We even called up the company that supplied us with paper and cleaning products and other club supplies. They also found ways for us to cut costs. In the end, we realized a $10,000 savings per month, plus they volunteered to go to our clubs and teach us how to use our cleaning products more efficiently, thereby saving even more.

It didn't matter how little the savings were—we rejoiced when we saved even a dollar. My motto was, "We don't know which dollar will save the company or put it out of business."

Even with all these improvements in cash flow, we were still underwater. I felt that we had to start laying people off, since that was by far our greatest expense.

I gathered our division heads and asked them where we should start cutting. We had over six hundred employees, and there had to be some waste out there, I thought. But our executives, who incidentally were mainly my partners and also had everything to lose if we went broke, all said the same thing: "We will do whatever you ask us to do, but whatever we save in wages will more than cost us in revenue."

I ranted and raved a little about how they were too close to their key people and had lost their objectivity. In the end, I said I would think about it over the weekend, and we would resume our meeting on cutting payroll on Monday.

I flew up to Seattle to see my family for the weekend. I was living almost full-time in Arizona—about twenty-four days per month. My wife and I went to see our favorite football team play, the Seahawks. As we walked through downtown Seattle toward the stadium, I discussed with her how I needed to cut $35,000 a month off of payroll, but I didn't know where to cut without hurting the overall well-being of the company.

We stopped to get a cappuccino at a cafe, and just as the barista handed me my coffee, an idea hit me. We would all take a 5 percent cut in wages, beginning with me and going all the way down to the janitors. I wasn't sure how this was going to go over, but like my mother had taught me many years ago, running a business is not about trying to win a popularity contest.

Monday morning, I declared to my executives that no one would be laid off, but that we would all take a 5 percent cut in our wages, starting with us. They weren't exactly overjoyed, but they agreed to make the change.

Surprisingly, this step created unusual enthusiasm within the company. It was partly relief, because many had seen their friends in other companies lose their jobs due to the recession; but I think for the most part, they felt a brotherhood developing among all of us, from top to bottom. We recognized we were all in the same situation, and we needed each other to get out of this alive. In the end, we saved over $45,000 per month by everyone sacrificing a little for the greater welfare of the company.

Next, I starting wondering if there was a way to reduce the rent we paid on our buildings. We had perfect credit and a great reputation with all of our landlords, since we had never missed or been late with a rent payment. But I was afraid of ruining our good name with our landlords and hurting our credibility in the community. Again, my mother's words rang in my mind: "It takes a lifetime to build a good reputation and only moments to destroy it."

Still, I couldn't get the idea out of my mind of somehow getting our rent reduced at least for a short period of time, until things got back to normal. So I asked God to help me write a letter to our landlords. In the letter, I expressed how much we appreciated them, how we were struggling financially due to the recession, and how my wife and I had put $4 million of our own money into the company and were prepared to contribute more if necessary. Then I wrote that I would appreciate a $5,000-per-month reduction in our rent payment for two years (a savings of about 10 percent). I prayed over the letter for God's favor, then sent a copy to each landlord.

To our amazement, our landlords received our request very favorably. Overall, we received a $35,000 reduction in rent costs. Our landlord in Scottsdale, a wealthy man named Gary Herberger, even asked us to take back the rent check we had sent in a few days earlier and issue a new one for $5,000 less. I will never forget his graciousness. He didn't even want to look at accounting records or anything that would verify the truthfulness of my letter—he trusted us. The humility and care he showed toward me in a time of financial need is an example of true greatness that many wealthy people leave behind once they become rich.

All of our competition had suspended their advertising to save money. We were tempted to do so as well, since we were spending about $125,000 per month on it. Instead, we decided to negotiate harder with our sales representatives, especially in television, recognizing that they, too, were in a bind after losing so many clients.

Rick Clark, my dear friend and longest-standing employee (I originally hired him in 1975), cut $50,000 off our advertising budget and simultaneously increased first-time guest traffic by 50 percent over the year before. He did an amazing job through creativity and strong negotiations.

Together, Rick and I came up with an advertising campaign that seemed ludicrous at first. We decided to run an eleven-year-anniversary special: monthly dues of just $19. This was a lower rate than we had charged thirty-five years earlier, and now we had ten times the facilities and services.

We figured that one thing we had was a surplus of space, since we had lost so many members—now over a quarter of them. We decided to just see what would happen. I remember thinking that we couldn't do any worse in driving new member sales.

We made a television commercial for about $3,000. For reference, in the past we had spent over $50,000 to make commercials. This one didn't show beautiful facilities or pretty faces or bodies. It just screamed out, "Join now for zero, pay just $19 per month, and quit anytime you want!"

The results were outstanding! Guest traffic more than doubled in some locations, and enrollments went from about 150 new members per month per club to 400; and that rate continued long-term.

In those tough times, people realized that for just $19 they could burn off some tension and get in shape. Many of our old members came back. In less than six months, we gained back the $200,000 a month in dues we had lost over the previous couple of years.

We also made a huge dent in picking up market share in our industry. Our biggest competitor, a large and successful international company, made a strategic mistake by choosing to keep their price structure the same and make very deep cuts in costs, especially in their management team. As a result, they lost many key managers to us, and their sales were cut in half in some of their locations as we continued our membership drive at ridiculously low prices.

The lesson here is worth spelling out. Make sure the expenses you cut don't adversely affect your revenue. Anyone can take a butcher knife to their budget, but if your income decreases at the same time, you will go into a downward death spiral. In our clubs, we both decreased expenses and increased revenue. We became more efficient and more productive at the same time—the ideal combination.

To Survive or to Flourish

There is no substitute for winning. All the pretty speeches in the world cannot hold a candle to putting up wins. Our managers, salespeople, and trainers all started to make great money again. To our amazement, we took a company that was on the brink of disaster and in just six months made it profitable again, even though the overall economy had not improved in the slightest.

It's hard to say what changed. Practical and spiritual laws work together, and there is never just one key to success. Success comes from doing a lot of things right at the same time. It's like a baker mixing various ingredients to produce the perfect pastry—every ingredient is important.

We had somehow captured that invisible thing called momentum. To this day, I can't put a finger on how to achieve momentum, but I can certainly tell when we are working against it—it is like a strong wind trying to blow us over. But when we have it, nothing can stop us!

Perhaps the biggest key was deciding to flourish, not just to survive, regardless of our economic environment. We didn't want to live forever with a survival mentality. We realized that we couldn't just live defensively.

We made a point of spending on outreach, advertising, and giving. It was during this economic storm that we decided to set up the charitable foundation I mentioned earlier that is dedicated to fighting childhood obesity. My daughter Rachael and son-in-law Jason Michalski headed up the new foundation, which we named The Future Generation Project.

In the middle of a deep recession, my partners and I invested over a quarter of a million dollars into the fight against childhood obesity. I can't put a dollar amount on the return, but I am convinced it was money well spent. The project built enthusiasm in our employees and members and impressed the entire community. NBC even heard about it and did a positive news story on us. People saw our company genuinely caring—for free—for kids in need. There is something about generosity that triggers momentum.

On a personal level, my wife and I continued to tithe as if we were making the same amount of money that we were accustomed to making. Technically it wasn't tithing, since tithing is figured as a percentage of your income, and for nearly three years we made no money from our business and endured many losses on outside investments. But we agreed to keep our giving at this level because we believed the Holy Spirit moved us to do so. I am not suggesting that everyone do this, of course—it has to be an individual decision based on how God leads you.

In addition to this, we gave a couple of large, sacrificial gifts to different ministries that had moved our hearts. Gina and I had decided years ago that if or when we got into trouble financially, we would give boldly. That way we would continue to depend on God rather than our limited resources.

In general, I think Christians suffer more from fear than greed. People hold back from giving not because they want to hoard it all and grow rich, but because they are afraid they won't have enough. The best way to overcome this fear is to give.

Weathering the Storm

In 2010, the economic storm was still raging, but at least we could see hope on the horizon. Slowly but surely, our problems began to be resolved. I can't take the credit for the turnaround. It was the wisdom and favor that God gave us that got us through.

It would be misleading of me to minimize the hard work and significant losses we incurred in the process. The road to victory was not always comfortable.

One of the two buildings that had been abandoned, a Seattle club owned by a partner, his children, and me, had to be sold for a $400,000 loss. The other abandoned club, which was in Everett, fared even worse, at least at first. We signed a new lease with some club operators that had little experience. We put in over a million dollars to renovate the club, and we gave them nine months of free rent. They ended up making only one rent payment and then defaulting on the lease. It took us another $250,000 to get them to vacate peacefully.

Eventually, though, my partner Leon Doris and his wife Loretta chose to come up from Arizona and run the club. Leon has worked with me for twenty-six years and is a dear friend and highly accomplished businessman. The Everett club is hugely successful today because of Leon's and Loretta's hard work and dedication.

During that time period, we also forgave a $165,000 note owed by the attorney who bought our club and was threatening a lawsuit. In exchange, he signed an indemnification agreement absolving us of blame in the original sale agreement. It was complete extortion from my point of view, but I was in my most pragmatic, problem-solving mode. In the end he failed anyway, and I was able to help facilitate a positive transaction between the attorney and some quality operators that had worked for me previously and had started their own fitness company. It is my understanding they are doing quite well with their new club.

Regarding the lawsuit by my ex-partner, after over a year of painful and expensive preparation, we settled in arbitration on paying her over a million dollars, plus attorney fees. It was a good but expensive lesson for me to always do the right thing at the right time, regardless of the situation. My decision to terminate our partnership was the right decision, but I didn't handle it properly. I paid a dear price for that, in more ways than just money. I lost the respect of a good friend and partner.

Ironically, the stroke I had experienced ended up improving my health. For over fifteen years I had battled acute back pain. I had tried everything to find relief, with no success. It turned out that my stroke left only one permanent effect: it completely numbed a major nerve that runs from my neck down the left side of my back and into my left leg and foot. This eliminated my back pain without affecting anything else in my body. Yes, God moves in mysterious ways!

Our newfound successes were encouraging, but we still needed to find a solution for the $2.5 million mortgage that our bank had refused. Incidentally, I was disappointed, but not too surprised, by the bank's actions. I knew from my experience in the early 80s that banks can do and will do stupid things when under pressure from upper management, including destroying good, paying, long-term customers.

I started cold-calling banks and giving one presentation after another. Each one politely turned me down, until a bank that I had done business with many years before, Columbia Bank, came to my rescue and agreed to refinance our building in Everett. I am very thankful for the wonderful VP that I worked with, who went out of her way to get the deal for me. It helped that I had borrowed a large amount of money from this bank in the past, had never missed a payment on the loan, and had paid it off early. Still, taking into consideration the negative banking climate, I am grateful for her and her bank's assistance at a critical time in our business.

Soon after, we had a three-hour showdown with our lead bank. I had a prior verbal agreement from the bank that they would term out a significant line of credit. Now the bank refused to term it out unless my wife and I signed an additional covenant that would give them the right to make decisions in all of our future expenditures, including personal ones. It was ridiculous, especially since we had never missed or been late on a payment and we were operating within all of our bank covenants. I knew that if we gave in to this additional covenant, they could move negatively against us for almost any reason. So we stood our ground, even though they promised up and down that it was just a formality and that the last thing they wanted to do was run our business or personal lives. In the end, they reluctantly scratched out the new, all-encompassing covenant and extended the lines of credit to a five-year term agreement. It was a win for the home team. Proverbs 22:7 says, "The borrower is servant to the lender," and that is very true. Use credit wisely and cautiously.

Throughout all of these negotiations, the most important asset we had was our war chest of money. This helped support our companies during the years of negative cash flow, it allowed us to pay off several difficult situations so we could concentrate on our business, and it gave us bidding power with our banks. If not for our savings, we likely would not have made it through this destructive, perfect storm.

Saving money is like being on a constant diet. It gets easier as you get used to it, but it is never completely comfortable. However, when a storm hits—whether due to your mistakes, economic recession, or unexpected tragedy—you will be prepared. Remember, "Do your best, prepare for the worst—then trust God to bring victory."

Happy Trials to You

I have never met anyone who enjoys trials, yet the Bible tells us in James 1:2–3, "Count it all joy when you fall into various trials, knowing that the testing of your faith produces patience" (NKJV).

The Message version of James 1:2–5 brings even more clarity to this passage: "Consider it a sheer gift, friends, when tests and challenges come at you from all sides. You know that under pressure, your faith-life is forced into the open and shows its true colors. So don't try to get out of anything prematurely. Let it do its work so you become mature and well developed, not deficient in any way. If you don't know what you are doing, pray to the Father. He loves to help you. You'll get his help and won't be condescended to when you ask for it."

In another passage, 1 Peter 1:6–7, Peter also comments on enduring challenges. "In this you greatly rejoice, though now for a little while, if need be, you have been grieved by various trials, that the genuineness of your faith, being much more precious than gold that perishes, though it is tested by fire, may be found to praise, honor, and glory at the revelation of Jesus Christ" (NKJV).

We must recognize that through the trials of life, God develops us into the people we were meant to be. That doesn't mean he is out to cause us harm—life takes care of that on its own. Rather, God uses what could have destroyed us to make us better. By definition, growing through trials is not a comfortable process. It is human nature to avoid pain, but it is God's nature to use every means possible to bring us closer to him and to increase our maturity and wisdom.

Realistically, trials and suffering will be part of our lives as long as we are here on this earth. Heaven will mean an end to these things, but in the meantime, we must learn to not only endure pain, but to rise above it with supernatural joy. James calls this a sign of maturity.

If we focus on the pain and difficulty in a given situation, we only get bogged down in our own fears. When we take our eyes off ourselves and set them on Jesus, the perfect man, and reflect on the sufferings he went through for our benefit and the promises he has given us in the Word, we find joy and peace that surpass human understanding.

Change of Plans

We had managed to survive the economic storm, but it had not been easy. Between 1999 and 2010, I had made over five hundred trips between Seattle and Phoenix. My wife was supportive, but it had taken a toll on the whole family.

Gina and I knew, however, that the only way out was to press on. We had to be victorious—some way, somehow. Both financially and emotionally, we were fully committed.

We decided that the only way to win this war once and for all was to build at least six deluxe, ten-million-dollar clubs in Arizona. We had already built three clubs in the deepest part of the recession, and we knew we could get deals that were almost too good to be true. Developers were hungry, construction costs were down 40 percent, and common sense and faith told me that America had suffered through the worst part of the storm. Things would get better. Now was the chance to capitalize on our new momentum.

Gina and I brainstormed on how she could again get more involved in the business now that our youngest child, Ian, had graduated high school. Gina has an incredible creative ability in design, and she brings elegance and beauty to whatever she does. We decided she would work with our architect to design these new super clubs. We prepared to sign leases with developers for the first three.

Together with our partners, we were willing and determined to take our company to the next level, even though we knew it would likely dominate the next ten years of our life. To be honest, it wasn't how we had visualized spending those years. We had dreamed of getting more involved in our church and in teaching business and spiritual principles to young businesspeople. We wanted to mentor them regarding how to capture their dreams and how to be effective and prosperous in the marketplace. We also found great joy traveling to other churches around the world, speaking about using generosity and wealth to extend the kingdom of God. But we saw no successful way out except to go all in.

One typical, scorching-hot day in Arizona, as I was heading toward one of our clubs, my cell phone rang. I recognized the two voices on the other end of the call. They were from LA Fitness, our number one competitor in Arizona and one of the best and most profitable fitness companies in the world. We were their biggest threat in that region. Years earlier, I had spent many hours with these two individuals negotiating the sale of some of our Seattle clubs.

Now, they expressed interest in buying our Arizona clubs. It was not unusual for them to call me once in a while, especially during rough economic times, to see if I was interested in pretty much giving our company away to escape disaster. I hate to admit it, but there were times back then when I was tempted to take them up on their offer. We always turned them down, though.

I told them that the price I would accept for our company was far beyond what they were willing to pay. I wasn't bluffing: I knew their formulas for evaluation, and even though we had showed a remarkable turnaround, we had not returned to our pre-recession profit levels.

They asked me to name my price and terms. I told them confidently what I wanted, and their response was what I expected: based on my revenue numbers and profitability, my asking price was entirely too high.

I told them I agreed, and we ended the conversation amicably.

Two days later, they called back. They told me that they could come close to my offer.

It was a big number, but not the number I wanted. Again, I politely declined their offer.

The next day they called back and said they had decided to accept my offering price.

Over the phone, I outlined carefully the rules of engagement in selling the company. I had been left at the altar once before, but I was more experienced now in negotiating the sale of a company.

Just like that, our plans were turned upside down. The irony of business is that you have to be a decisive person with an iron will, but at the same time you have to be open to changing your plans if you are going the wrong direction. The Bible says in Proverbs 16:9, "We can make our plans, but the Lord determines our steps."

My philosophy is to knock on every door of opportunity I find, knowing that most will not result in anything. That doesn't bother me. I have learned not to attach my ego or emotions too deeply to my ideas, especially at first.

When I find an open door, I go through it decisively and wholeheartedly. Weak-willed people often second-guess the open doors and beat themselves up over whether the decision is right or wrong. I don't see any benefit in that. Of course, you must analyze all the options rather than acting impulsively or ignorantly. But allowing fear of failure to paralyze you is simply bad business.

Once I step through an open door, I inevitably face obstacles that I need to push through or find a way around. In these instances, my stubborn nature comes in handy!

But on some occasions, despite my best efforts, it becomes clear that the door of opportunity has closed. In those cases, I choose to believe God is protecting me, and I don't resent the change in my plans. While it may take some time for me to wrap my mind around the reality that what I had dreamed of and fought for is not meant to be, once I recover my emotions and thoughts, I move on.

We began the long, complicated process of selling our company. Selling a business is the most difficult exercise I have ever been a part of. Although I have been successful in closing every major sale I have attempted, it is common knowledge that less than half of attempted sales actually close. My attorney told me that in this recession, where sellers so highly outnumbered buyers, I had maybe a one in five chance.

You would think selling a company would get easier after doing it a number of times, but it still strains your emotions and mental capacity to the breaking point. It almost forces you to become two people. You have to continue business as if the sale is not going to happen, because in all reality it probably will fall through, yet you have to put on hold anything long-term: signing or renewing leases, hiring general contractors to build new locations, extending advertising contracts, and hiring new executives. Instead of focusing on the future, you must shift all your energies to executing on the present. If your employees find out that you are considering selling, it can create a contagious panic. People fear change and the unknown.

In most cases, it has been my strategy to tell our key executives that there was a possibility we would sell, and to arrange a specific, generous bonus for them if we were to sell. Their responsibility was to focus on driving current revenue and keeping costs down. This psychology works, but it is truly mind-bending.

I think it is doubly hard on my CFO and me, because 90 percent of our time is spent either in negotiating the intricacies of the asset purchase agreement or performing various due diligence activities.

In this case, the sale was particularly difficult because we had to negotiate with our landlords for releases from our long-term leases. They needed to not only release the company and us personally from our contracts, but they had to allow the buyer to shut down the clubs and "go dark," or continue to pay on the space even though it would not be occupied. Landlords generally hate empty space because it hurts overall traffic flow to their malls.

One of the hardest parts of selling a company is the constant back-and-forth you experience between thinking the sale will go through and thinking it won't. It takes months to jump through all the hoops—first an oral agreement, then a detailed letter of intent, then the asset purchase agreement with contingencies, then the sale, and finally the closing when they actually deposit their money in your bank account and you hand over the keys. During the process, the sale usually blows up at least five times.

The emotional stress is really beyond understanding unless you have gone through this miserable exercise. In the back of my mind, I knew I was allowing my biggest competitor to review every part of my company and to learn my strengths and weaknesses. I also know that because I had put all plans on hold for an extended period of time, I most likely would lose that elusive thing called momentum if the sale did not close.

Because they were experienced negotiators, I'm sure they knew this is what I was feeling. And as we got closer to the closing date, they ratcheted up the pressure by becoming more and more demanding, hoping to break us down mentally and emotionally.

I kept my mental and emotional fortitude all the way through the negotiations, but four days before closing, I was done. I was emotionally burned out. If the sale didn't go through, I knew how hard it would be to pick myself up and re-engage in running our company.

It was a strange conflict of the heart. On one hand, deep inside, I knew the sale would happen because it had clearly come from God. I did not plan it or manipulate it. My wife, my partners, and I were going full speed ahead with our ten-year plan. Then without warning, God stepped in and said in essence, "You are going to go a different direction."

On the other hand, the doubts, fears, and sheer exhaustion were overwhelming. I didn't know if I could push through.

I remember watching an interview with Muhammad Ali, the greatest heavyweight fighter of all time, when he discussed his famous fight with Joe Frazier. They had finished fourteen grueling rounds. Both of them were beaten and weary when they headed back to their respective corners, awaiting the final, fifteenth round. The bell rang, but Joe Frazier didn't get up. Ali said in the interview that had Frazier gotten up, he wouldn't have.

That was how I felt four days before the sale closed—if the buyer would have come back with one more demand, I think I would have given in, just to end the struggle.

I had prayed and trusted God throughout the process, but it was at this point that I truly surrendered the sale to God. I meditated on the verse that says, "My strength is made perfect in weakness" (2 Corinthians 12:9). The opportunity had come from him in the first place, and if he wanted it to happen, he was more than able to finish the process.

In the end, the sale was successfully completed, and in November 2010, we handed over the keys to our clubs. Our net profit was beyond what we could have hoped for, especially considering the economy.

We had endured the perfect storm, and we came out of it financially blessed. Best of all, in tough times we did not turn against each other. We stayed friends to the end. My marriage and my partner's marriages endured the trying years as well. Now, we look forward to our next challenge.

I encourage you to keep the faith, regardless of how difficult your circumstances might seem. Always remember, we serve a good God. He will not allow us to go through trials beyond our abilities or strength, and he will never leave us. Keep fighting—keep moving forward.

13

Building a Solid Foundation

Flash back to 1996, eight years after I had gone broke for millions of dollars. We had rebounded from those dark days, but it had required sacrifice and patience.

Gina and I had kept our living expenses down throughout those years, saving at least 50 percent of what had grown to be a very high income. The only thing we didn't scrimp on was our children's schooling. They always went to the best private schools, because we looked at our children as our greatest single investment. It took a lot of discipline to drive old cars and live in an old house when we could have bought pretty much whatever we wanted.

Meanwhile, most of my managers were living in new homes and driving expensive new cars. I remember having one manager and his wife over for an informal dinner at our house. While we were preparing the hamburgers, the wife remarked good-naturedly that eating at the Schobers' house was like going camping, because none of our utensils or dishes matched. It was true, but to be honest I didn't appreciate her candor at the time!

By the grace of God, we had been able to save our home, which sat on a beautiful acre of lakefront land that I bought early on in my career for $205,000. It wasn't much of a house to begin with, and now, almost twenty years later and with four children and my mother-in-law and father-in-law living with us, we needed to upgrade. For years, we had dreamed of demolishing the old house and building a luxury home on this property for all of us to enjoy, especially our kids and their friends.

Our goal was to build it with cash. Every month, I would take my savings and buy stock, mainly Microsoft. During the late eighties and early nineties, Microsoft stock increased in value dramatically, up to 400 percent, if I remember correctly. Looking back, it probably wasn't wise to invest such a large percentage of my savings into one company, but I wasn't as risk-averse at forty years old as I am now, and it more than worked out.

Finally, we saved enough to begin the construction process. Unexpectedly, the building department told us that we would have to build and sink forty-three pilings thirty-five feet into the ground. In essence, our new house would sit on a block of concrete that extended thirty-five feet deep.

We argued vehemently that our old house had sat just fine for almost fifty years without that much foundation work. We were more than 300 feet from the lake, and never in all the years we had lived there had the water risen higher than our retaining wall, which was 290 feet from our house.

But the geologist insisted that the earth was too soft to hold a house the size we wanted to build, and that without the pilings, it would be like building our house on sand.

I remember driving up after the foundation was complete and looking out over the topmost four feet of this massive block of concrete, the only part visible above the ground. Then I read the invoices for completing the foundation work. To my distress, the foundation cost me more than what I paid for my entire land and house twenty years ago. I realized that before I even started building, I was over budget by $200,000.

When our new home was completed, many of our friends wanted tours. Whenever we showed people the beautiful house and furnishings, with its expensive paintings and Oriental rugs, I always wanted to take them down into the crawl space and show them what a cool, expensive foundation we had. We now owned one of the most beautiful houses on the lake, with a new boat and wave runners at our dock and luxury cars in our driveway—but what meant the most to me was that expensive foundation.

A Costly Foundation

Sometimes God speaks to us in strange ways. This expensive foundation was an object lesson that has stayed with me ever since. In everything I build, I must invest in a proper foundation.

In business, having a solid foundation means things like careful planning and adequate capitalization. But in life in general, you need more than that.

Without a doubt, the solid foundation in my life is Jesus. It's been thirty-seven years since I first believed in Jesus as my Savior and Lord. As I look back over nearly four decades of God's involvement in my life, I can't overstate the importance of knowing him personally.

I don't pretend to be a theologian, but I know what God has done for me. I owe him my financial success, my restored marriage, my health, my changed character, and most of all, salvation and eternal life. His goodness is irrefutable proof that he loves me and that serving him is the best thing I could ever do.

The God I know is a God of extravagant love, so much so that he sent his only son to die on a cross for our sins. Jesus didn't sin—we did. But he took our place and our punishment.

Sometimes I wonder why he had to die such a horrific death at the hands of his own creation. Often, in my early morning devotions, I have reviewed this horrifying death that Jesus endured for us. He was beaten with vicious whips to the point of death, every part of his body covered with stripes of blood inflicted by his torturers. They crowned him with thorns and dressed him in a robe to mock and demean him. They spit in his face and beat him. Yet, even when asked to defend himself, he offered no defense. He simply said they could do nothing to him unless he allowed it.

Then he was nailed to a cross, one of the most agonizing methods of execution ever invented. Incredibly, at the moment of his death, he cried out to his Father in heaven, "Father, forgive them, for they don't know what they are doing" (Luke 23:34).

When I remember this awful death that Jesus endured for us, I realize that often we don't fully understand the seriousness of our sins. In the sacrifice of Jesus, God demonstrates both his infinite love for man and the severity and grotesqueness of evil. The foundation that Jesus purchased for us was truly costly, more than we will ever know.

Before his death, Jesus told his apostles that there is no greater love than to lay one's life down for a friend. Jesus gave his life for us, demonstrating God's love and his desire to be in relationship with us. Now, he asks us to recognize his gift of eternal salvation and submit to his authority as Lord.

This is not about blind faith. There is more evidence that Jesus was and is the Son of God than anything else we believe in.

I say this respectfully but with great conviction: if you do not believe that eternal life can be obtained through Jesus and Jesus alone, you owe it to yourself to research the matter. No one knows when their life on this earth will end and eternity will begin. And while we have thousands of days to live here on earth, that is but a vapor compared to eternity.

If you are struggling with believing, I suggest you read *Mere Christianity*, by C.S. Lewis. For years, the author was a self-proclaimed atheist. He decided to answer what he believed to be the most important question of all: what happens after we die. In the book, he approaches his research from a strictly rational point of view. He ends up concluding that Christianity is not only plausible, it is the only logical conclusion. His reasoning and logic are beyond contradiction. Ultimately, though, he states that we must take a step of faith, like a little child jumping off a tabletop into his father's loving hands.

If you took that step of faith long ago, I urge you to always remember the value of the foundation you have in Jesus. Never forget or minimize the gift of forgiveness and eternal life. His sacrifice should not be taken lightly; rather, it should inspire us to give our lives back to him as a sacrifice of love.

If you have not yet taken that step, why not do it now? This is not religion or ritual—it is a heartfelt recognition that Jesus died for your sins and a decision to let him lead your life.

When winds, storms, and earthquakes come at us, we might be shaken. But like my house with its firm foundation, we will be secure and strong forever.

Well Done

The greatest moment in our lives is when we give our hearts to Jesus. Nothing is more important, and nothing we do in life can equal this gift that God offers everyone. All we must do is open our heart and accept it.

This is just the starting point, however. God has a life of adventure and purpose designed specifically for each of us. Strangely, Christians often become so heavenly minded that they idle away their precious time on earth. They are throwing away their God-given purpose, gifts, and opportunities.

When the Bible speaks about keeping our mind on heavenly things, it doesn't mean checking out of our responsibilities on earth, nor does it mean living sloppy, mediocre lives. Quite the opposite—it means living this life with excellence, knowing that our earthly actions have eternal significance, both for us and for those whose lives we bless through the resources we gain.

We have the responsibility to pour ourselves out passionately to accomplish what God has in store for us. Remember, God saved us for *his* purpose. He has a goal for us, and it is far more important than we might think.

Within the sphere of influence, grace, and talent God has given us, there is tremendous room for growth and creativity. As in the parable Jesus told, some of us have one talent, others have two talents, and a few have five talents. As we capitalize on what we have been given, God gives us more.

It is pointless and unproductive to compare our gifts or accomplishments to those of other people. There will always be people smarter, more talented, or richer than us, and conversely there will always be someone less smart, talented, or rich than us. Compete with one person only: yourself. In every area and endeavor, ask the simple question, "Did I do my best?"

It is our responsibility to catch a vision from God and then take the land he has set before us. I think many Christians would be shocked at what they could accomplish with their lives if they followed this principle wholeheartedly. I've seen people with little apparent talent accomplish much more than highly-talented people because they had the faith to attempt great things.

Christians are often perplexed by the success that many non-Christian businesspeople achieve. Believers rationalize it by branding unbelievers as wicked, immoral, or unethical, but it has nothing to do with that. Unbelievers are usually successful because through their own power, drive, and desire and by adhering to God-created principles, they outperform Christian businesspeople. They don't recognize the creator of these principles, but they have discovered it is profitable to adhere to them.

A very successful businessman once said to me, "I believe in nothing but making money. I am ethical and honest and I treat people well because it yields great profit." Sadly, though he has accumulated great wealth and helped many others achieve success in business, unless he acknowledges Jesus as his Savior and Lord, he will miss out on the greatest reward of all.

How could we as Christians, who have the Holy Spirit working in us, be out-competed in the marketplace? We should have the advantage. The answer is that God has established principles or laws that govern the universe. If we are not careful to follow them, we will experience limited success.

This does not contradict the principle that we are saved by grace. True grace doesn't just cover the past—it also motivates us to a higher standard of living in the present. Many Christians, because they know that they will end up in heaven sooner or later, become too self-forgiving or sloppy in their lifestyle.

God's moral and spiritual principles are every bit as absolute as his physical laws. In the physical realm, cause and effect are so closely attached that we learn quickly to adhere to these laws. They are absolute and undeniable. We learn not to touch burners and stove tops at an early age because we instantly experience pain. Toddlers are introduced to the law of gravity from their first attempts at walking and running. Most of us realize that if we overeat and do not exercise, we will gain weight and have health issues.

Moral or spiritual principles are harder to learn, however, because we don't immediately feel the negative effects of breaking them. But over the course of our lifetime, the consequences are undeniable.

Unfortunately, that doesn't mean we always learn from our mistakes. Some people choose to deny, rationalize, or refuse responsibility for their wrong actions. They blame their negative circumstances on everyone but themselves.

We must learn from God how best to conduct our lives. His commands were designed to save us from experiencing pain. They are not burdensome—they are life-giving. If we accept and obey them by faith, we will see the benefits in the long run.

God exhorts his people in Deuteronomy 28:1–2, "If you fully obey the Lord your God and carefully keep all his commands that I am giving you today, the Lord your God will set you high above all the nations of the world. You will experience all these blessings if you obey the Lord your God."

Biblical history teaches us that when God's chosen people followed his principles, they more than prospered; but when they didn't, they destroyed themselves and their entire culture.

If we walk outside of God's commandments, we in essence walk outside his protection and power. God's laws are absolute. They were designed to run the universe and to help man live a life of abundance, joy, and peace of mind.

As Christians, we have a distinct advantage in capturing a life of abundance. God lives in us and promises to give us the power and guidance we need.

God has given us the gift of purpose. He has destined our life, our time, and our income to accomplish good things and to be a blessing to others. His purpose gives us significance.

Someday, in heaven, we will see God face to face, free from sin and pain. We will give him a full account of what we have accomplished, and we will hear him say, "Well done!"

14

Take Your Land!

Over the years, I have made a hobby of studying great leaders in different fields throughout history. The individual that I think most clearly epitomizes the qualities a leader should possess is Joshua, whose story is found in the Old Testament. In about 1450 BC, Joshua led the nation of Israel as they took possession of the Promised Land, which was the territory God had told them they would possess.

I believe that the leadership principles Joshua demonstrates transcend time, culture, and occupation. Understanding these principles will aid us greatly in achieving success in the marketplace, while ignoring them will almost certainly lead to failure.

In the next few pages, I will go through his story, drawing out points that are particularly relevant for the business leader. These are principles that resonate deeply with me, because I have watched them work for forty years.

Perspective

Like the rest of the nation, Joshua was born into slavery and lived as a slave under the harsh rule of the Egyptians for many years. He witnessed the miracles of God that freed him and his people, including the plagues against Egypt and the parting of the great Red Sea, when the entire Jewish nation escaped Egypt into the desert.

While most of the Israelites reacted to difficulty in the desert by complaining and rebelling, Joshua had a different perspective. He realized that although their situation was far from perfect, it was better than living in slavery.

As a result of his perspective, he didn't overreact to temporary discomfort. He focused on the vision rather than resenting the present. And when the time came to enter the Promised Land, he was mentally and spiritually ready to face the challenge.

Vision

Moses chose Joshua and eleven other leaders, one from each of the twelve tribes of Israel, to spy out Canaan, the "land flowing with milk and honey" that God had promised them. Moses instructed them to study the size of the cities, how well they were fortified, and what kind of people inhabited the land.

After forty days, they came back with their report. Joshua and one other leader, named Caleb, had a faith-filled vision. They had brought back samples from the harvest, proof that the land was in fact flowing with abundance. They declared boldly that with God on their side, they would defeat their enemies.

The other ten leaders, however, were full of fear. They said that the cities had great, fortified walls and the people were giants. They summed up their report by saying, "Next to them we felt like grasshoppers" (Numbers 13:33). Their fear became negativity, which spread to the people who listened to them. Soon, the people rebelled completely against Moses and God, blaming them for taking the nation out of Egypt and into a land where—they imagined—their enemies were going to consume them.

All twelve leaders had seen God work on their behalf time and time again, protecting them and defeating their enemies. Yet only Caleb and Joshua stood strong in their faith.

The greater the vision God gives us, the greater the obstacles we must defeat in order to fulfill the vision. Unfortunately, like the ten fearful spies, our dreams are often defeated before we even start, because we exaggerate the obstacles. We sabotage our courage and faith just when we need them the most.

God will not give us a vision that we cannot accomplish. He gives us the exact gifts and power we need. It's up to us to believe the vision and act upon it.

He will be faithful to fulfill the vision he has put in our mind and heart, but we must not sacrifice our integrity along the way. If we can learn not to take matters into our own hands when we run into obstacles that are too big for our strength and resources, we will see miracles in our life. Trust God, and he will clear the way.

Timing

Sometimes we have both vision and faith, yet because of circumstances outside of our control, the accomplishment is delayed. In this case, the dream Joshua and Caleb had of acting on God's promise to take the land had to be postponed forty years because the people lacked the faith to overcome their obstacles.

Most successful leaders don't have any trouble moving forward toward their goal. What drives us crazy, though, is when we are forced to wait, especially through no fault of our own. The urgency to move forward and satisfy the burning desire God has put in our heart must be balanced with patience in order to move in God's proper timing.

I knew it was God who gave me the desire to start a new company in Arizona. But instead of trusting that he would sooner or later move on my wife's heart to confirm the vision, I moved forward without her blessing. That premature decision almost ruined our greatest dream of all—creating a wonderful family.

I am sure Joshua and Caleb were frustrated with the lack of belief their fellow leaders and relatives demonstrated after spying out the land, but instead of losing faith in their God-given vision, they used the next forty years to their advantage and became awesome leaders.

Joshua became Moses's loyal assistant who was allowed to travel partway up Mount Sinai, where Moses received the Ten Commandments from God. Over the next forty years, God developed Joshua into a man of the highest character and honor.

Unlike other biblical characters, from the prophets to the kings, we never see Joshua falling into serious sin. I am sure he learned and obeyed the Ten Commandments and other laws and rituals that God introduced to his chosen people in that time. He witnessed God's wrath when his friends and relatives lost faith and disobeyed God, bringing punishment on themselves. But Joshua proved over time that Moses and, more importantly, God himself, could trust him.

It's worth noting that Joshua didn't respond to the delay by rebelling against authority and taking matters into his own hands. I've seen many leaders limit their success because they never learned how to submit to authority. Most leaders are naturally hard-headed and know-it-alls. But if they can't learn to submit to authority, they can't be part of a team.

A related truth is that you attract who you are. If you are a rebel, you will attract rebels. By learning to submit to authority, you will attract people that will submit to your leadership.

When it came time to enter the Promised Land, Joshua was nearly eighty. He had been wandering around the desert eating manna for nearly forty years. Still, he held tightly to his dream of taking the land that God promised him and his people. What an example of patience and persistence!

Faith-Filled and Courageous Leadership

Soon after leaving Egypt, Moses instructed Joshua to choose soldiers to fight their first real battle. They were facing the Amalekites.

After four hundred years of slavery, the Israelites probably knew little about the ways of war. They did not possess the best fighting equipment or know the latest battle tactics. Yet Joshua inspired, equipped, and trained thousands of ex-slaves to fight like no other group of warriors at that time in history.

Since this was their first real battle, they had no past victories to look back on for encouragement or strategy. Joshua's troops were fortified by the courage that Joshua instilled in them and by the prayers of Moses as he watched the battle from a nearby mountain, with his hands raised toward heaven.

The battle began. As long as Moses had his arms raised to heaven, signifying that the source of victory was God's strength, the Israelites prevailed; but when he lowered them, the enemy prevailed. I believe that Joshua's men could see their leader and drew emotional and spiritual strength from his arms being lifted up to God.

Against all odds, Joshua's army defeated the enemy. Their faith that God was going before them and their trust in their leaders carried them to victory.

For the businessperson leading a team into battle in the marketplace, I can't overstate the importance of faith-filled and courageous leadership. Success doesn't come from having the best team assembled for battle or all the needed resources. Faith creates courage and a winning attitude, enabling the leader and his or her army to overcome apparently insurmountable odds.

Self-Identity

Moses began the process of mentoring Joshua before he sent him to spy out the Promised Land. Moses even changed Joshua's name from Hoshea to Joshua, which means "The Lord's Salvation." I believe he saw a young, talented leader with huge potential, but he wanted him to see himself as greater than the sum of his own talents and strengths. So, Moses made his point by adding God's purpose to Joshua's name.

Though he was an Israelite, Moses was not brought up as a slave, but rather as a prince in Pharaoh's household. He was educated and trained. People viewed him with respect. All of this produced self-esteem and confidence.

Moses likely realized that a slave mentality was his greatest obstacle in developing a new generation of people who would have the courage to capitalize on God's promise. Moses knew that if he could change how Joshua saw himself, Joshua's great leadership abilities could change a nation of slaves into a nation who knew they were special because God had handpicked them to be his people.

Delegating Authority

The Lord told Moses that because he had sinned, he would not lead the people across the Jordon to take the Promised Land. Instead, Joshua, his loyal assistant, would.

We can all sympathize with Moses. After steadfastly doing the will of the Lord for so many years, he made one crucial mistake that kept him from setting foot in the Promised Land. But instead of feeling discouraged or rebelling against God's will, Moses reacted like the great leader and mentor he was.

The book of Numbers describes in detail how Moses empowered Joshua to be the next leader. Numbers 27:18–23 says:

> The Lord replied, "Take Joshua son of Nun, who has the Spirit in him, and lay your hands on him. Present him to Eleazar the priest before the whole community, and publicly commission him to lead the people. Transfer some of your authority to him so the whole community of Israel will obey him. When direction from the Lord is needed, Joshua will stand before Eleazar the priest, who will use the Urim—one of the sacred lots cast before the Lord—to determine his will. This is how Joshua and the rest of the community of Israel will determine everything they should do. "
>
> So Moses did as the Lord commanded. He presented Joshua to Eleazar the priest and the whole community. Moses laid his hands on him and commissioned him to lead the people, just as the Lord had commanded through Moses.

Then in Deuteronomy 31:7–8, Moses encourages Joshua:

> Be strong and courageous! For you will lead these people into the land that the Lord swore to their ancestors he would give them. You are the one who will divide it among them as their grants of land. Do not be afraid or discouraged, for the Lord will personally go ahead of you. He will be with you; he will neither fail you nor abandon you.

Leaders often make the mistake of delegating responsibility but not granting the authority to get the job done. This sets their subordinates up for failure. They are usually insecure leaders more interested in control than in accomplishing objectives.

True, delegating responsibility to unqualified employees can be disaster. But after carefully mentoring them and analyzing their performance as they learn to do the task independently, you must let them fly on their own.

A great leader finds and develops leaders around him that can execute their job even better than the mentoring leader. This is the only way that the organization can become stronger and more effective as it grows.

Once Moses knew Joshua was going to be the next leader, he acknowledged the promotion in front of all the people who would be his followers. He laid hands on him and transferred some of his authority to Joshua, so the people would know that rebelling against Joshua was the same as rebelling against Moses.

Listen and Obey

Most eighty-year-olds have been retired for years and are living in rest and comfort. Not Joshua. His vision and destiny had finally arrived. He had prepared himself for this season of conquest for over forty years.

God finally told Joshua and Israel that it was time to enter the land. In Joshua 1:2–5, God says:

> The time has come for you to lead these people, the Israelites, across the Jordan River into the land I am giving them. I promise you what I promised Moses:

"Wherever you set foot, you will be on land I have given you. . . ." No one will be able to stand against you as long as you live. For I will be with you as I was with Moses. I will not fail you or abandon you.

Most of the time, at least for me, God speaks in a very soft voice. Some might even call it intuition. It is a pushing or a nudging to go here or do this. Occasionally, he speaks loudly, almost audibly, and I know exactly what God is commanding me to do. I believe this was the case with Joshua. He had no doubt that the time has come, that magical moment when he and God would work together, taking back the land that his people had lost over four hundred years earlier.

Joshua may not have had the physical strength that he possessed when he first spied out the land nearly forty years earlier, but his inner man was strong. He knew he could do it because God was with him. Yes, his army had been trained and had won some key victories, but he knew the real difference-maker was God.

God reminds Joshua three times to be strong and very courageous. He tells him to observe all of the law and not to turn to the right hand or to the left. God states that if Joshua will do what God has been teaching him all these years, things will go smoothly for him and his men of valor, and they will take the land.

At the end of chapter one, Joshua's men also urge him to be strong and courageous. They assure him that if anyone rebels against him, they will put him to death.

Joshua was empowered by God and by his men to lead, and he was ready to take the land. God knew he had the right man in place. Joshua had proven his love for God by keeping his law; he had been faithful to him for many years; and he had diligently developed a war machine of around forty thousand troops.

Miracles happen when excellence in the supernatural meets excellence in the natural. For Joshua, an invisible momentum was about to arise like history had never witnessed before.

God often takes many years to prepare us for what appears to others to be an instant miracle. He spends a long time sharpening the tool, so to speak, so that we are ready to accomplish great things when the time is right. When we allow God to build character, experience, and wisdom into our lives, he can accomplish more in a day than we could in our own strength in an entire lifetime.

God knows how fragile and volatile our minds and emotions can be from one moment to another. Even a wise and experienced man like Joshua could become filled with fear and be thrown off track. Instead of adhering to God's commands, he might take matters into his own hands. That is why God encouraged him so many times to be strong and courageous and to spend time studying his word. His exhortations to Joshua underlined the importance of not getting lax in anything so that God could do the miracles he had planned.

It is imperative that all of us, especially leaders, spend time focusing on God. One way we do this is through worship, which helps set our hearts and spirits right before God. Another key is reading and saturating ourselves with God's word in order to renew our minds.

In our fast-moving, competitive culture, many businesspeople think extended times of worship, prayer, and Bible reading are a waste of time. But just look at what Joshua accomplished in a relatively short period of time. Spending adequate time in God's presence is far more efficient and effective than working harder on our own.

The accomplishments described in Joshua are so amazing that it would be easy to write them off as divine acts, independent of man's participation. That would be an incomplete understanding of the story. They were divine miracles, of course, but the response of Joshua and the Israelites to God's direction was critical. They listened, believed, and obeyed, and God did the miracles.

God has a plan that includes—even depends—on our participation. He can do things on his own, of course, but in the Bible and in my own experience, I see that he prefers to involve us. If we align ourselves with his principles and wait for his timing, God will create amazing miracles through us.

I have seen this happen countless times in my life. I am still learning to listen to God and move in harmony with him, even at nearly sixty years of age.

Joshua sent two spies across the Jordan River and into Jericho, a walled and fortified city. The spies returned filled with faith, saying that the people of the city were afraid and knew that the Israelites camped on the other side of the Jordan were coming to destroy them. The people had heard how God parted the Red Sea and defeated Israel's enemies. Rahab, a harlot from Jericho who befriended the spies, said of the people of Jericho, "Our hearts have melted in fear." They were in a state of near panic, even though they completely outnumbered the Israelites and had a huge wall around their city. What a difference from the report Moses received from his spies forty years earlier!

The next step was to take the entire nation across the Jordan River, which was at flood stage. God had a plan to accomplish this.

In John 10, Jesus, using the illustration of a flock of sheep to describe our relationship with God, says that sheep recognize the shepherd's voice. If another shepherd calls, they will not respond. We should be able to distinguish God's voice and his direction over other voices we hear in our mind. The closer we grow to God, the easier it is to recognize his voice and prompting.

After years of walking with God in love and obedience, Joshua was able to hear God's voice clearly. God gave him a supernatural plan to cross the Jordan that must have confused many people. The priests were to take the Ark of the Covenant, which represented God and his power, and step into the Jordan River, with the people following a specific distance behind.

When the priests took their first step into the water, the river parted, and the Israelites easily reached the other side of the Jordan. God told Joshua to build a memorial out of twelve stones to remember this miracle.

Imagine the level of faith and courage Israel now had to conquer Jericho. They were confident that God was with them. They trusted and respected their leader, who had many times proved he could hear from the Lord and accomplish the impossible.

On the other hand, imagine the panic in the people of Jericho when they heard that the Jordan had mysteriously parted, and the Israelites had crossed through unharmed.

Team Building

The Lord then told Joshua to circumcise all his warriors. No one had been circumcised since Israel left Egypt forty years earlier. An entire generation had grown up in the desert, where their fathers, due to their sin and unbelief, had been sentenced to die without setting foot in the Promised Land.

This ceremony represented once and for all that they were no longer slaves—they were a nation that God had chosen. Around this time, the manna that they had survived on for forty years stopped, and they ate produce from the land.

Think about the significance of this ceremony. Forty thousand men participated together. I don't mean to be sacrilegious, but what a bonding experience!

Over the years, I can remember a number of bonding exercises we took our leaders through to create group unity, cohesiveness, and centralized purpose. We wanted to create a mastermind, or one great group mind.

In any organization, the components of diverse talents and team unity must go hand in hand. Diversity without unity results in power struggles, misunderstandings, and offenses. Unity without diversity means blind spots are not discovered and weak areas are never strengthened. Great leaders seek out and value diversity, and they know how to use both good times and bad times to produce unity of purpose and singleness of mind.

Submission to God

Joshua's men recuperated after a few days, then prepared to attack Jericho.

Imagine how pumped up Joshua was now that he was ready, after all these years, to begin his conquest of the Promised Land. Moses, his leaders, and God himself had told him time after time to be strong and courageous. He had just witnessed God miraculously stop the waters of the Jordan River. His army was full of courage and united like no other army of the day.

One day, near Jericho, a great warrior with a sword in his hand appeared to Joshua. Joshua confronted him. "Are you friend or foe?"

He replied, "Neither one. I am the commander of the Lord's army."

Joshua realized this was an angel of the Lord. He immediately got a hold of himself and fell with his face to the ground in reverence. "I am at your command. What do you want your servant to do?"

There is a fine line between confidence and arrogance. This is an example of what a wise and powerful leader Joshua had become. There was no doubt in Joshua's mind about who was in charge. He knew this battle was not his, but the Lord's.

Joshua had submitted to Moses' authority for forty years. Even though he was now the leader of Israel, he understood that his authority and success came from God, and that without God he was weak, fearful, and easily defeated.

Creative Problem Solving

All great leaders have one thing in common: they are able to solve problems that few, if any, in their organization can solve. They know how to catch a vision, create a strategy, and overcome obstacles as they arise.

A leader gets a reputation for being a genius when he creates an unusual strategy that goes against conventional thinking—and it works. Think about the strategy Joshua laid out to his men of war. For six days, they would walk around the city walls of Jericho once per day, not saying a word. Seven priests would walk ahead of the Ark, blowing horns. On the seventh day, they would walk around the city walls seven times in silence, but after the last time around, there would be a long blast on the horns and everyone would shout loudly. Then, the Lord would give them the city. These men must have believed completely in Joshua to buy in to such a strange war strategy.

After the final shout, the city walls imploded and mysteriously fell to the ground. Many have contemplated what caused this unusual occurrence, or whether it even happened. Personally, I think that the massive number of people who were inside the walls of Jericho were so stricken with fear, and the army of Israel was so faith-filled, that the sudden shout of an army of courageous men created an energy force that caused these walls to crumble. It was obviously a miracle, but I think there was a metaphysical and even physical force involved as well.

When a large number of like-minded people share a strong belief, something powerful happens. I watched it happen in Arizona with my Pure Fitness company. When faith replaced fear, first in me and then in my team, problem after problem began to be solved. It was amazing, mysterious, miraculous—and very real.

Passion for Integrity

God commanded Joshua to destroy Jericho. Joshua warned his men that no one was to take anything for himself. Since this was the first city to be conquered in the Promised Land, all the silver, gold, and other valuables would be collected and deposited in the treasury of the Lord.

The defeat of Jericho was so complete and unbelievable that Joshua's fame spread throughout the land. Joshua and his army seem to have been impressed by their own victory, because in the next battle they faced, they acted in presumption and arrogance, without seeking God's plan.

They focused their energies on Ai, a much smaller city than Jericho. Joshua's leaders counselled him to send only three thousand warriors. To the Israelites' shock, they were routed and chased down the mountains by their adversaries. They lost thirty-six of their soldiers.

When Joshua heard the news, he and his elders prostrated themselves before the Lord and cried out, not understanding why the Lord would allow such a humiliating defeat to come upon his people.

Finally, God told Joshua to stop crying and get up. He said the people had sinned—someone had taken some of the spoil from Jericho. Joshua and his men searched until they discovered who had broken the command: Achan, one of the soldiers.

Although Joshua handled the situation with humility and gentleness, he had to have the man and his family stoned to death. A monument was erected to memorialize the consequence of his sin.

God is teaching us that tolerance of wrong or evil behavior inside an organization has negative effects. We have to ensure that our culture does not dilute our conscious to the point of tolerating behavior that is dishonest, deviant, sloppy, immoral, or deceptive. I must admit that over the years, I have been too lenient in tolerating wrong behavior in business if the person was getting the job done in an excellent fashion. Consequently, I have never had the success that Joshua had.

Equally important is that God holds the leader of an organization responsible for his subordinates' actions. Many times leaders try to wash their hands of the wrong actions that are done by those under them, but even our society and our laws recognize the responsibility of leadership to oversee the actions of employees and representatives of the company.

After building a number of successful organizations, I am more challenged than ever to learn what Joshua learned: to show my love toward God by giving myself wholeheartedly to accomplish his vision for me. As I do that, I believe I will see miracles in my life as well.

Ultimately, Joshua earned fear and reverence not only from his enemies, but from his own army. The fear immobilized his enemies, but it inspired excellence within his organization as he laid out the laws and the consequences of disobedience.

Joshua knew that his men had been defeated because of disobedience to God's orders and, possibly, because they were overconfident after their previous victory. As a result, they had not sought God or created a winning strategy to defeat the city of Ai.

After making sure the sin had been dealt with, Joshua sent all forty thousand troops with a specific battle plan. They set an ambush for Ai and won a resounding victory.

Joshua and his men regained their confidence that God was with them. They learned the importance of following all of God's commands, and Joshua learned to carefully appraise his leaders and troops.

From top to bottom, Joshua had created a pure flow of thought and obedience: from God to Joshua, and from Joshua to his leaders and loyal soldiers.

Miracles

Over the next few years, Joshua and his men of valor won one battle after another, defeating armies that sometimes hugely outnumbered them. On one occasion, the Gibeonites, known as some of the strongest warriors of all, were so afraid of Israel that they agreed to become slaves rather than fight them in battle.

Joshua's battle strategies became more and more complex as he became a more experienced general, but whenever he needed assistance, he called out to God, who moved on his behalf. In one battle against the Amorites, God helped defeat Joshua's enemies by raining huge hailstones on them. In another instance, Joshua prayed that God would extend the day by stopping the sun from setting so he would have more time to defeat his enemy, and God did it.

Together God and Joshua did the impossible, whether through conventional tactics or supernatural ones. Because of Joshua's faithfulness to God's law and purposes, he was invincible, regardless of the odds facing him. In the end, the Promised Land was divided between the tribes of Israel, and the nation prospered just as God had promised.

Obedience produces miracles—not because we deserve or earn them, but because God delights in showing his power on behalf of faithful men and women.

Loving Obedience

I am reminded of a promise God makes in Jeremiah 29:11. "For I know the plans I have for you," says the Lord. "They are plans for good and not for disaster, to give you a future and a hope."

God's love, grace, and goodness were evident in every step of Israel's journey. If we are paying attention, we can see his hand at work in our lives, too. He desires the best for us. Even when we make mistakes or are outright disobedient, he doesn't give up on us.

Obedience to God's commands is a natural response of love. The more we get to know God, the easier it is to do what he asks.

Obedience is usually more for our sake than for God's. His commands are not difficult, illogical, or unreasonable—they are designed to protect and bless us.

Joshua 1:8 says, "Study this Book of Instruction continually. Meditate on it day and night so you will be sure to obey everything written in it. Only then will you prosper and succeed in all you do."

Jesus says in John 14:21, "Those who accept my commandments and obey them are the ones who love me. And because they love me, my Father will love them. And I will love them and reveal myself to each of them."

Obeying God brings blessing. Disobedience, or sin, brings suffering. That is true in the home, at church, or in business. In American culture today, many people are offended if you even refer to wrong behavior as sin. They view the concept of sin as judgmental and intolerant.

As Christians, we understand that Jesus died for our sins. He paid the price for our past, present, and future failures. We are fully accepted by God, because when he sees us, he sees his son, Jesus.

But we also understand that obedience is the natural result of a relationship with Jesus. If we love him, we will obey him. We take holiness seriously because we understand the purity of God and the destruction that sin brings.

We are not on our own in the resistance against sin. God gives us both the desire and the power to overcome sin. When we need grace, the Bible encourages us to approach God boldly in prayer, asking for his help.

As business leaders, I can't emphasize enough the importance of both walking in grace and walking in holiness. Don't allow pressures, stress, busyness, fear, temptation, or anything else to pull you away from your commitment to God. I've done that, and I never want to do it again.

Like Joshua, take time each day to center yourself in God and to gain his perspective. Let the Holy Spirit review your motivations, attitudes, and actions. Gain courage as you hear his voice. Your Promised Land is there for the taking!

Training the Next Generation

Joshua made one significant mistake that should serve as a warning to us. He did not train up a great leader to replace himself. Because of this, the next generation began to lose their way for lack of godly leadership. Judges 21:25 says, "All the people did whatever seemed right in their own eyes." As a result, much of what Joshua and the nation accomplished was undermined and eventually destroyed by succeeding generations.

Ultimately, our challenge is not so much about what we accomplish while we are on earth, but about how successfully we set the next generation up for success.

Joshua was truly a godly leader. He led his people courageously into the fulfillment of God's promise to his people. Not once did he take individual credit for his victories, but he accepted responsibility for his men's actions even when they rebelled against his orders. Every time a miracle of God occurred, he went out of his way to build a monument to God, memorializing how God had moved on their behalf to bring them victory. He led by near-perfect example, and he continuously taught his people to be faithful to God by following God's commandments.

At the end of his life, he charged his people to continue in complete adherence to God's law. I think his life is best summarized by a phrase from that speech: "But as for me and my family, we will serve the Lord" (Joshua 24:15).

At the end of my life, I want my legacy to be, like Joshua, that my family and I served the Lord with all our heart. Wealth is temporary and fame is fleeting, but a relationship with God and a family that loves each other are priceless.

Conclusion

As this book goes to press, I am actively preparing for the next chapter of my life. I have no intention of retiring any time soon. I have several business ventures in the works, and I'm looking forward to new challenges and growth.

I am also excited about a new ministry I am leading at my church, called the School of Generosity. Like this book, the goal of the school is to equip people, especially businesspeople, to earn more, save more, and give more. I am passionate about helping people achieve success and become generous.

I hope the principles and examples I have presented in this book help you on your path in life. If my failures and successes can inspire a younger generation to know God better, to believe in themselves, and to persevere with passion and excellence until they take hold of true success—that's a legacy I can get excited about.

Many of us have seen the movie Braveheart, which tells the story of how William Wallace led the Scots in revolt against England. He was a champion who inspired his countrymen to stand up against their enemies. Although he was brutally killed by the English, he gave his people hope for a free Scotland. His famous cry of "Freedom!" as he was being martyred is one of the most powerful moments I've ever seen on film.

Deep inside, I think we all want to be champions, to make our life count for something. What motivates someone to give his life to save others? The answer is a burning love that goes beyond self.

Jesus willingly offered himself on the cross for our freedom. His love for us motivated him to pay the ultimate price. Because of his death, we have access to eternal life. He is our hero, our champion.

I have covered many topics related to personal and financial freedom, but ultimately, everything begins and ends with Jesus. I don't say that just to sound religious—I know it is true. As we make our relationship with God our first priority, he reveals himself to us. His destiny for us brings us a life of joy, and everything begins to fall into place.

God tells us that he knows the exact number of hairs on our head. He knows our thoughts before we think them. He passionately longs to give us the desires of our hearts. All we have to do is trust him completely, and he will produce one miracle after another in our life.

Then, the burning desire that lies deep in our hearts to be a champion, to have true purpose, will be fulfilled.